POLITICAL

ANALYSIS

Series Editors: B. Guy Peters, Jon Pierre and Gerry Stoker

Political science today is a dynamic discipline. Its substance, theory and methods have all changed radically in recent decades. It is much expanded in range and scope and in the variety of new perspectives – and new variants of old ones – that it encompasses. The sheer volume of work being published, and the increasing degree of its specialization, however, make it difficult for political scientists to maintain a clear grasp of the state of debate beyond their own particular subdisciplines.

The *Political Analysis* series is intended to provide a channel for different parts of the discipline to talk to one another and to new generations of students. Our aim is to publish books that provide introductions to, and exemplars of, the best work in various areas of the discipline. Written in an accessible style, they will provide a 'launching-pad' for students and others seeking a clear grasp of the key methodological, theoretical and empirical issues, and the main areas of debate, in the complex and fragmented world of political science.

A particular priority will be to facilitate intellectual exchange between academic communities in different parts of the world. Although frequently addressing the same intellectual issues, research agendas and literatures in North America, Europe and elsewhere have often tended to develop in relative isolation from one another. This series is designed to provide a framework for dialogue and debate which, rather than advocacy of one regional approach or another, is the key to progress.

The series will reflect our view that the core values of political science should be coherent and logically constructed theory, matched by carefully constructed and exhaustive empirical investigation. The key challenge is to ensure quality and integrity in what is produced rather than to constrain diversity in methods and approaches. The series will provide a showcase for the best of political science in all its variety, and demonstrate how nurturing that variety can further improve the discipline.

POLITICAL ANALYSIS

Series Editors: B. Guy Peters, Jon Pierre and Gerry Stoker

Published

Jon Pierre and B. Guy Peters
Governance, Politics and the State

Forthcoming

Colin Hay
Political Analysis

David Marsh
Political Behaviour

David Marsh and Gerry Stoker
Theory and Methods in Political Science (2nd edn)

Political Analysis Series
Series Standing Order
ISBN 0–333–78694–7 hardcover
ISBN 0–333–94506–9 paperback
(*outside North America only*)

You can receive future titles in this series as they are published by placing a standing order. Please contact your bookseller or, in case of difficulty, write to us at the address below with your name and address, the title of the series and the ISBN quoted above.

Customer Services Department, Macmillan Distribution Ltd
Houndmills, Basingstoke, Hampshire RG21 6XS, England

Governance, Politics and the State

Jon Pierre
and
B. Guy Peters

First published 2000 by
 MACMILLAN PRESS LTD
Houndmills, Basingstoke, Hampshire RG21 6XS
and London
Companies and representatives throughout the world

ISBN 0–333–71847–X hardcover
ISBN 0–333–71848–8 paperback

A catalogue record for this book is available
from the British Library.

This book is printed on paper suitable for recycling and
made from fully managed and sustained forest sources

10	9	8	7	6	5	4	3	2	1
09	08	07	06	05	04	03	02	01	00

Printed in Hong Kong

Published in the United States of America by
ST. MARTIN'S PRESS, INC.,
Scholarly and Reference Division
175 Fifth Avenue, New York, N.Y. 10010

ISBN 0–312–23176–8 (cloth)
ISBN 0–312–23177–6 (paper)

Men should be governed in such a way that they
do not regard themselves as being governed,
but as following their own bent and their own free
choice in their manner of life; in such a way, then,
that they are restrained only by love of freedom,
desire to increase their possessions,
and the hope of obtaining office of state.

— **B. de Spinoza**, *Tractatus Politicus*, 1677

What you need around here is a government
that aint afraid of doing a little governing.

— **Peter Sellers**

Contents

Acknowledgements

Several colleagues have generously offered advice, critique and support throughout this project. The late Vincent Wright at Nuffield College and Rolf Solli at Förvaltningshögskolan in Gothenburg have provided opportunities for us to meet and discuss early drafts. Steven Kennedy and two reviewers offered extensive comments on previous drafts of various sections of the book which significantly helped us sharpen the arguments. Also, our work was very much inspired by the discussions at a conference on theories of governance at the Ross Priory outside Glasgow in 1997. The conference was financially supported by the University of Strathclyde and the ESRC Local Governance programme.

We are also indebted to the many colleagues and friends at the University of Pittsburgh, University of Strathclyde and University of Gothenburg who listened patiently as we struggled to explain what governance is all about and why we think it is important. The KLM Royal Wing Lounge at Schiphol Airport in Amsterdam provided seclusion and a relaxed environment that we like to think advanced our thinking on these and related issues.

Most importantly, Sheryn Peters and Monika Pierre offered the kind of support without which any academic project is doomed to fail.

Gothenburg   JON PIERRE
Pittsburgh   GUY PETERS

Introduction: What is Governance?

In the last decade of the twentieth century the concept of 'governance' has emerged from virtual obscurity to take a central place in contemporary debates in the social sciences. The concept has come to be used frequently, but often with quite different meanings and implications. A key reason for the recent popularity of this concept is its capacity – unlike that of the narrower term 'government' – to cover the whole range of institutions and relationships involved in the process of governing. The aim of this book is to elucidate this concept in its various meanings and to demonstrate how thinking about governance can contribute to our understanding of the contemporary political world. Although we will be discussing a variety of meanings, our focus is on the capacity of government to make and implement policy – in other words, to steer society.

Part of the appeal of governance as a concept is that it links the political system with its environment, and may complete the project of making political science more policy-relevant. Thinking about governance means thinking about how to steer the economy and society, and how to reach collective goals. The debate that has arisen is whether government is the only way of deciding upon those goals or not, or even if it remains an effective way of performing those tasks. The weakened position of governments then forces consideration of how their role can be strengthened, and of alternative modes of political governance. It also points to the different ways in which countries have coped with changes in their international and domestic environments. Thus, governance addresses some general questions but also provides a means of asking questions about comparative politics.

Despite its recent prominence, governance is actually a rather old term. It was known in French (*gouvernance*) in the fourteenth century although it quickly came to refer to royal officers rather than to the

1

process of governing or 'steering'. In this volume we will be concerned with the more contemporary question of the relationship of government to governance, and the fundamental question of whether governments can continue to govern their societies successfully by making and implementing policies. Providing direction to society, whether directly or indirectly, is the central governance activity. Several decades ago the capacity of governments to provide that governance would have been axiomatic in the industrialized democracies. At the end of the twentieth century that capacity has become a hotly contested issue.

Governance and government

The concern with governance represents a closing of the circle of the rapid, if not turbulent, political development during the twentieth century. The first decades of this era saw the consolidation of democratic government throughout the western world. In Western Europe, and slightly later in the United States, the early post-Second World War period witnessed the second phase of political change. Governments took a higher profile, embarked on political projects of regulation, economic redistribution and, more generally, an expansion of the political sphere of society (Maier, 1987). What in the United States was labelled 'The Great Society' and in Sweden was heralded as 'The Strong Society' – two very different national contexts – essentially meant growing government, including increased public spending on public services and welfare state programmes and – albeit with substantial national variation – a growing political intervention in the market. These were the times when government was seen as the appropriate, legitimate and unchallenged vehicle for social change, equality and economic development.

In the third phase, illustrated excellently by the Thatcher and Reagan eras in Britain and the United States respectively, much of this development was effectively turned around in an astonishingly short period of time (Rockman, 1998; Savoie, 1994). Government was now increasingly defined not as the solution to societal problems but instead as the very root and cause of these problems. Through privatization, deregulation, cut-backs in public spending, tax cuts, monetarist economic policies, radical institutional and administrative reform, and the introduction of a distinctly market-based philosophy in public service production and delivery normally referred to as the New Public Management (Hood, 1991), Britain and the United States – with countries like Australia and New Zealand following suit (Boston *et al.*, 1996; Halligan, 1997; Zifcak, 1994) – attempted to reverse the growth in government in order to allow the market to play a leading role in society. However, countries like France and Germany – and until quite recently Japan – have been reluctant to embark on these types of reform, something which suggests that national contextual factors such as political culture and traditions make a difference with regard to reforms of state restructuring.

The fourth and final phase, which dates back to the early 1990s onwards, highlights the emergence of a partially new model of government. This emerging model of government draws on new ideas about what is, and what should be, the role of government in society; new perspectives on the process through which governments implement their programmes; and new approaches to the perennial issue of how elected and accountable government is to conduct a coordinating role in a society which is increasingly prone to follow market ideals. Thus, in some respects the political economy of the 1990s looks remarkably similar to that of the interwar period when governments played a fairly modest role in society with regard to the limited range of public services provided and the presence of the state in markets.

The key question addressed by governments, civil servants and citizens in the 1990s is how democratic government – which we rightfully expect to be able to exert some influence, control and coordination – is to be able to perform these roles in the political climate and the economic and fiscal situation of the 1990s. Even at the end of the twentieth century much thinking about government and its role in contemporary society remains very traditional. Although any reasonably keen observer can identify change occurring throughout the public sector, the traditional ways of thinking about government remain deeply entrenched. The public sector is still conceptualized (especially in Anglo-American democracies) as largely independent from the private sector, and government is often thought to have the capacity to control easily, and directly, activities within the private sector, as and when it feels it necessary to impose that control.

Similarly, democracy is still conceptualized in terms of elections and voting, with governments presumed to have substantial latitude for action between those elections. We will note below (Chapter 7) the extent to which the latitude for government action is now constrained by participatory mechanisms, as well as by an increasing legalism in many cultures. If they are to be successful in governing, democracies will have to devise means of accommodating more continuous forms of participation while still being able to supply the needed direction to society.

There is also an assumption that 'good government' implies uniformity of services across the entire political unit, both geographically and personally. Devolution and decentralization are making that assumption about governance appear increasingly quaint.

Finally, governing is still discussed primarily in terms of national governments which exercise authority throughout the territories within their national boundaries and which can exert substantial control over international influences on their domestic policies and institutions (for example, national markets).

However, following the budget cut-backs and the dismantling of many public services, we can identify signs of a changing perspective on governments and what governments are expected to do and how they should do it. In this introductory chapter we suggest that the new emerging way of thinking about government is characterized by three general ideas or concepts. First, there has been a gradual shift in focus among the political and administrative elite as well as among social scientists from input control towards outcomes and output control. This is not to say that institutions should be of any less interest than hitherto. Throughout the western world the past decade has witnessed numerous and extensive structural and institutional changes which suggest that institutions still matter a great deal. Also, constitutional issues remain to the fore as devolution and other regional reforms in the UK and experiments with alternative channels of citizen engagement in policy-making and policy advice in Canada suggest. In public service production and delivery, however, institutional forms as such appear to have become less important than efficiency and productivity.

Second, there has been a shift in perspective with regard to state–society relationships and dependencies. Previously, government enjoyed an unrivalled position in society in that it was the obvious locus of political power and authority. True, states have nearly always been engaged in some type of negotiation with other significant structures in society but even then the dominant role of the state was never questioned. In the current perspective, the state evolves as an actor which remains in control of some unique power bases in society such as executive and legislative powers and the enforcement of public policy. At the same time, however, states are becoming increasingly dependent on other societal actors. This is because it lacks the resources to deliver public service, or it lacks the legitimacy, or because it faces an environment which is becoming increasingly 'ungovernable'.

This type of governance problem gained much attention among political scientists in the 1970s and 1980s (Birch, 1982; Crozier *et al.*, 1975; Lowi, 1979). In the 1990s the governance problems are different from the 'overload' noted in the 1970s, meaning the continuing expansion of government and its confrontation of both fiscal limits and problems that would not respond to the 'tools' available to government. In contrast, the main governance problem has become how to redefine the relationship between the political and administrative branches of the state in order to allow for market-based models of administrative reform.

Finally, throughout the western world there has been a growing critique of the role which governments have acquired during the postwar period. Public sectors are increasingly seen as rigid and bureaucratic, expensive, and inefficient. Not least during the 1980s and 1990s such critique has surfaced in many different forms and expressions. Parties of the political left in Western Europe which played a leading role in the development of the welfare state came under intensified attack by Conservative and Liberal parties and, indeed, often saw themselves placed in opposition, as happened in the Scandinavian countries, Austria, Germany and the Netherlands. In the USA, the Reagan administration launched an attack on the federal civil service and a large number of the programmes it was delivering. Furthermore, throughout western Europe parties of right-wing social and political protest gained political support at an almost unprecedented pace (Taggart, 1996). The most prominent examples of these types of parties include the Danish and Norwegian Progress parties, Le Pen's Front Nationale in France, and nationalist parties in a number of countries.

Taken together, these developments were proof that the political formula of the early postwar period had lost much of its electoral support. The political climate of the 1990s is such that the traditional model of public policy and public services is less efficient and no longer unconditionally supported by public opinion. Even when more familiar political parties are in power their approach to governing is radically different than it had been in the past. The clearest piece of evidence on that point is 'New Labour' in the United Kingdom. The heyday of the strong state is gone and we now need to think about what can come in its place.

These changing perspectives have – with, as we will discuss later, substantial national variation – been embraced by elected officials, public bureaucrats and social scientists alike. This is not to suggest that these fairly radical ideas enjoyed immediate support from all political camps and the public bureaucracy as a whole. What does seem to be clear, however, is that for many of these officials the new way of looking at the role of government provided a formula which could help resolve several acute problems. First, it helped redefine the role of elected officials. In light of the growing discontent with and disbelief in politicians throughout the western world this seemed to be an urgent task. In particular, the new ideas, emphasizing action over words and results over commitments and promises, suggest that government believes itself to be capable of responding to the *Zeitgeist* of the 1980s and 1990s, heralding the market, individualism and free enterprise.

Second, this new image of the government and the public sector helped give the state a partially new and more contemporary image at the same time as it provided some degree of support and legitimacy to further cut-backs in public expenditures; as Stoker (1998:39) puts it, 'governance is the acceptable face of spending cuts'. In a fashion not too different from the 'lean and mean' ideal of the competitive firm in the 1990s, this new perspective on government presents the public sector essentially as the functional equivalent of a mean and lean business in the private sector. By the same token, new forms of citizen engagement which could be seen as a reaction to widespread frustration with traditional models of governance have quickly gained massive attention on both sides of the Atlantic (Pierre, 1998b).

Finally, it is an image of politics and government which, although the heyday of 'big government' clearly seems to be gone for ever, suggests that some societal functions traditionally accorded government are just as important as they have always been and that, indeed, government remains the system of institutions which is best geared to assume these responsibilities. These traditional roles refer to some of the core definitions of government such as law enforcement, some level of social security, national defence and so on. In addition to these basic roles of government, the public sector has also, historically speaking, played important roles with regard to economic development. National governments throughout the western world have been instrumental in the development of a capitalist economy by regulating markets, defining the basic rules of the game for private businesses, and developing trade rules and tariff systems which, from time to time, have protected the domestic industry from foreign competition (Polanyi, 1941; Shonfield, 1965).

These new perspectives on government – its changing role in society and its changing capacity to pursue collective interests under severe external and internal constraints – are at the heart of governance. The concept of governance is notoriously slippery; it is frequently used among both social scientists and practitioners without a definition which all agree on. To be sure, even within each of these groups there are many different definitions and connotations of governance. Throughout the book we discuss 'governance theory' which might be slightly misleading. The current academic governance debate is still to a large extent concerned with defining key concepts. Thus 'governance theory' refers to a proto-theory but remains basically a set of observations looking for a more comprehensive theory. We also discuss different types of 'actors'. 'Actors' includes real actors such as presidents, prime ministers and bureaucrats; in other instances, 'actors' is more amorphous. That is, they may be structures, interests, international regimes or policy networks. We are trying not to anthropomorphize the many entities such as regimes and networks. Still, these entities do have political influence over policy and governance.

Furthermore, governance refers to slightly different phenomena in the United States and Western Europe; in Europe the term refers to 'new governance' ideas of the involvement of society in the process of governing, while in the USA the term retains much of its original steering conception. While the debate on governance has been much more dynamic in Western Europe than in America, this does not mean that governance is not just as common in the United States as in Britain or the Scandinavian countries. Finally, as mentioned earlier, governance has in some countries emerged as a politically attractive alternative to government and the idea of strong states in society.

Outline of the book

The book is divided into three parts. Part I focuses on conceptual and theoretical problems in understanding governance; Part II first discusses governance between different institutional levels of the state and then proceeds to outline three different models of governance, or three scenarios of state roles in governance; and in Part III, finally, we bring together the conceptual discussions and the empirical analyses into an analysis of the trajectory of state development in different regions of the world.

In Chapters 1 and 2, we discuss in more detail a number of conceptual and theoretical aspects of governance. While some aspects of governance are fairly novel to the western political culture, it is also true that governance understood as a reliance on the private or 'third' sectors in policy formulation and implementation are established practices and traditions. However, the compounded effect of the financial crisis of the state, the globalization of the economy and the growing importance of transnational institutions such as the European Union (EU), the North American Free Trade Association (NAFTA), and the World Trade Organisation (WTO) has been a profound challenge to the traditional model of states and what constitutes state strength. Chapter 3 looks at these changes and how they, each in its own different way, pose challenges to the state.

As we move into Part II, Chapter 4 takes this discussion one step further by discussing how the traditional powers and capabilities of the state have been diluted both 'from below' as subnational governments claim more autonomy from the state and engage in overseas networks and 'from above', as international regimes enjoy increased leverage *vis-à-vis* the state.

Chapter 5 presents the first of our three scenarios in which the state, instead of surrendering to global and subnational political and economic pressures, seeks to reassert some of its lost control. States have historically played a critical role in the economy by resolving different types of collective action problems which economic actors have not had any incentives to resolve on their own (Pierre, 1997a) and there is little to suggest that the current economy would be any less bothered by such problems than previous capitalist economies. More importantly, states still have considerable powers and resources which can be employed to enhance their influence in society and in markets. Also, states can rely on a brokerage role to maintain some control over their environments.

Chapter 6 presents almost the opposite scenario; here, states surrender significant parts of their capabilities to transnational systems of institutions (EU, NAFTA, WTO, ASEAN (Association of South East Asian Nations) and so on) in order to help develop public control, albeit at a higher institutional level. At the same time, regions position themselves autonomously in the world economy and 'the global community'. The state, in sum, conducts a low-key type of governance while allowing for other regimes to increase their control.

In Chapter 7, the third scenario is outlined. Here, the focus is on communitarianism and social capital as alternatives to state – or public – control. These models have gained considerable attention during the 1990s both as political theories (in the case of communitarianism) and as a theory of the social underpinnings of economic development (which is at the heart of theories of social capital). In both theories, collective solutions are redefined from matters of the state to spontaneous forms of collaborative actions which are believed to be more attractive and more appropriate to resolve the collective problems of the 1990s when the public sector is too weak and too poor to play its former role.

In Part III, finally, we examine the trajectory of modern states in order to tease out what explains changes in state strength. In Chapter 8, we apply a historical perspective in order to investigate why some states seem to gain strength while others become weaker. Theories of governance challenge our traditional understanding of what constitutes state strength. Rather than relying on their legal and constitutional capabilities, states in a governance perspective derive their strength more from coordinating public and private resources, broadly defined. Traditional, legal 'powers over' are replaced by contextual 'powers to' (see Stone, 1989; Gourevitch, 1986). These alternative ways to think about state strength are elaborated in Chapter 9 which is the concluding chapter of the book.

Part I

Perspectives on Governance

Introduction

Governance has become a popular if not trendy concept in much of the contemporary political and academic debate. Such rapid increase in popularity often tends to cause confusion about what the concept in question stands for, and the recent debate on governance is no exception to this rule. That is why the first two chapters present different ways of thinking about governance at some length. Governance as an analytical perspective is still emerging and there are contending views on what is the most rewarding approach to governance. It is therefore appropriate to present different views on what governance is and how it is best understood.

Our own approach to governance is a state-centric approach. We believe that although governance relates to changing relationships between state and society and a growing reliance on less coercive policy instruments, the state is still the centre of considerable political power. Furthermore, emerging forms of governance depart from a model of democratic government where the state was the undisputed locus of power and control, hence we cannot think of any better 'benchmark' than the image of the state as it is portrayed in liberal-democratic theory. For these reasons mainly we look at governance as processes in which the state plays a leading role, making priorities and defining objectives.

Chapters 1 and 2 present extensive conceptual and theoretical analyses of governance. Chapter 3 places that discussion in a political context and teases out a couple of explanations of why governance has drawn so much attention in the late twentieth century.

We see governance as the articulation and pursuit of collective interests in the "post-strong state" era. Two decades or so ago, most Western European countries were governed by governments powerful enough to intervene in the economy to pursue goals of redistribution and social justice. Today, those countries pursue a much more modest agenda; the governing state has been replaced by an enabling state that governs to a large extent by coordinating and facilitating other powerful actors in society. That having been said, however, governing the state and society is still a highly politically charged process and, we argue, the state remains the only creature in society that can play that political – and democratic – role. Markets may be efficient in allocating resources but they can never play the same role as political actors or arenas. When the state exits the stage, so do responsive government and democracy.

1

Different Ways to Think about Governance

Governance can be a confusing term. It has become an umbrella concept for such a wide variety of phenomena as policy networks (Rhodes, 1997), public management (Hood, 1990), coordination of sectors of the economy (Campbell *et al.*, 1991; Hollingsworth *et al.*, 1994), public-private partnerships (Pierre, 1998a), corporate governance (Williamson, 1996), and 'good governance' as a reform objective promoted by the World Bank and the IMF (Leftwich, 1994). Furthermore, there is a tendency to confuse governance as an empirical phenomenon with theories about how this phenomenon operates and can be understood.

Given the possible confusion about the term, we need to examine and evaluate the different ways to think about governance and the different definitions of that concept existing in the contemporary political science and economics literature. Chapter 2 will address these issues in more detail. Here we will discuss governance as structure and process. We begin with four common governance arrangements that have existed historically as well as at present: hierarchies, markets, networks and communities. In addition we will discuss governance as the processes of steering and coordination, which are two dominant dynamic perspectives in the current literature.

Governance as structure

We will begin by thinking about governance in structural terms. That is, one reasonable assumption about the variety of political and economic institutions that have been created over time is that they were designed (or evolved) to address problems of governance. Each of the four structural arrangements we will be discussing addresses the problem of providing direction to society and economy in its own way. Each appears effective in solving some parts of the governance problem, but each also has its weaknesses. Further, each of the 'solutions' is bound in cultural and temporal terms so they may be effective in some places and at some times, but may not be a panacea for all problems.

Governance as hierarchies

Governance conducted by and through vertically integrated state structures is an idealized model of democratic government and the public bureaucracy. In the bureaucratic sphere, the Weberian model of the public service characterized most of the advanced western democracies for more than a century if not longer. This was essentially governance by law; instead of bridging the public–private border, this type of governance strictly upheld that distinction. The state – conceived of as the epitome of the collective interest – was thus distinctly separated from the rest of society but governed society by imposition of law and other forms of regulation. Other institutions of the state were also entangled in a hierarchical system of command and control. Subnational government enjoyed some degree of autonomy but the state never surrendered its legal authority over these institutions which, while 'autonomous', remained creatures of the state. Thus, hierarchy characterized both the state's exchange with society as well as its internal organization and *modus operandi*.

Much of the current governance literature is dismissive of hierarchy as a model of governance. Hierarchies, critics contend, were an appropriate institutional order in the days of highly standardized public services, a 'Fordist' economy, domestically controlled markets and unrivalled state strength. With most of these factors profoundly altered, so must hierarchies fall, the argument goes. The emphasis now is instead on smaller scales, flexibility, diversification, informal exchange rather than formal control, and 'sharing power' between state and market (Kettl, 1993) rather than maintaining a strict division between the public and the private.

Further along this argument, western society is said to be

becoming increasingly horizontal (SOU, 1990:44). Networks bringing together a variety of actors are emerging as increasingly powerful coalitions of interests. Such networks are sometimes even said to be powerful and cohesive enough to sustain pressures from the state and to perform an autonomous regulatory role within their sector (Rhodes, 1997). While some of these accounts of policy networks may exaggerate the powers and capabilities of these coalitions, it nevertheless suggests that hierarchies no longer reflect power relations in society. Governance, so the argument goes, must therefore depart from another model of social and political organization. The hierarchical state is believed to be 'too big to solve the small problems in life and too small to solve the big problems' (Bell, 1987).

Also, the state is said to be too weak to maintain the same control it exercised only a couple of decades ago. This is partly due to the shrinking resource base of the state and partly because of changes in the state's external environment. The globalization of financial and other markets during the 1990s has to a considerable extent reduced the state's control over its economy. The more precise nature and extent of the changes brought about by globalization are topics of a heated current argument (Boyer and Drache, 1996; Camilleri and Falk, 1992; Evans, 1997; Hirst and Thompson, 1996; Scott, 1997). It is difficult to argue that nothing has changed, but it is also easy to assume that everything has changed, so this debate must be considered carefully.

Critics of the globalization thesis argue that states have responded to the market globalization by developing transnational institutions and organizations which exercise effective control over the deregulated markets, such as the EU or the WTO (Helleiner, 1994; Mann, 1997; Peters, 1990; Strange, 1986). However, the leverage which these transnational institutions control is to a significant extent surrendered by the nation states. Therefore, the emergence of transnational institutions tend to pull in the same direction as globalization to the extent that they reduce nation-state sovereignty and autonomy. As will be argued later in this book, however, linkages upward towards transnational governance institutions and downward towards subnational government should be more thought of as state strategies to reassert control and not as proof of states surrendering to competing models of governance.

In addition, actors in the state's environment are said to be increasingly reluctant to conform to the state's interests and objectives. Previously, the state was an attractive target for organized interests not least because they controlled vast economic resources. Current nation states face considerable economic and fiscal problems and hence are less interesting in the eyes of most societal actors. Societal actors may indeed now invest more effort in avoiding involvement with the state than in pursuing such involvements as they may have at one time. That having been said, however, there are still areas of economic and social action in which government remains a crucial actor.

Finally, a keystone argument against hierarchies as a mode of governance holds that cities and regions are acquiring more effective autonomy at the expense of the state. To some extent, this process has been propelled by the state-driven decentralization which has taken place in most of the advanced democracies, such as France, the United States, the Scandinavian countries and the Netherlands (Sharpe, 1988; Smith, 1986). In addition, in regions like Quebec in Canada and Catalonia in Spain, ethnic and cultural sentiments have played an instrumental role in driving demands for increased regional autonomy (Keating, 1996). The argument goes beyond this diffusion of political power, however, and asserts that subnational governments are becoming the most appropriate form of political organization in the 'post-strong-state society'.

Thus, conventional wisdom has to a large extent become the critique against hierarchies, but dismissing formal hierarchies as systems of governance is unfortunate, for several reasons. First of all, much of the alleged development towards 'horizontalization' of institutions and organizations – and indeed of political life more generally – has been a spontaneous and organic development which has yet to be confirmed by changes in legal and constitutional frameworks. The discrepancy between these frameworks and actual political and institutional behaviour cannot be sustained over an extended period of time.

Second, governance through hierarchies is the benchmark against which we should assess emerging forms of governance and we therefore need to examine the nature of hierarchical governance in some detail. In parts of the current literature on governance there is a tendency to equate traditional modes of governance with a sterile view on political institutions and their exchanges with the surrounding society, and reserve the concept of governance for the new or emerging forms of such exchange. We believe this to be an unfortunate way to think about governance. Governance, strictly defined, is as old as government. What is novel – and what is the overarching theme of this book – is recent changes in governance. For these reasons, hierarchies should be thought of as one of several different modes of governance. It is not likely to disappear in the foreseeable future although it is increasingly being accompanied by other forms of governance.

Finally, governance through hierarchies still plays an important role in a surprisingly large number of national and institutional contexts. In Britain, state–local relationships remain contested and politicized and central government still exercises tight political control over local authorities (Goldsmith and Newton, 1993); some ideas of the Labour government, for example the increasing use of audits (Power, 1997), are tending to centralize power even more. Similarly in Germany, although the federal government has withdrawn some control over public services, allowing for greater regional and local control (Derlien, 1995), it is possible that the federal government, if it so chooses, can resume such delegated powers. In Japan, a growing interest in local government is considered 'progressive' and a 'politics of participation' (Muramatsu, 1997:6) because it challenges the hegemonic power of the central state. Even in the Scandinavian countries where local government and local autonomy have always been extensive and have indeed increased over the past decades, the state retains significant control through legislation and grants. Thus, hierarchies still play a very important role indeed in the political and institutional organization of the advanced western democracies. It could well be that horizontal networks are becoming more important but they are still less significant than the hierarchical relations between institutions and actors.

Governance as markets

If our image of hierarchies is that of prematurely dismissed structures of governance, then the contemporary image of markets is almost the opposite. The market as a governance mechanism is very much in vogue, indeed so much so that it is probably believed to be the solution to more problems than it can resolve. The market has come to be seen as everything Big Government is not; it is believed to be the most efficient and just allocative mechanism available since it does not allow for politics to allocate resources where they are not employed in the most efficient way.

Markets are also believed to empower citizens in the same way as we exercise powers as consumers. Instead of having elected officials – who may or may not be responsive to their constituencies – make decisions about what services the state should provide and at what cost, introducing a market-like situation for such services allows clients to choose directly, hence the final say on public services rests with the public.

The concept of the market has many different meanings in the context of governance. One understanding of markets is that of a resource-allocating mechanism, or, more broadly, the employment of monetary criteria to measure efficiency. In its idealized form, neither elected officials nor managers actively make any detailed decisions; instead decisions are made within the framework of over-arching policies.

Another meaning of markets in the governance context is as arenas for economic actors. Here, governance emerges as a problem because of the atomistic and anonymous nature of the market and its actors. The self-interest which is typical of economic theory generates problems since it cannot resolve problems and needs which all actors share but in which no one can see an economic incentive in resolving individually. Governance, here, refers to various mechanisms in which economic actors can cooperate to resolve common problems without distorting the basic mechanisms of the market.

We need to be aware of the difference between markets as a governance mechanism and the governance of markets. In the latter case, actors in markets, although they compete against each other, share problems of coordination. Companies in an industrial sector, for instance, share a need for coordination in order to have some collective control over prices, foreign competition and production volumes (Hollingsworth *et al.*, 1994).

Governance as networks

One of the most familiar forms of contemporary governance is policy networks. Such networks comprise a wide variety of actors – state institutions, organized interests and so on – in a given policy sector. Networks vary considerably with regard to their degree of cohesion, ranging from coherent policy communities to single-issue (or issue-specific) coalitions (Rhodes, 1997). Policy networks facilitate coordination of public and private interests and resources and, in that respect, enhance efficiency in the implementation of public policy.

Networks are by no means novel features of contemporary political life. 'Iron triangles' and 'policy communities' comprising actors with common interests in given policy sectors have been reported for a couple of decades (see, for example, Jordan, 1981, 1990). Similarly, the state has always had some form of continuous exchange with key actors in their environment, either in the form of corporatist models of interest representation or on a more *ad hoc* level. What is more novel, however, is that – in the extreme form – these networks are said to have become sufficiently concerted and cohesive to resist or even challenge state powers; they are essentially self-regulatory structures within their policy sector (Marsh and Rhodes, 1992).

Networks in the 'new governance' thus regulate and coordinate policy sectors more according to the preferences of the actors involved than with consideration to public policy. There are several important consequences of such governance. Public policy becomes shaped more by the interests of self-referential actors in the network than by the larger collective interest. Furthermore, policy change initiated by the state will be obstructed by the networks which try to insulate the policy sector from cut-backs. In addition, while networks effectively control the policy sector, citizens still hold the state accountable for what happens in the sector. Networks, in this perspective, short-circuit the democratic process by separating control and responsibility.

The relationship between the networks and the state could be described as one of mutual dependence. From the point of view of the state, networks embody considerable expertise and interest representation and hence are potentially valuable components in the policy process. However, networks are held together by common interests which tend to challenge the interests of the state. The development from government towards governance – the decreasing reliance on formal–legal powers – has clearly strengthened the position of the policy networks. One of the dilemmas of the contemporary state is that while it needs networks to bring societal actors into joint projects, it tends to see its policies obstructed by those networks.

Governance as communities

A fourth general model of governance which has generated a great deal of debate in the social sciences over the past decade or so departs from the socio-economic homogeneity and common interests which characterize small communities and raises the question of whether government is at all required to resolve common problems. The general idea is that communities can – and should – resolve their common problems with a minimum of state involvement. Care of children and the elderly, the argument goes, is better and more efficiently organized more or less spontaneously at the community level. In a broader perspective, communitarian governance builds on a consensual image of the community and the positive involvement of its members in collective matters. The state – or, for that matter, local government – is believed to be too big and too bureaucratic to deal with these issues. More importantly, communitarians argue that government which emerged as an instrument for the management of political conflict now breeds or encourages such conflict over matters which in and by themselves are not controversial. Thus for communtarians government generates at least as many problems as it resolves. The communitarian solution to this problem is to organize governance without government.

Interestingly, this communitarian view on governance is supported both by those who think that there is too much and by those who think there is too little government. For the former, communitarianism is an attractive alternative to having government at different levels decide on matters which are better resolved by members of the community whereas for the latter it is a means of introducing some sense of collective responsibility into the community. Communitarian governance seems to resolve common problems and foster a civic spirit in the community without breeding large public bureaucracies. It is a political theory which purportedly has found the third standpoint between the state and the market. It rejects both of these models of governance.

This view on what the members of a community can accomplish when acting in a humane, concerted and enlightened way may appear overly idyllic and philanthropic and, much as we regret to say it, to a great extent it is (but see Etzioni, 1995). Individuals have frequently proved to be less inclined to make personal sacrifices to the common good than communitarians would like to think they are. Also, for all its consensual virtues, communitarian governance has problems enforcing the common will on those who oppose specific proposals to that effect. Most importantly perhaps, communitarianism tends to exaggerate the blessings of consensus and the evils of disagreement; conflicts over specific issues would not be seen as something negative but rather as something refreshing by most observers of local politics. In Chapter 7 we will discuss this approach to governance in much more detail.

Dynamic views of governance

The above four ways of thinking about governance have emphasized the impact of structures and institutions. The assumption is that if you want to get governance 'right' you need to manipulate the *structures* within which it is presumed to be generated. The alternative assumption is that governance is a *dynamic outcome* of social and political actors and therefore if changes are demanded then it is those dynamics that should be addressed. This view, like that of the structuralists, provides some insights into governance but also leaves some aspects in doubt.

Governance as process

The governance approach is often argued to focus more on process and outcomes than on formal institutional arrangements. This is largely because governance, with its encompassing and contextual approach to political behaviour, often is less concerned with institutions than with outcomes (Peters and Pierre, 1998). However, institutional arrangements remain important not least because they determine much of what roles the state can actually play in governance. Even so, thinking about governance in a process perspective is important because governance is not so much about structures but more about interactions among structures. We should expect governance to be dynamic with regard to both configuration and objectives: the inclusion and influence of different actors could well change over time and across sectors.

There seems to be an increasing interest in many countries in altering the policy process. For instance, a number of western democracies are experimenting with new models of policy consultation. Such experiments include citizen engagement in the policy deliberation process, an increasing reliance on consultants and think tanks, and websites where anyone can present their views on public policy (Pierre, 1998b). At the same time, traditional models of interest representation seem to have been weakened over the past decade or so, arguably as a consequence of the fiscal crisis of the state. For these reasons, perceiving governance as a dynamic process is essential: we need moving pictures more than snapshots.

Governance as steering and coordinating

The conception of governance as 'steering' is at the heart of much of the current research in governance in different subfields of political science (Pierre, 2000). Lexicographically, 'governance' derives from the Latin 'cybern' which means 'steering', the same root as in 'cybernetics', the science of control. (For a political application, see Deutsch, 1963.) The notion of the state as 'steering' society is still central to theories of governance (see, for example, Kooiman, 1993, 1999). What is at issue here, however, are two related problems. First, the governance perspective typically argues that states are still indeed capable of 'steering' society, only now its authority is less based in legal powers and more due to its control over critical resources and its Gestalt of the collective interest. The second question is towards what objectives states can 'steer'. Much of the governance literature has been fairly quiet on who defines the objectives of governance; its main concern has been with the relationship between the actors involved in governance.

Governance sometimes refers to coordination of a sector of the economy or of industry (Hollingsworth *et al.*, 1994), and sometimes to the process through which a government seeks to proactively 'steer' the economy (Gamble, 2000). In either of these manifestations, governance is still being considered in a dynamic manner, seeking to understand how actors, public and private, control economic activities and produce desired outcomes. Both views see government as having a central role in producing economic outcomes and as helping to manage the tensions of modern economies in the global environment.

Analytic framework

Finally, we can move from more output-oriented views of governance to consider it strictly in intellectual terms. That is, as well as being 'something', governance is a way of viewing the world of politics and government. It makes us focus attention on things that happen and the ways in which they happen. By so doing it moves the study of politics away from formal concerns and to some extent returns us to the classic question raised by Lasswell (1935) – 'Who gets what?'

Governance as analytical framework

A common source of confusion in the governance literature is that between governance as phenomenon and governance as theory or analytical framework. It is unfortunate, in some ways, that governance has been given this dual meaning. Much as we are aware of this problem, we acknowledge that the concept may be given different meanings in different contexts. Unfortunately, introducing a new concept to replace that of governance in one of the two meanings is not a viable strategy.

The analytical framework in theories of governance differs in several important aspects from traditional political science frameworks. In governance theory many political science postulates concerning political institutions and their capacity to govern are not accepted at face value. The extent to which they do exercise such powers is, we argue, largely a matter of context. While political science has a natural interest in political power and assumes that such power rests exclusively with political structures, governance theories are more wary of political power as a base for governing. Instead, in governance, leverage is frequently derived from entrepreneurialism and political skill.

The importance of governance

The perspective on governance outlined in this book is focused on the state: on its role in governance and how the emergence and challenge of governance affect the state in different respects. The choice of analytical perspective is not chosen arbitrarily. We pursue a state-centric model of analysis because the state, despite persistent rumours to the contrary, remains the key political actor in society and the predominant expression of collective interests. We believe that the role of the state is not decreasing as we head into the third millennium but rather that its role is transforming, from a role based in constitutional powers towards a role based in coordination and fusion of public and private resources (Evans, 1997; Payne, 2000).

Furthermore, the ongoing globalization challenges the traditional model of the state but is not necessarily a threat to the nation state as such. States have proved to be surprisingly resilient and innovative in meeting a variety of challenges, for example financial constraints, powerful organized interests or even political protest and legitimacy crises. We should expect to see various forms of transnational cooperation become increasingly important as markets become global. The process of state reorganization as a response to changes in their external environments is about as old as the state itself and we cannot think of any reason why that process would not continue.

Most importantly, however, we argue that in order to be able to understand the full nature of governance and its effects on the established structures and processes of power and control in society, we must depart from the state of affairs before these challenges emerged. We have already discussed the dangers in dismissing the state as the source of political authority and financial resources. Understanding the causes and consequences of governance requires some kind of 'benchmark' against which these changes can be assessed. The most obvious 'benchmark' in such an analysis is the world as it was prior to the emergence of the contemporary interest in governance.

These transformations in the role of the state are a key research problem for political scientists. Approaching the state in a governance perspective helps us understand the new or emerging roles of the state. Different forms – or modes – of governance will characterize the pursuit of collective interests in the foreseeable future much more than alternative forms of the exercise of formal, constitutional powers. The gradual shift from 'government' towards governance has significant ramifications both within the state (see, for example, Peters and Savoie, 1995; Peters and Pierre, 1998a) and its relationship with the surrounding society (Rhodes, 1997). This book seeks to stimulate our thinking about these changes and how we are best to understand them.

Process and outcomes: the state as independent and dependent variable

As mentioned earlier, this book considers governance from a state-centric perspective. Some might object that if one of the defining characteristics of governance is the downplaying of the state in the pursuit of collective interests, focusing on the state is an awkward approach. However, in order to understand the role of the state which we see emerging in various modes of governance, and before dismissing the state as a leading actor in this governance, we must have a clear picture of the historical role of the state. The state-centric perspective allows us to look at the state as either the independent or the dependent variable. In a less positivist language, we can look at the state either as a cluster of factors which explain governance, or we can observe how emerging modes of governance affect the state in different respects.

In the first perspective the role of government in governance is, in fact, one of the key aspects of governance. The role of the state in governance can vary from being the key coordinator to being one of several powerful actors. To be sure, we can think of governance processes in which the role of the state is close to non-existent. Also, as subsequent chapters will discuss in detail, the role of the state in governance derives to a significant extent from the role which the state has played historically in society and the institutional strength of the state.

The role which the state plays in governance depends on a large number of factors such as the historical patterns of regulation and control of the particular policy sector; the institutional interest in maintaining control; the degree to which governance requires legal and political authority; and the strength of societal organizations and networks. The actual role which the state plays in governance is often the outcome of the tug-of-war between the role the state wants to play and the role which the external environment allows it to play. In the political economy literature on governance we find several examples of persistent self-regulation of market sectors and a common interest among corporate actors to minimize state presence in the governance of industrial sectors (Campbell *et al.*, 1991; Hollingsworth *et al.*, 1994). Similarly, the network approach to governance substantiates the capacity of cohesive networks to fend off state interests in the governance of policy sectors (Marsh and Rhodes, 1992).

The alternative research strategy – looking at the state as the 'dependent variable' – raises questions about how the emergence of governance alters the powers and capacities of the state. The increasing reliance on various forms of public–private coordinated projects, or on voluntary forms of joint action with subnational government, or the challenges posed by transnational forms of governance, put tremendous strain on the institutional arrangement of the state and the management of these institutions (Kooiman, 1993). This is primarily because political institutions are significantly constrained by the 'due process' and can not move financial resources as easily as corporate actors. While public-private partnerships aim precisely at granting institutions such discretion, this is often used as an argument against such partnerships (Keating, 1998; Peters, 1998d). Thus, while partnerships may be a comfortable way of increasing the state's points of contact with the surrounding society it also feeds back into the state apparatus and causes strain between the 'due process' and the need to be as flexible as the other partner.

For the state to be able to engage in different forms of governance, many of the traditional models of public sector command and control need to be replaced by more relaxed and decentralized management models. Furthermore, the extensive decentralization programmes which have been implemented in a large number of western democracies over the past decades have helped facilitate governance at the local level. Even if the traditional assumptions are relaxed, we should remember that it is still the state which is the actor

Obviously, whatever perspective on the state we choose, it is clear that when it is observed over time we need to incorporate elements of both approaches. The role which the state can play in future governance is to a considerable degree explained by how past governance has impacted on the state and its institutions.

2

Conceptual and Theoretical Perspectives on Governance

This chapter will elaborate the nature of the concept of governance and particularly the variety of theoretical perspectives in the social sciences that can be brought to bear on this subject. As well as elaborating the concept itself, this discussion of the existing literature will identify a number of ways of explaining observed variations in governance. We will be able to see very clearly that there are perhaps as many different views about governance as there are scholars interested in the subject. As a consequence of those differences a great deal of clarification and definition is necessary when beginning any discussion using this term.

There are, however, several very basic questions about governance that appear in a number of different settings. One of these questions is the role of governments in governance and the countervailing powers of civil society in governing. A related question is whether it is still appropriate to think of the major locus of governance as the nation state, or whether globalization and the growth of international regimes in a number of policy areas (Rittberger, 1993; Krasner, 1983). Another related question is the extent to which the *governability* of the society is as important as the *governing capacity* of government itself in producing governance. Finally, we need to know how government is to govern if indeed it is capable of doing so. If it is not, how is the society and economy to be steered, or are we willing to permit these more or less unstructured forces to dominate? These are hardly simple questions, as they go to the heart of the relationship between government and society, and between government and individual citizens.

Role of government in governance

The words 'government' and 'governance' have the same root but they need not, and indeed should not, be taken to mean the same thing. The role that government plays in governance is a variable and not a constant, and, as we will point out, there are models of governance that are state-centric and some that are more society-centric. Rather than as a sharp dichotomy, however, it makes more sense to conceptualize the role of government and the state in governance as a continuum. Different governments and different policy areas are located at different points along this continuum, with a major analytic issue being understanding why those differences exist and what impact they have on the effectiveness of governance.

There is a tendency to discuss the apparently increased influence of non-governmental actors in governance as a change from a traditional past, and to some degree it is. However, that having been said, it is also easy to overestimate the capacity of governments in former times to govern with more or less absolute control. In particular, the seemingly powerful governments of the post-Second World War period in western countries may be the historical aberration, not the periods of weaker and more constrained government. For example, although the growth of global markets is argued to reduce the capacity of government, the current level of international trade is actually a return to levels of trade that existed prior to the First World War (Hirst and Thompson, 1996). It is certainly true that the freedom of movement of capital is higher than ever before, but even capital to some extent remains national as well. Thus, it appears that the differences observed are more those of degree rather than kind, with the role of government remaining crucial.

To some extent the recognition of the role of non-governmental actors in governance is just that – the recognition of a fundamental pattern that had been functioning for some time. Even the most state-centric analyst would find it difficult to deny the role that international forces now play in national policies. They would, however, also have to accept that this role is long-standing. The struggles of the British government to maintain the strength of sterling in the decades following the Second World War are but one of many such instances of the role of international economics in policy (see Brittain, 1975; and Stephens, 1997).

Nor could that analyst deny the role that interest groups have played in governance decisions for decades, and perhaps centuries. For example, some of the early economic regulations in the United States in the nineteenth century were referred to as the 'Granger Laws', recognizing the centrality of that early agricultural interest group in having them adopted. We now have better ways of identifying and conceptualizing the role of non-state actors, but those actors were influential even before social scientists had the right words to capture their involvement in the process.

From the perspective being advocated in this volume, the very adoption of the governance concept enables the analyst to understand better the role that non-governmental actors play in producing policy outcomes. Just as the implementation framework (Pressman and Wildavsky, 1973) enabled researchers to identify more clearly when actual policy outcomes deviated from the intentions of the 'formators' (Lane, 1983) of those policies, so too the governance perspective forces analysts to think about what perfect control from the centre of government might look like if it were ever achieved. With that almost 'ideal type' model in mind we can then ask about the root causes of any deviations from that centralized steering model. The degree of deviation will be variable depending upon the country, the policy area and the particular issue.

Thus, as well as being a useful way of describing a great deal of the activity surrounding the development and execution of public policy, 'governance' can also provide a crucial analytical perspective. It provides a standard against which to compare outcomes and actual policies. That standard may be somewhat unrealistic – as any ideal type will be – but it does provide scholars with a place to begin the analysis. We can identify what a governance process determined by the 'central mind of government' (Dror, 1986) might look like, and can then see where international, intergovernmental or societal pressures have forced deviations from the predicted pattern. We will argue that beginning with those two types of external pressures to assess the outcomes of governance processes does not provide any comparable standards or predictions against which to compare the performance of the system.

We have been arguing that government plays a major role in governing, but just what is that role? We will be arguing first and foremost that the role of government is to provide a set of goals for governing. A conventional definition (Easton, 1953) of the political process is the 'authoritative allocation of values for a society'. In this view the most important thing that governments can do is to take all the valid, but conflicting and expensive, wants and demands from society (see below) and convert those into a set of more or less coherent policy statements. Of course there are always political questions and the choices made by government are less than coherent and coordinated across policy areas (Peters, 1997b, 1998b). Still, within each area there does tend to be a more or less clear set of ideas about what constitutes 'good' policy.

It is important to note that the more amorphous actors somehow involved in governance, including the international market and networks, have a difficult time making these types of statements about priorities. In the market the coordinating device is a 'hidden hand' emerging out of the self-interest of all the participants. Likewise, network approaches tend to either define away conflicts by restricting a network to groups and individuals having common values (Dowding, 1995), or they provide limited means for resolving conflict. Politics is inherently conflictual, although it involves mechanisms for compromise as well as for clear victories. Thus, if we want to understand governance we need to understand the ways in which the political process copes with conflict and produces decisions.

We also need to understand how government implements the decisions it has made in order to comprehend governance. Again, the implementation literature has done some of the necessary work here by pointing to the need to trace the effects of policies and programmes through to their final effects on society, and to judge how well the ostensible policy goals were achieved. The governance perspective links that set of concerns even more directly with the process of policy-making and with policy formulation. In governance all these components are seen as parts of the same integrated process rather than as discrete aspects or stages of policy.

Further, rather than necessarily conceptualizing each point in the process as a 'decision point' or a 'veto point', the governance perspective is willing to adopt a more consensual, cooperative perspective and think about more creative ways of avoiding potential blockages. Adrienne Hertier (1998), for example, has been examining how the many potential blockages in European politics are overcome on a routine basis by more creative modes of managing governance. The 'joint decision trap' (Scharpf, 1988), for example, that is assumed to present such a major barrier to effective policy-making, appears to be overcome quite readily in this analysis.

Is governance then really any different from political science as a whole, or more particularly from the study of comparative politics? What then do we gain from using this term? One answer to that question is that using the governance perspective highlights not just the institutional interactions usually associated with public policy-making (Jones, 1984), it also points to the relationship of society to governing. Further, it makes these linkages in the context of the overall goals for society chosen and pursued through the political process. Conventional comparative politics is able to do some of these things, but its tendency to focus on the input side of the polit-ical system (Dalton, 1996) and on components of the process rather than on the process as an integrated pattern of action has reduced its capacity to see the larger picture of governing.

The role of society

Society performs complementary, and occasionally competitive, functions in the process of governance. The obvious role of members of society is to present their 'wants and demands' to gov-ernment and to press for the adoption of their own agendas through the political process. Of course, participants in the public sector themselves are not without ideas about what government should do, with each agency having its own perspective on the 'real priorities' (see Seidman, 1998). This blending of societal demands and internal agency priorities and perspectives helps to shape the agenda for government and for governance.

Society also has other roles to play in the process of governance. When we discussed the implementation process above we argued that society can be a major implementer, just as is government itself. Governments use organizations in society to implement pro-grammes for a variety of reasons, not least being that if these groups do the implementation it will save government money and also make the public sector appear less intrusive. Further, implementa-tion through social groups enables governments to utilize the expertise of those groups to make better decisions. Last, but not least, the use of groups to implement also coopts those groups so that they and their members are less likely to oppose the policy.

The basic question which emerges from these various roles is the degree of 'governability' of the society. The most effective government in the world might be of little consequence if the society with which it is faced is inherently difficult. For example, the government of France can be seen as having been for years technically excellent, populated by the 'best and brightest' from the society and basically well-organized (Ashford, 1982). On the other hand, it was faced with a society that for decades had raised *incivisme* to an art form (Seigfried, 1940; Tilly, 1985). The net effect was a government that worked reasonably well on a day-to-day basis but which often failed when confronted with major challenges.

The governability question now tends to be raised more with respect to less-developed societies. The argument often made is that governance, and particularly democratic governance, depends upon the development of the appropriate forms of civil society rather than the actions of governments themselves (Putnam, 1993; Gyimah-Boadi, 1996). The most important thing to do if one wants to improve the capacity for steering and management for the government, therefore, would be to strengthen the self-governing capacities of segments of society. Putnam's research has argued that it is virtually irrelevant whether the groups developing such capacity are manifestly political or not; what matters is the generation of organizational capacity and the movement of interest and identification beyond the family.

Linkages between state and society

To this point we have been discussing society and the link between state and society in relatively general terms. We should, however, look at different models of that linkage and examine the implications that each of these has for governance. Further, we must be careful to differentiate between intellectual models of these patterns and the reality of the relationships. It may be that the understanding of reality becomes a function of the intellectual tools used to describe those relationships, rather than fundamental differences between the patterns. This may be especially true for network models that can be sufficiently vague as to include almost any other pattern.

There are three conventional models of the relationships between government and society – pluralism, corporatism and corporate pluralism – that dominate the discussion of this topic. Each of these models contains its own implications for governance, and each is more or less compatible with different interpretations of socio-political interactions. These models by now have become extremely conventional, but it may still be useful to discuss them briefly in the specific context of governance, as opposed to the usual manner in which they are discussed as merely the mechanisms of structuring inputs into the political system.

For North Americans the most familiar model of state–society interactions is pluralism, assuming that government is relatively little involved with interest groups directly (Dahl, 1961). Rather, government establishes the arenas through which the groups work out their own political struggles and establishes a set of 'rules of the game' about how decisions will be made. In this theoretical position no single group is considered dominant but all groups have relatively equal chances of winning on any issue. Further, groups move in and out of the policy process relatively easily, with impunity, and largely at their own initiative.

The pluralist model is quite consistent with traditional, top-down notions of governance. In that view government is relatively autonomous from interest groups and therefore can choose to let the groups more or less battle it out among themselves. There is, of course, some influence of groups on policy, but that influence is not institutionalized or formalized. Just as the groups move in and out, so too government can pick and choose the groups with which it wishes to interact, and can be highly selective in how it uses its authority in interacting with society. Indeed, this view is the most compatible with the traditional view of governance, treating society as a largely disorganized and incoherent set of groups with little systematic impact on policy.

Corporatist models, in contrast to the pluralism discussed above, assume a much closer linkage between state and society, and some official sanctioning of interest groups by government (Schmitter, 1974). In corporatism particular interest groups are accorded a legitimate role as representatives of their sector of the economy or society. There are a number of different varieties of corporatism

(Cawson, 1986; Lehmbruch, 1979), as well as various interpretations of the basic pattern, but the fundamental point is that only a limited number of actors can play the game, and those that do are bound closely with the power of the state.

Although the corporatist model may appear to give society greater influence and to be less compatible with the top-down conception of governance, in some ways this model strengthens the state. It strengthens the decision-making capacity of the state by limiting the number of societal actors which can be involved in making policy, and by closely binding those groups with the state. In this model the state may appear to lose some autonomy (the 'semi-sovereign state' as described by Katzenstein), but in many ways societal actors lose even more autonomy – they are effectively coopted into the realm of the state.

Finally, there is the corporate pluralist model that, as the name implies, falls somewhere between the other two models (Rokkan, 1966; Olsen, 1987). The basic logic of this model is that like pluralism there are a large number of actors involved but like corporatism those actors are given a legitimate status for influencing public policy. The pattern observed in Norway, and to some extent in the other Scandinavian countries, is the involvement of a large number of interest groups in government through advisory committees, petition processes and a variety of other participation mechanisms (Micheletti, 1994; Olsen, 1987). These groups are formally recognized as legitimate participants in the policy process, and they tend to establish stable relationships with formal actors in the public sector, particularly the ministries.

The corporate pluralist model of state and society comes closer to the putative 'governance without government' paradigm, but by no means does it actually advocate such an approach. The basic approach is that of using these groups as means of governing through state institutions, rather than presenting alternatives to those institutions. So, the corporate pluralist structures are means of making inputs into the governing process, or perhaps means of making implementation easier for government. Further, these structures force the participants in the process to confront each other's demands and to negotiate the priorities and the coordination that are central to governance.

Changing models

Although the above models are well-entrenched in the political science literature, there are also a number of emerging models, notably the various derivatives of the basic network model. The full elaboration of each of these alternatives might require another whole volume. In this context, however, it is important to consider the influence that different structures of groups may have over the capacity of governments to exercise control, just as do the other more familiar models of governing.

The most important difference among the various sub-models in the network family is the difference between communities and networks. The former models assume a much higher level of agreement among the participants than do the more formalistic interactions assumed in networks. Although both versions tend to assume some uniformity of perceptions among the participants, the community approach tends to assume a high degree of common values. For example, the 'epistemic community' (Haas, 1992; Zito, 1998) version assumes that there is a common scientific or professional background that creates a very clear differentiation of the community from other groups.

Another important distinction to be made about networks is the extent to which they involve government actors. As the governance process increasingly involves decentralized or deconcentrated public sector actors then these actors need to be directly involved with the process if there is to be any coherent policy formulation and implementation. The traditional models of state–society relationships (even corporate pluralism) place public sector institutions in dominant positions, deciding who will be involved and/or making the ultimate decisions about policy. In the network models, however, government is being conceptualized as more differentiated and as being just another component, or components, of the complex patterns of interaction. Indeed, if anything the state institutions appear subordinated to the capacity of actors within networks to evade and avoid the (presumably) authoritative decrees of government.

State and society are linked in the process of government. They always have been, with some of the difference in the ways in which we as political scientists conceptualize the relationships and these in turn affect the way in which we conceptualize the process of governance. In particular, the more amorphous network conceptualization of that relationship means that governance also becomes a somewhat more amorphous commodity, and that this very vagueness may in turn make governance less effective. At a minimum it makes the analysis of governance more difficult by not offering clear predictions of expectations of outcomes.

Theories of governance

Governance is a useful concept not least because it is sufficiently vague and inclusive that it can be thought to embrace a variety of different approaches and theories, some of which are even mutually contradictory. While it is true that all these approaches do contain some general idea of supplying direction to the economy and society, the number of different ways in which this is seen to occur means that when someone says that he or she adopts a governance perspective, this is the beginning, rather than the end, of the discussion. At this point we should identify the most important of these varieties of governance approaches and point out some of their relative strengths and weaknesses.

Traditional authority

The starting point for a consideration of governance theories is the traditional notion of 'top-down' authority vested in the state. Stated simply, government, as the legitimate embodiment of the general will, or the Crown, or whatever the source of authority is assumed to be, is the only possible source of governance in these models. Law and coercion are the instruments of this style of governance, and attempts to undermine the power of government must be assumed to be unacceptable usurpations of state powers. Indeed, in some conceptions of the authoritative state, even the attempts of interest groups or political parties to influence the actions of government border on the illegitimate. This more extreme pattern of thinking is characteristic of some Jacobin thinking about the state in France, and of some American constitutional theorists such as Madison, albeit for rather different reasons.

This traditional authoritative position of government is associated with pre-democratic regimes, whether in Europe in the eighteenth century or in developing and transitional societies at the beginning of the twenty-first. This hierarchical view of governance has also been central to communist regimes (see below) during that phase of development in which there had to be a 'dictatorship of the proletariat'. Some of this hierarchicalist (Hood, 1998) thinking even tinges the constitutional norms of countries such as the United Kingdom in which there has been a sense of the almost unrestrained power of the Queen in Parliament. For example, some of the concern of Rhodes (1997) and others (Saward, 1998) with the development of the 'new governance' is a function of the deeply ingrained conception of the powers of the Crown (and government) in most Westminster systems.

As well as these broad questions concerning political regimes the traditional top-down view also comports (at least in part) with a legalistic conception of governing. For example, the *Rechtstaat* system so central to the role of the state in the Germanic tradition assumes the acceptance of law and the capacity of government to govern through law with only minimal opposition. In practice this freedom to govern from above is constrained – and the state therefore is only 'semi-sovereign' (Katzenstein, 1987) – by both constitutions and the power of groups in society that are given legitimate powers to participate.

The top-down view is perhaps less compatible with the patterns of governing encountered in the smaller European states where histories of compromise, coalition and conflict management mean that any attempt to rule through centralized mandates is likely to be questioned. Further, the notion of centralized power is not compatible with patterns found in federal regimes or in presidentialist regimes with separation of powers. Thus, despite its relevance as a point of intellectual and analytical departure, we need to think about most forms of effective control from the centre as the exception rather than the rule in real political life.

Autopoesis and network steering

An alternative view, and at the opposite end of a continuum of power assumed to reside in the state, is characterized by literature in the European sociological tradition arguing that government is increasingly powerless in relation to society. The argument here is that society and markets have developed the capacity for self-organization and for eluding any attempts on the part of government to control them. This self-organizing power is especially evident in societies such as the Netherlands that have a very rich organizational universe and a government that has a history of accommodation to social interests.

This approach does use the concept of 'steering' developed above, but does so within the context of the inability of government to steer independently. To the extent that governments can steer, it must be 'steering at a distance' (Kickert, 1994). In this view the most that nominally legitimate actors can do is to establish a framework for action within which the more or less autonomous societal and economic actors are able to pursue their own goals. There may be some influence by government here, but little or no direct governance for society from the centre.

Another way to think about the power and importance of society in governance is to think of the literature on 'civil society'. Robert Putnam (1993) has argued that democratic governance tends to be most effective when there is a strong civil society to support its activities. A strong civil society is perhaps most important for the democratic aspects of governance, but is certainly not unimportant for the effectiveness of the process as well. For example, strong organizations can be used to develop partnerships and to provide an infrastructure through which government can operate (Pierre, 1998a). In this view, however, rather than being competitive with government the structures in civil society are seen to be complementary and cooperative.

The obvious critique for this self-organizing approach to governance is that governments establish the basic parameters within which markets, and even social groups, function. Markets cannot exist without the rule of law and clear statements of property rights, as the experiences of countries in Eastern Europe have demonstrated after the collapse of the Soviet bloc. Likewise, although many associational groups exist independently of politics and government, for many groups the opportunity to influence policy is their justification for existence and others could not survive without direct and indirect support from the public sector, for example tax exemptions for charities. There may be substantial interaction between legal parameters and the pressures coming from autonomous actors in society, but it is very easy to underestimate the influence of state actors, as well as the extent to which law creates the niches within which social groups function.

Cybernetics and steering

Another way of thinking about the steering process within governance is as a cybernetic process. That is, we can conceptualize the institutions involved in making governance decisions in systemic terms, and as being highly responsive to their environment. In this view government (or possibly other public organizations) will be responsive to changes in the environment and attempt to maintain some sort of equilibrium levels for certain key indicators – the obvious analogy being with a thermostat that regulates the temperature of a building, striving to keep that temperature as constant as possible. Cybernetics and governance share a common etymological root, and hence linking the two appears to be a logical process.

Karl Deutsch (1963) developed a full-scale model of government as a cybernetic system. He argued that governments should attempt to become more cybernetic and be more responsive to the environment, with an implicit assumption that governments could indeed steer themselves and society rather well if they simply developed the information-processing capabilities. Deutsch then proceeded to invest a great deal of his academic time in the development of indicator systems that would support such a pattern of governing.

Many critics have questioned the concept of government as cybernetic, on both empirical and normative grounds. First, empirically there are a number of questions about the existence of social indicators that are anything near as reliable and valid as is temperature for our thermostat example above. A good deal of progress has been made with social indicators, but they are still rudimentary when compared to the type of data that would be used in engineering applications of cybernetics. Further, the capacity of governments to collect and process these data in a sufficiently timely fashion would limit the cybernetic capacity of government. For example, we have rather better economic indicators than we have indicators about other aspects of socio-economic life. Even here, however, we do not really know what the level of GDP growth or inflation or whatever is until months after it has happened; in cybernetic language there would be a great deal of 'lag' in the system. There are also some 'leading indicators' for the economy, but their validity and reliability are not as high as for the other, *ex post*, economic indicators.

The normative objections to the cybernetic idea are at least as

strong as the empirical ones. The argument here is that the cybernetic model is too oriented toward the status quo, especially given
the central place of equilibrium and the maintenance of equilibrium in the model. The obvious way around this objection, central
in the social cybernetics literature, is that there is actually a moving
or a dynamic equilibrium rather than the single fixed-equilibrium
value as one might find with a thermostat. Even with that modification, the approach can still be considered as excessively concerned
with stability, and as excessively mechanical for the contemporary
world of policy-making and governance.

Associated with the homeostasis critique is the absence of goal-
seeking in such a model of policy-making. In a cybernetic view the
goals being sought are primarily simply a return to the *status quo ante*,
or in other words a return to a stable state that existed prior to the
disturbance of that stability. Steering in this sense can only be considered as extremely minimal. This view can also be rescued somewhat by a concept of dynamic equilibrium in which there is some
goal-seeking provided that some equilibrium in the other parameters of the system is maintained. Even in that construction, however,
the steering notion of governance appears to be subordinated to the
equilibrium concept, and hence cybernetics does not appear to
provide as rich.

Policy instruments

A third way to think about how government can steer society is to
think about the instruments that it has at its disposal (Salamon and
Lund, 1987; Hood, 1984; Peters and Van Nispen, 1998). This perspective tends to assume that governments can govern, and then
proceeds to consider that it can govern most effectively and efficiently. Further, some scholars writing in the instruments, or 'tools',
literature also take into account the political consequences of instrument choice. In the contemporary political environment this political factor means primarily that governments will select the least
intrusive instruments (Woodside, 1998).

The basic argument of the tools approach is that the means
through which governments choose to govern will not only affect the
outcome in the policy area, but will also have a number of secondary effects on the economy and society. The choice of instruments will also have an effect on government itself. Some

policy-makers tend to be committed to particular tools, for example, lawyers to regulatory instruments, and economists to market-like instruments. and to use those even when they are probably not the most appropriate. What is needed, but not yet available in the literature, is some sort of algorithm for matching tools and policy problems.

Unlike the first two approaches to governance, the instruments approach does not appear to ask any sweeping questions about the relationship between state and society. Rather it assumes that there is a government process in place that is making choices about policy goals and the means that will be employed to implement those goals. In this way the tools approach links governance with the large body of public policy research in political science and public administration. Governance is in many ways about the capacity of governments to make policy and put it into effect. Tools capture that basic question and provide a means of understanding one of the variables central to success.

This more operational view of governance, however, does highlight the capacity of government to implement those choices and the multiple characteristics of any instrument selected. For example, even though an instrument, such as tax expenditures (Howard, 1997), may be politically palatable and relatively inexpensive to administer, it may not be as effective as others in ensuring that all eligible citizens are accorded its benefits. Other more intrusive instruments may be needed for that purpose, and government will have to decide how important it is to ensure equality and coverage. For example, tax expenditures depend upon private incentives to be successful and therefore may not be suitable for achieving goals that are more collective.

The tools approach also tends to assume that all tools are available to all governments, and that simply may not be the case. Some of the tools, for example, moral suasion, may depend upon government being legitimate and respected by the population. Also, some governments have more money than others and hence can afford to spend in order to achieve their aims whereas others may be restrained by weak economies or tax resistance among the population. Finally some governments can use coercion more readily than others, although in the end this is an inefficient means of achieving all but the most basic policy objectives.

Critics of the tools approach, however, argue that this begs the question of the ability of governments to govern. They argue that any tool that government invents can be evaded by the 'self-organizing' capacities of society. In other words, in this view government can govern only to the extent that the society is willing to let it govern. Although this is phrased as a fundamental critique of the instruments approach, it may only be a restatement of the political point made above: the less intrusive an instrument is the more likely it is to be acceptable to the public, everything else being equal. This view of the efficacy of governing by stealth runs counter to contemporary views about transparency in the public sector, but does indicate that less visible instruments do tend to be more successful in the contemporary world.

Institutional analysis

Another approach to the question of governance is to examine the role that institutions play in the process. One of the dominant questions in this area is the role that the choice of presidential or parliamentary institutions plays in determining the capacity of governments to govern effectively (Weaver and Rockman, 1993; Sartori, 1994). There has been a great deal of normative analysis (Riggs, 1988) in this area, as well as a growing body of more grounded analysis. There are other substantive institutional questions raised also, for example, the role of non-majoritarian institutions such as courts (Majone, 1994), bureaucracies and central banks.

As well as the empirical questions about the impact of institutions on governance, there are also analytical questions about how to understand institutions. March and Olsen (1989), for example, conceptualize institutions as sets of norms and 'logics of appropriateness' that provide guidance for policy-makers. In such a view, attempts to exert governance can be understood only through the logics being utilized, and therefore to some extent through regimes' norms. On the other hand, rational choice institutionalists (see below; also Shepsle and Weingast, 1995) would argue that governing involves the manipulation of incentives for the participants, and if those are adjusted properly governing becomes a relatively simple exercise. Historical institutionalists (Thelen, Longstreth and Steinmo, 1992) would view governing as path-dependent, so that programmes that have worked in the past would be likely to continue to be successful in the future: governance is largely inertial (see also Rose and Karran, 1994).

Another institutional question arises in relation to the civil society literature discussed above. This question is whether the best strategy for individuals or groups attempting to improve the governance capacity of their regimes is to build civil society or to construct the institutions of governance. The institutionalist answer is, of course, that the more effective course of action is to emphasize building the institutional structures needed for governance. This choice does not necessarily deny that civil society may be important for governance; it only argues that the more effective strategy for producing change in governance is to build the institutions first. This strategy is likely to be effective if for no other reason than that institutions are probably more malleable than is society. We know that institutions do have a number of defences to resist change. However, they can be altered structurally rather easily by political leaders (Pollitt, 1984), and function may follow form after those structural changes. Further, societies may have even more defences to change being imposed from outside.

Rational choice

Rational choice theory based on the utilitarian logic of economics has become an important, if not dominant, approach for the social sciences (Dowding and King, 1995; Tsebelis, 1990). What does this approach say about governance? One answer can be taken from principal–agent views of public bureaucracy (Horn, 1995; Wood and Waterman, 1994). This becomes in some ways another way of stating the traditional, top-down view of governance in that the assumption is that a principal – for example, a political executive of some sort – is attempting to control his or her agents through contracts or other arrangements. These agents – usually agencies or individual bureaucrats – have incentives to pursue their own goals and to 'shirk' control from the principals.

The linkage of rational choice to authoritative management of the state should be obvious. The assumption behind that linkage is that the principals represent the legitimate policies of the government and therefore any shirking by the agents is a deviation from those legitimate wishes. Again, this perspective is very similar to the implementation literature in that it begins the analysis with the policy intentions formulated at the centre of government and then proceeds to identify deviations from those intentions. The difference from implementation analysis is that there is an assumption of some sort of contractual relationship existing among the parties. Further, there is an assumption that the selection of the correct set of economic incentives is capable of making the relationship function effectively.

Networks and policy communities

A major alternative to the top-down conception of governance is one that emphasizes the interactions among different groups in society with government, or even without direct government involvement. This set of ideas is variously labelled 'modern governance' (Kooiman, 1993) or 'new governance' (Rhodes, 1997; see Demers, 1998). In this view governance is an emergent property of interactions rather than the imposition of control from above. The argument is often extended to imply that any attempts on the part of government to impose its authority will be met with resistance and evasion, and further that this evasion is likely to be successful (in 't Veld, 1993). Society is presumed to be capable of self-organization to avoid the attempts of government to impose its own organizational imperatives on society.

The changing nature of the state and of the management of public sector activities lends a great deal of credence to this approach. Governments may not have moved completely from 'hubris to helplessness' (Downs and Larkey, 1986) but there is certainly some loss of self-confidence, and a much greater loss of public confidence (Nye, Zelikow and King, 1997). They are less likely to believe that they are capable of doing everything that needs to be done to govern effectively. Governments have increased their use of partnerships and a variety of other relationships with the private sector for the delivery of public services, so that the sense of top-down authority exercised through state actors has been diminished or lost. They also have become more active in seeking out advice and in consulting widely with societal groups before acting.

This conception of governance may be applicable to a number of settings, but there are differences across policy areas and across countries in the extent to which government has altered its role in the process of governance. Some policy areas have extensive networks that do indeed contribute to the process of governing and that can supplement, if not supplant, the authoritative actions of governments. It should be remembered, however, that often these networks are composed of other levels of government, or quasi-government actors, so government may not be out of the picture entirely. Other policy areas, however, remain very much the domain of government itself: despite external concerns monetary and fiscal policy remain largely governmental. Similarly, some political systems, for example, the Low Countries and Scandinavia, have well-developed interest-group structures with long-standing cooperative relationships with government while in others interest groups are still regarded with some scepticism.

Neo-Marxism and critical theory

Finally, neo-Marxist theory also contains a view on governance. As noted above, some of this perspective arises from traditional Marxist conceptions of the need for a strong state to counteract the power of capitalist, imperialist states. Neo-Marxist theory is somewhat ambiguous over the role of the power of the state in governing, but there is some sense that the function of the state is to govern. Central to conceptualizing the role of government in this body of literature is the 'legitimacy crisis of late capitalism', and the extent to which the presumed reduction of legitimacy minimizes governance capacity.

The basic argument of this approach is that the capitalist state has been constructed around the need to facilitate the accumulation of capital and the associated need to legitimate that action. The welfare state was seen as a means of building that legitimacy through public expenditure. The capitalist economy tends to produce significant inequalities in income and life chances, so the welfare state was developed to raise the level of living of the lowest groups in society sufficiently so that they would not challenge the continuation or appropriateness of capitalism.

The literature on the crisis of the state argues that the loss of legitimacy in capitalist economies and the consequent loss of governing capacity have resulted from strains on the spending capacity of government and that this financial constraint will lead to the downfall of those systems (O'Connor, 1973). While some of the Marxist rhetoric in this literature now appears quaint after the fall of the Soviet Union, the basic logic of government's capacity to govern being dependent upon its ability to legitimate its existence is basic to the governance process. Interestingly, neo-Marxist and Conservative analysts have both stressed the role of high taxes, and popular reactions to those taxes, as a major part of the process of delegitimating the political system.

Nation states embedded and embedding

If we now return to the role of nation states and their formal government structures in the process of governing, we can see that nation states constitute important linking structures. On the one hand the nation state is embedded in a number of aspects of the international economic and political systems, and is an actor in many of the interactions in those systems. On the other hand, any number of actors, governmental and non-governmental, are embedded in the national government and derive some of their power and meaning from that relationship. The state serves as a means of protecting sub-state actors such as firms from the power of international systems and at the same time attempts to press the demands of those actors on that system.

Peter Evans (1995) has advanced the argument that nation states are embedded in the international system. He was making that argument primarily with reference to the newly industrializing countries (NICs), the economies of which depend upon the international market perhaps more than other countries. The international market has provided viable niches for these countries, and to some extent the substantial power of these national governments is a function of the role that they play in the world economic system. Without that economic role the political role, and especially the relatively authoritarian nature of many of the regimes, might not be understandable. Further, the role that government plays tends to strengthen their governance capacity, rather than weaken it as some globalization scholars tend to argue.

The relationship between economic and political factors for governments in the NICs is a chicken-and-egg problem to some extent. That is, strong governments have been important for economic management and development, and at the same time the effectiveness of the economies has strengthened the governments. That having been said, however, the most important point for governance theory is that a substantial exposure of a country to the international market-place does not inherently produce weaker governments. Rather, there can be cases in which governments can, and indeed must, develop greater capacity in order to cope with those market forces.

On the other hand, governments and their policies also create the niches for a number of domestic groups, and even subnational governments, to exert their influence on a wider canvas. In governance terms the embedding of these groups in the state at once constrains and empowers the state. On the one hand these actors require governments to play 'two-level games' (Putnam, 1988) in international politics. They cannot negotiate international agreements autonomously but must always be thinking of the reaction of domestic political forces. On the other hand, if these groups can be brought on board their support empowers governments in international organizations. For example, having labour unions and human rights organizations supporting governments in European countries directly involved in questions of child labour in poorer countries lets the target countries know that, even if the state is not a unitary actor, in this debate at least some parts of the public are involved in the issue and can be relied upon to support the government.

As with the international dimension of governance, there is not necessarily a zero-sum game here. Government and the interest groups can be in conflict, but they can also work in a positive-sum, cooperative manner to achieve common purposes. To some extent the possibility of creating such cooperative arrangements depends upon the pattern of interaction between state and society, with corporatist and corporate pluralist arrangements being more conducive to those relationships than are pluralist interactions. This possibility for stable and cooperative interactions also depends in part upon general cultural elements, as well as the extent to which steering from the centre of government remains an acceptable activity.

From government to governance: institutions and governance

The emerging governance relationships between state and society present a rather fundamental paradox, and that in turn presents real questions for those who would attempt to manage these relationships. On the one hand the public appears still to demand that government exert some control over the process and outcomes of governing. Government is still about governing, at least in the minds of most of the public, so that any government that appears weak or indecisive may be punished by the public – the difference between the Thatcher and Major styles of governing may be instructive in this regard.

On the other hand, the public also appears to resist control from government. This resistance need not be just the rather negative conception of evasion and overt resistance found in some of the literature discussing autopoesis and the 'decentred' style of governing. It also can be more positive statements about the role of the public as a source of policy ideas and the need for broader citizen engagement in making policy. If anything, the 1990s have been a period in which the reform of the public sector, as well as being driven by market ideas, has been directed towards opening government to greater participation by the public. This has not necessarily meant that society has been put in charge of governing. It does mean, however, that there is demand for real influence.

The creation of a more participatory style of governing does not mean that government is in reality less powerful. It does mean, however, that state and society are bonded together in the process of creating governance. If anything, the state actually may be strengthened through its interactions with society. The state may have to abdicate some aspects of its nominal control over policy, especially at the formulation stage of the process. On the other hand, it tends to gain substantial control at the implementation stage by having in essence coopted social interests that might otherwise oppose its actions. The ultimate effect may be to create a government that understands better the limits of its actions and which can work effectively within those parameters.

3

Why the Concern with Governance Now?

Governance has become a political catchword during the 1990s. Practicians and political scientists alike in a number of subfields and political–administrative contexts have embraced the idea of governance as a new way of thinking about state capabilities and state–society relationships. Together with the IMF and the World Bank, the United Nations has initiated a large-scale campaign promoting 'good governance' as the new reform objective in the Third World (Leftwich, 1994; Peters, 1998a). In the urban politics field the British Economic and Social Research Council (ESRC) launched an extensive research programme on 'local governance' (see, for example, Stoker, 1998a). In policy analysis, much of the previously dominant literature on policy networks has been reformulated and reinterpreted into a governance framework (Rhodes, 1997). A great deal of recent EU-focused research has also been shaped by theories of governance or multi-level governance owing to the negotiated nature of the relationship between local, regional, national and transnational institutions. Furthermore, in international relations, there has been a rapidly growing interest in 'global governance' (Rosenau and Czempiel, 1992; Rosenau, 2000). In political economy, finally, public–private exchange has become conceived of as 'governance' and numerous studies drawing on extensive research projects have investigated the role of government in coordinating sectors of the economy.

We will look more closely at how governance plays out in these different analytical contexts in the next chapter. Here, our principal concern is what has caused this fairly sudden fascination with the concept of governance, or with governance as a reform objective. More specifically, we discuss different explanations of why governance has gained such widespread attention at this time. In addition to the perennial changes in academic fads and fashions political scientists have for some time been searching for theories that capture significant changes in the state's environment and the state's response to these changes. That said, our concern here is not so much the academic developments as what changes in the state and society could have contributed to the growing interest in governance. Thus, we believe that this interest is much more a reflection of the changing condition of contemporary states and societies than merely a changing fad among social scientists. This does appear to be a case of art imitating life.

To some extent, the emerging theories of governance are a reconceptualization of a phenomenon which is as old as government itself; the pursuit of collective interests through political institutions but also through different arrangements which transcend the public (Maier, 1987). In the political science literature the same basic problem has been cast in different conceptual frameworks in different time periods. The general systems theory which dominated political science in the 1960s was primarily concerned with the decision-making process of the state but even so it had problems delineating what made the state 'authoritative' and what were the social and political underpinnings of authority (Easton, 1979). The 1970s saw an extensive debate on 'overloaded government' – incidentally a conceptual remnant from systems theory – and the 'ungovernability' of society (Scheuch, 1976; Crozier *et al.*, 1975). The 1980s, finally, were characterized primarily by a recurrent interest in the state, only to find that properly understanding stateness and state capabilities is to a large extent a matter of understanding how the state manages its exchange with its environment. Thus, the state could not be understood without understanding its political economy and its civil society.

The recent debate on governance, and the present analysis in particular, draws on all of these previous discourses to the extent that we are putting the state at the centre of our analysis in order to understand what changes in the state have triggered the need for developing new forms of governance. However, as should be clear to the reader, we also acknowledge that governance has become important due to changes in society, too, and that the new governance is a strategy to link the contemporary state to the contemporary society. In that respect, the current thinking about governance is distinctly different from previous conceptualizations of the state and state–society relationships.

The financial crisis of the state

Perhaps more than anything else, the emergence of the new governance has been propelled by the decline in state capabilities, particularly its financial resources, during the 1980s and 1990s (Damgaard *et al.*, 1989). Comparing the economic condition of western states in the 1960s and 1970s with that of the 1990s the difference is truly astounding (Rockman, 1998). In the 1960s, most of the Western European governments enjoyed relatively stable economic growth which generated growing tax revenues. There was also, generally speaking, believed to be room for further tax increases to finance the growing number of commitments of the state and local governments. True, the economic situation was not altogether rosy throughout the western world – the British government had to negotiate an IMF loan in the wake of the collapse of sterling in 1976 (Gamble, 1994:174). There was, however, an apparent belief that the government exercised considerable control over the development of the economy.

Twenty years later, the same states were rapidly accumulating budget deficits and debts beyond political control. Economic growth had slowed and become uncertain, and indeed in some cases transformed into negative growth. Interest rates on the state debt alone had become an expenditure at the same level as that of core policy sectors such as education or defence in many countries. Also, a growing number of governments experienced crises sustaining the value of their currency. Most of these were the less developed countries, but even some wealthy countries experienced these problems, perhaps most notably the Japanese government in the late 1990s (Cargill, Hutchison and Ito, 1997).

This is not the place to go into any deeper discussion about the roots and causes of this financial crisis. We will only discuss two of what appear to have been among the more important causes of the economic plight of most western states and which also highlight governments' difficulties with governing their economy. The first major source of the economic crisis was the automatic increase in public expenditures. Many state service programmes have had their expenditure levels more or less automatically adjusted for inflation. The same mechanism has often been used for public sector employees' salaries. Abolishing programmes altogether has only rarely been a political option because of powerful opposition from constituencies and the bureaucracy.

It has become painfully obvious to western governments how much of their public expenditure is 'structural', that is, not politically or otherwise manageable in the short term. Instead, most states have conducted a slow and incremental restructuring of the state expenditure. This economic restructuring has been exceedingly expensive to the state; programmes which the state can no longer sustain have been financed with borrowed money, something which has quickly driven a staggering deficit. This problematic appears to have been most noticeable for traditional welfare states such as the Scandinavian countries, the Netherlands and Belgium. However, the United States also generated a massive budget deficit during the 1970s and 1980s with a mixture of high defence expenditures and a modest but expanding welfare state (Kettl, 1992).

The second overarching explanation of the fiscal crisis of the state which is relevant in the present context is failing or stalling state revenues. By the 1970s taxes in many countries had reached a level beyond which they could not be raised further. Growing political protest, increasing incentives for tax evasion and impaired economic growth all seemed to prohibit further tax increases (Peters, 1992). During the 1950s and 1960s many governments diversified their revenue system by introducing taxes on general consumption – the value-added tax. But not even those strategies could conceal the fact that the overall tax level was reaching its effective maximum. Going beyond that level would probably be counter-productive, with the flight of capital and increased citizen incentives to avoid and evade taxation.

The management of the financial crisis of the state has highlighted the tremendous inertia associated with changing both revenue structures and expenditures. Another component of this problem has been the waning political support; the public's reluctance towards further tax rises is surpassed only by its resistance to cut-backs in public spending. In a governance perspective, we see governments essentially unable to transform the economy; expenditure patterns are politically sensitive and administratively 'locked in' while taxes and other revenues must be handled with great political caution. Governments have not been totally inert. They have found that consumption taxes provoke less resistance than do income taxes, and they have also found that fees and taxes linked to specific expenditures are palatable to the public, but the state still encounters public scepticism about raising revenue.

In this perspective it is little surprise that the economic crisis has encouraged the development of new instruments of governance. Governance has become an attractive philosophy and political strategy for three main reasons. First of all, by involving private actors and organized interests in public service delivery activities, governments (state and subnational) have attempted to maintain their service levels even while under severe budgetary constraints. This has been the case in different areas of public social care as well as within the culture and leisure sectors.

The second aspect of governance which explains its increasing popularity in times of budgetary constraints lies in its participatory nature, especially the inclusion of private sector actors and management thinking into the public sector. By blurring the public–private distinction, the state's problems in managing its affairs are portrayed more as a matter of the tasks and challenges the state is facing rather than a consequence of poor public management. Governance, in this perspective, is used 'to provide the acceptable face of spending cuts' (Stoker, 1998b:39).

The third factor, finally, relates to the legitimacy of public service production and delivery which has come under attack during the economic crisis of the state. In an era when 'government' has increasingly become equated with slow bureaucracy and a collectivist political thinking, incorporating private sector management thinking and diversifying public service delivery have emerged as an attractive strategy. Also, the notion of the state operating in concert with societal actors, instead of imposing its will on them, corresponds well with the political *esprit du temps* of the market-oriented 1990s.

The economic crisis has forced the state to become less self-reliant and more inclined to operate through networks and other forms of public–private joint action. Unable to provide the financial and organizational resources necessary to sustain the previous level of public services, the state now seeks to play a coordinating role, bringing together public and private resources at little direct cost to the public budget. The crisis has also had a profound effect on the design of the public service: there is now much more emphasis on consumer choice and diversification. Finally, we also need to think about administrative and institutional reform in this context (Peters and Savoie, 1998). The overall transformation of the public sector since the 1980s is the combined effect of a development towards governance, a redesign of public services and administrative reform to accompany those changes.

The ideological shift towards the market

The second set of explanations for the growing interest in governance is the shift from a collectivist to an individualistic political culture, or, more generally, an ideological shift from politics towards the market. This shift has been noticeable throughout the western world – and indeed also in former Eastern Europe – but has been most prominent in the Anglo-Saxon countries. The Reagan and Thatcher administrations in the 1980s that capitalized on and strengthened this rejection of the state and politics as a vehicle for change heralded the market and portrayed the government not as a solution to societal problems but rather as a problem in itself.

It is important not to equate this political philosophy with other political sentiments on the right side of the political spectrum. Xenophobic or populist parties are much less constructive and coherent in their critique of the established parties. For Thatcher and Reagan there was – with significant variations in details – a fairly clear diagnosis of where the problems were located and how they should be attacked (see Savoie, 1994). For Reagan, the federal bureaucracy was an overregulated, and overregulating, body impairing or obstructing economic growth. Mrs Thatcher shared Reagan's belief that economic prosperity was hampered by too much political control and regulation of markets. For both, unleashing the market was an overarching political goal. Conventional government had had its proverbial day in the sun but had, in their view, proved incapable of resolving the problems it was supposed to solve.

Mrs Thatcher and Ronald Reagan obviously did not initiate the ideological shift towards the market but rather capitalized on and sustained that movement. Their political mission was a drastic reduction of the political sphere in society. Certainly, throughout the period after the Second World War, private businesses have put forward similar demands (Wilson, 1990). The difference was that now the market advocates had conquered 10 Downing Street and the White House. If the political style did not change as a result of outside pressures it should change from within.

As was the case with the discussion earlier about the economic crisis of the state, we are not interested in what drove this development but rather primarily with how it came to enhance the collective interest in new forms of governance. The ideological shift towards individualism and the market posed a major challenge to the state. The state is the epitome of the collective interest and is built on the normative image of collective action as the superior model of defining the goals of societal transformation. The ideological shift during the 1980s essentially discounted and rejected this role of the state. Politics was not part of the solution but part of the problem. The support for collective action was eroding. The state somehow had to redefine its role in society if it were to maintain an effective role.

The notion of 'steering' in some ways squared the circle because it acknowledges that the state in itself is not the source of economic dynamics and growth at the same time as it maintains that political institutions are the only actors who can define goals and make priorities on behalf of the polity. 'Steering' entails a redefinition of both the state and elective office. Political leadership in this perspective operates at arm's length from the 'operative' elements of the public sector. 'Steering' also implies concerted public–private action instead of an adversarial relationship between the state and private business; indeed, conflict, in the *Zeitgeist* of the 1980s and 1990s, is typical to politics and (hence) counter-productive and unpopular. It is interesting to note that there is very little in the governance literature which points at the democratic problems associated with the state's moving closer to private capital; two decades ago such suggestions would have triggered a massive critique from the political left.

Globalization

With only slight exaggeration, globalization has become the leading social science mantra in the 1990s and is used to account for almost all changes in Western European and North American politics. Thus globalization purportedly explains tax cuts and the abolition of welfare state programmes, persistent high unemployment, political inability to control private capital, growing problems with international crime, and so on. Globalization has become a catchword for almost all types of international impositions on national sovereignty, be they political or economic, bilateral or multilateral, or driven by the state itself or by 'the market'. The tenor of the debate on globalization has been largely to bemoan globalization, arguing that it undercuts national political control and sovereignty (the tacit assumption being that states were 'sovereign' before globalization began); that domestic institutions can no longer exercise control over financial markets (the tacit assumption being that states exercised effective control over the economy prior to globalization): and that states are invariably forced into a 'race to the bottom', that is, a competition for private investment that dictates tax cuts and drastic cut-backs in public spending (the tacit assumption being that states did not compete with each other for private investment before globalization (see Martin, 1996; see also Vogel, 1995).

The initial literature on globalization painted a bleak and depressing picture of the future of the nation state and the options for autonomous domestic policy choice (Boyer and Drache, 1996; Camilleri and Falk, 1992; Moses, 1994). Later accounts have tended to question both the actual extent of globalization and actual change (Hirst and Thompson, 1996; Scott, 1997) as well as its consequences on the state (Evans, 1997). As a result, we are left with a fairly confusing, and sometimes even contradictory, account of globalization according to which the extent of change in much of the debate is exaggerated but at the same time there is sufficient change for states and social scientists to address its consequences. We also seem to be moving towards a more empirically and less normatively based debate on globalization; while the normative side of these developments certainly needs to be debated it has been unfortunate that that debate has been conflated with the debate on how to interpret empirical indicators on globalization (Hinnfors and Pierre, 1998).

We do not disagree entirely with most of the empirical assessments of globalization. Instead, our argument is that before we can pass judgement on the actual extent of globalization and its reverberations on the state we first need to elaborate on the different dimensions of globalization and, second, to examine these changes in a dynamic perspective. It would be naive to assume that states simply surrender to globalization; nation states have faced challenges not too different from globalization in the past and have proved quite resilient and capable of responding and adapting themselves to changes in their external environments (Navari, 1991). There is nothing in the present situation to suggest that states should be less adaptive to globalization than they have been to previous challenges.

Globalization has two basic dimensions, an economic and a political one. The two dimensions are closely intertwined: economic globalization has been propelled by a series of political decisions aiming at deregulating (or 'unleashing') the economy in order to remove political obstacles to growth (Helleiner, 1994). Interestingly, while the United States and Britian were the key promoters of this deregulative regime, it soon became embraced by transnational institutions such as the EU as an integral element of the political and economic harmonization of the Community. Thus already at this stage not only the economic sphere but also the political were increasingly shaped at the transnational level.

More importantly in the present context, however, economic globalization has presented a series of challenges to national governments which have prompted a wide range of counter-measures to adapt institutions, economic policy and transnational cooperation in relation to the new situation. Thus the political and economic aspects of globalization are to a significant extent each other's causes and effects. As a number of observers have noted, nation states led the deregulation and subsequent globalization of private capital and nation states retain the leverage to reverse this process (Helleiner, 1994; Peters, 1997a). True, not everyone subscribes to this proposition (see, for example, Moses, 1994) but even so we maintain that it would be premature to dismiss the significance of nation states in the governance of the economy.

Globalization has certainly had a wide range of direct and indirect consequences on government's traditional ability to steer society and the economy. Some of these have been fairly direct, knock-on effects, such as the transfer of authority from domestic institutions to international bodies such as the EU, the WTO, and to some extent to NAFTA. Other effects have been more indirect but no less powerful in the longer term, such as the transnational harmonization of regulations, taxes and social policies as is currently evolving in the EU. However, state responses to these effects have to a considerable degree aimed at not just ameliorating and mitigating the effects of globalization but also developing and strengthening transnational institutions through which states in concert pursue their interests *vis-à-vis* global capital. Many observers tend to forget that globalization has several positive components, too, from the point of view of the state and its capacity to exercise steering and control in the economy.

There are two issues which need to be sorted out here. First, how can we relate the growing interest in emerging models of governance to globalization? What are the linkages between these two almost parallel politico-economic developments? Second, is governance just the state's desperate attempt to reassert its few remaining sources of political control or, conversely, could new forms of governance be conceptualized as a set of strategies among and within states to adapt to the globalization of private capital?

We will answer these two questions in one and the same context because they refer very much to the same issues. There are several close linkages between globalization and governance (Peters, 1997a). One is related to the search for new techniques and strategies to create a political counterweight to private capital, not least the deregulated and volatile currency and financial markets. The growing leverage of transnational institutions such as those of the European Union or the WTO – which will be discussed in more detail in the next chapter – are manifestations of these strategies. Another linkage between globalization and governance refers to the changing preconditions for domestic policy choice. Globalization has also introduced a new element of uncertainty in domestic policy-making and for the civil service which makes these institutions more dependent on domestic and international expertise. One of the key roles for transnational institutions such as the EU and the OECD is to provide such expertise.

A third linkage between globalization and transnational governance is associated with the decreasing efficiency of traditional domestic instruments of control such as law and regulation. Corporate actors are, for reasons which space prevents us from elaborating, becoming less attached to a given locality. While there is a tendency to exaggerate the volatility of private businesses (Hirst and Thompson, 1996), it remains true that much of the contemporary industry has less interest in the locale where they are based compared to most previous industrial activity that tended to exploit natural resources such as the steel and mining industries. The increasing integration of the EU also lowers the threshold for companies to relocate. This means that governments tend to be more careful in using legal enforcement towards major corporate players and instead seek to influence them through more subtle, perhaps even cooperative, strategies.

This downplaying of traditional models of governance, such as law and formal political authority, is not just the result of the increasing mobility of major corporate players; those actors represent a relatively minor fraction of all private businesses in any given country. The need to develop closer but informal links with private industry is also driven by a strategy to manitain or increase the international competitiveness of the domestic industry, something which is in the immediate interest of both government and industry. Such competitiveness seems to a great extent to be contingent on integrated public and private strategies and actions where the public sector ensures that modern infrastructure and high-quality education are provided (Porter, 1990).

Globalization has clearly encouraged the development of transnational institutions for new forms of governance. However, it has also propelled a similar search for less complying and more negotiated forms of public–private exchanges in the domestic economy. Domestic institutions have less leverage over private capital in the 1990s compared to a couple of decades ago but it would be misleading to say that they are deprived all leverage over corporate actors. Some form of interdependence between the political and corporate sectors is still very much the case, not least because corporate development is contingent on policies and programmes which only the government can provide. Shared dependencies often tend to lead to shared powers and responsibilities. Therefore, it is difficult to say anything definite about the impact of globalization on domestic public–corporate partnerships because globalization entails both forces bringing these actors closer together and forces pulling them apart. Again, it is important to recognize both sides of the argument and not to rush into simplifying conclusions about the impact of globalization on the domestic political economy.

Failure of the state

A fourth explanation for the emergence of new governance stems from an assessment of the performance of the state over the 1980s and 1990s. Interestingly, in all major ideological perspectives the performance of the state during the period after the Second World War has been more or less disappointing. For Conservatives, the postwar period has witnessed an unprecedented expansion of the public sphere in society, with dramatically raised taxes and a redistribution of wealth through public policies. There has also been a socialization of functions which previously were managed by the family or the 'third sector' such as care of children and the elderly as well as a more general political encroachment of the family and the private sphere. 'Big Government' has been the topic of heated argument not just in the United States – where, ironically, the size of the public sector does not come near to that of most European countries – but also in most of Western Europe.

Most Liberals seem to be equally disappointed with the performance of the state. Some Liberals share the Conservative concern with the rapid growth of government. Others, with a more social–liberal political view, seem to be pleased with the expansion of public services at the same time as they share the Conservative critique against high taxes. Social Democrats in many Western European countries, finally, can rejoice at the advancements of the welfare state and the redistribution of wealth and prosperity. At the same time, however, many core policy goals of these parties such as equality, equity and equal opportunity have not been achieved. Further, critics on the left complain about the bureaucratization of the state and its failure to treat citizens more humanely.

The differences in how different ideological orientations perceive the performance of the state suggest that success or failure is to some extent in the eye of the beholder. However, we should also review the performance of the state on a level above and beyond different ideological or partisan perspectives. Most western democracies seem to share a dilemma between expectations among voters, elected officials and civil servants on the state as a vehicle for the transformation of society on the one hand and the limited governing capacity of the state on the other. Much of the postwar political *Zeitgeist* portrayed the state as a powerful set of structures and the undisputed locus of power and leader in the transformation of society (see Chapter 4). In the United States, notions of 'The Great Society' and 'War on Poverty' were predicated on this image of a strong government. In Britain and France – both countries with traditional 'strong' states and and an *étatiste* political and administrative culture – there was a similar strong belief in government, not least with regard to its role in the economy. In Austria, the Netherlands and the Scandinavian countries, government – frequently in concert with organized interests – assumed responsibility for the well-being of its citizens from the cradle to the grave.

Thus, the image of the strong state and the resulting high expectations of its capabilities were largely constructed by the state itself. The postwar trajectory in these respects did not represent a new path but should be seen more as a logical development of the state's role and responsibilities. State–society relationships were never significantly altered in these countries: the state did more but the bulk of economic activity and the vast majority of social activity remained private. These were mixed economies, with the mix generally remaining in favour of the private.

But the fiscal crisis of the state and growing popular frustration with 'big government' changed much of this. Voters supported parties promising tax cuts and more individual freedom; indeed, in many countries parties advocating more or less extreme but unspecified 'change' such as the 'Progress' parties in Denmark and Norway, the D66 in the Netherlands, the Austrian Freedom Party or why not Ross Perot in the United States became popular, in some cases almost overnight. What British observers tend to refer to as the postwar 'settlement' or 'consensus' came to an abrupt end as Mrs Thatcher challenged most established power relations in British politics and the economy (Kavanagh and Morris, 1994). The state was now seen as excessively big and expensive yet incapable of delivering appropriate services. There was a clear notion that the state somehow had failed: it had failed to live up to the expectations put upon it, it had failed to attain any of the ideological goals endorsed by different constituencies, and it had failed even by its own standards and idealized model to 'govern' society and the economy. Instead, it had become increasingly obvious how contingent the state was on the economy and actors in the markets, or on civil society and organized interests which, for widely different reasons, withdrew some of their involvement in the political process, as was the case with the 'depillarization' (Mierlo, 1986) in the Netherlands or the collapse of much of the corporatist arrangements in Sweden (Christensen, 1997).

Some of these failures are real, others are perceived. Most of them are derived from overly optimistic views about what the state can do. In order to be able to take this discussion further, we need a definition of 'failure' or some kind of benchmark against which we can assess the state's peerformance. An important element of such a benchmark should be the aspirations and goals of public policy. This is clearly not the time or place to go into a detailed analysis of policies in different national contexts. However, a common denominator across Western Europe is that public policy is based on a social constructionist theory with two key postulates. One postulate is that public policy is an appropriate instrument to resolve societal problems, or, slightly differently put, that government intervention can be designed in such a way that public policy can solve problems efficiently and without causing new problems in the process. Much of the recent policy analysis and research on public policy has called the validity of this postulate into serious question (Pressman and Wildavsky, 1973; Wildavsky, 1979; Cohen *et al.*, 1972).

The second postulate in this constructionist theory holds that the state controls the formal and legal powers, capabilities and knowledge required to play an intervening role in society. Even a quick glance at that statement suggests that public policy based on such a theory is not very likely to be successful. Much of the history of western democracies during the twentieth century highlights the plights of democratic government embedded in a capitalist economy in terms of governability and devising efficient control instruments. More recently, the globalization of the economy has exacerbated these problems further. Thus, using the state itself and its theories of social and political change, it becomes clear that the state has helped produce some of the failures with which it has recently been charged.

The new governance is in many ways a logical response to this critique of the state. The emphasis on public–private sharing of functions and joint mobilization of resources is one means of reducing the specificity of the state within society and, indirectly, to suggest that states are not as powerful and resourceful as the general expectations on it assume. The collective problems have not disappeared but government has, to a greater or smaller extent, proved unable to resolve them, hence the need to explore other solutions.

Furthermore, the emphasis in the new governance on market-based concepts (see more below) is not just a consequence of the fiscal problems of the state but rather could also be seen as a strategy to incorporate dominant values and norms in society.

Emergence of the New Public Management

A fifth explanation for the increasing interest in governance is the 'managerial revolution' in public service production and delivery in some countries summarized under the heading 'New Public Management' (NPM). The overall philosophy of this market-based reform of the public service has been described extensively else-where (Hood, 1991; Pollitt, 1990, Peters, 1996) so we will only focus on some specific aspect of the New Public Management in the present context.

The New Public Management approach to public service produc-tion and delivery runs counter to the bureaucratic tradition in most of the western world. It rejects the idea of a specific culture for public organizations and typically argues that such organizations should be managed in the same way as any private sector organiza-tion. Indeed, NPM advocates such as Osborne and Gaebler (1992; see also DiIulio, 1994) argue that the inertia and rigidity tradition-ally characterizing the public sector are largely attributable to the alleged specificity of the public sector.

The emergence of the NPM has propelled the new governance in two different ways. First, it presupposes that the state renounces some direct control over its organization. By 'letting the managers manage' the NPM accords a more peripheral role to elected officials compared to the traditional system of government. Politicians are left primarily with a goal-setting role, something which corresponds closely with the new governance thinking. Service production and delivery in the public sector should be conducted in as market-like a fashion as possible and at arm's length from the political elite. This arrangement will ensure increased efficiency and lower costs, the argument goes.

Second, New Public Management advocates less input control but more emphasis on evaluation and performance. This, in turn, requires different organizational models and interactions compared to the previous model of public administration. More importantly, since the criteria used in the evaluations normally are derived from private sector organizations more than from bureaucratic theory, this represents yet another blow to the claims for a political and cultural specificity of the public sector.

New Public Management and the new governance share some similarities but they also differ in many important respects (Peters and Pierre, 1998). The key similarity between the two philosophies is the argument that formal–legal state strength is becoming less and less important and that more or less temporary institutional arrangements across the public–private border provide institutional leverage and coordination. Perhaps the most important difference between New Public Management and the new governance lies in their different conceptualizations of the state. NPM is quite dismissive of the role of the state; to be sure, this model sees the state – at least in terms of a service provider – as more or less obsolete. Most – but not all – scholars in the governance field, on the other hand, take a much more positive view of the state as the epitome of the collective interest and its role in facilitating and coordinating governance. However, there is some kinship between the two perspectives and it appears clear that the recent interest in governance has, in part, been triggered by the increasing popularity of New Public Management and the idea of some generic forms of societal control.

Social change and increasing complexities

The sixth set of explanations for the current interest in governance has to do with the changing nature of the most salient issues in contemporary politics in Western Europe and the United States. It seems as if politics in these parts of the world have reached the 'third wave' in terms of which policy areas have dominated public policy. The first 'wave' was dominated by developing the institutional framework for political debate and the consolidation of political democracy, including parliamentary reform, extending the suffrage, and so on. In the second 'wave', the political elites were mainly concerned with distributive and redistributive political issues, including tax policy, health policy, social policy, and so on. In the current third 'wave', what are often referred to as 'postmaterial' issues play if not a dominating role – economic issues are still much to the fore in most western democracies – at least a very important role (Dalton, 1996; Inglehart, 1991).

The 'third wave' type of issues reflects contemporary social change, broadly defined, and includes issues like enhanced participation, environmental protection and gender issues. Some of these issues, such as gender politics, can be addressed in a national political context whereas others, such as environmental protection, need to be attacked domestically as well as internationally. Moreover, both sets of issues contain relatively new types of social change and social complexities which, in turn, present a new type of challenge to the government. Gender issues are played out on almost all levels of government, ranging from the intra-organizational level to the societal level. More importantly, an important component of managing these issues is not so much devising new policy instruments and institutional arrangements (although that certainly is a major challenge in itself) but more a matter of imposing or strengthening a new set of values on the governmental apparatus and society at large.

These increasing complexities also require new sources of expertise, something which makes government more dependent on external sources of knowledge. The new governance could be seen as a way for the state to develop more continuous exchanges with such sources of expertise and knowledge. There is a similar interest among those societal actors (for example, organizations in the environmental field or groups promoting gender issues) to move closer to the state because it gives them access to policy-makers and the civil service. Indeed, some critics argue that these groups have moved *too* close to the state and have been coopted by access to policy-making and even by funds to continue their activities.

New sources of governance

The seventh explanation for the current interest in governance relates to the growing importance of new sources of regional and international (or global) governance. As argued in the introductory chapter, the growing strength of regional organizations like the EU and international organizations such as the WTO and IMF is one of the most significant institutional developments in the postwar period. In the next chapter we will look more closely at these institutions and what appear to be the main drivers of their increasing strength and leverage. In the present analysis, we should note that these emerging institutions have propelled social scientists to look more conceptually at how regional and international institutions relate to states and sometimes also to subnational governments. Much of this analysis is cast in terms of governance, or multi-level governance. We do not yet have a good conceptual framework for such models of governance although much research is under way.

Legacy of traditional political accountability

The eighth and final cluster of reasons why governance has become so much debated recently is the apparent tension between these new forms of political coordination and steering on the one hand and a powerful legacy of channels and instruments for political accountability on the other. Democratic theory posits that power and accountability must rest with the same actors in order for some form of electoral control to be real and meaningful. Governance to some extent confuses that linkage by inviting non-accountable actors into the political process. Even if there is a clear intention to maintain lines of accountability, the complexity of the emerging relationships between the public and private sectors may make it difficult for the average citizen to understand how accountability functions.

The problem is not quite as novel as it might seem. In corporatist systems of interest representation the dilemma of organizations' influence over public policy for which they cannot be held to account is very familiar, indeed. But the new governance presents a slightly more complicated situation. In modern society, government is still responsible yet at the same time it is less capable of acting alone. Interestingly, the New Public Management, which displaces political power much more than the new governance does, has little difficulty in resolving these problems. In the New Public Management, citizens can exercise accountability through other channels than the traditional ones, for instance through consumer choice or 'stakeholderism'.

The shift towards governance: fifth element or fatal attraction?

We have now briefly identified what seem to have been the most important explanations for the current interest in governance. Each of these trends and developments are long-term, gradual shifts which over time have amounted into profound value changes in society. In closing we should therefore ask two general questions about the nature of these changes. First, how much of the current theories and practices of governance is 'hype' more than substance? Is governance merely a way of wrapping government in a new paper which is more palatable to the public, or does the idea represent something qualitatively new and different compared to western democratic government in the earlier parts of the twentieth century?

A common denominator in the discussion in this chapter about what has driven the increasing interest in governance is that the state no longer has a monopoly over the expertise nor over the economic or institutional resources necessary to govern. However, the state remains the key vehicle for the pursuit of the collective interest in society and what we are witnessing is a transformation of the state to fit the society of the late twentieth and early twenty-first century. Thus the new governance, we suggest, does indeed represent something new and different compared to traditional systems of government at the same time as the basic rationale or the *raison d'être* of the state – to promote and pursue the collective interest. The new governance, we reiterate, does not mean the end or decline of the state but the transformation and adaptation of the state to the society it is currently embedded in. In particular the state remains crucial as a goal-setting structure if not always as an implementing structure.

The second question refers to how many political and institutional bridges were actually burnt in the rush towards governance. If the state itself to a greater or smaller extent orchestrated the development towards governance, does that mean that it also has the capacity to reverse that trend and reclaim its traditional power bases, or is its traditional authority lost once and for all? The answer here is probably 'no' with the amendment that if we assume that states – like all organizations and systems – need to adapt to their environment then reversing the development towards governance, would really not make much sense since society is slowly developing towards a system which can only be governed through these emerging forms of steering, coordination and goal-setting which we call the new governance.

Regardless of our views on these issues, it is clear that different forms of governance are becoming increasingly important and prominent on different institutional levels. It is virtually impossible to make any clear generalizations about governance; it must always be contextualized and nuanced to be useful in describing particular settings. The next chapter looks more closely at how governance is played out in modern society locally, nationally and globally.

Part II

Models of Governance

Introduction

One of the interesting aspects of governance is how differently it manifests itself at the local, national and international levels and what different roles political institutions play in governance at these levels. These differences can to a large extent be attributed to the history and tradition of cooperative behaviour among key players. Thus most countries have a long history of different models of public–private concerted action at the local level whereas cooperative behaviour among states at the international level has often been more contested and difficult to attain. Additionally, governance is increasingly often portrayed as 'multi-level governance' where international, national and subnational processes of governance are interlinked in a negotiated fashion.

Chapter 4 discusses three different types of shifts in political power. First, power has been shifted downward in the political system, to regions and localities. Second, there has been a shift upward to transnational organizations such as the European Union and the World Trade Organization. Third, control has been shifted outward, towards institutions operating at arm's length from elected officials. These different displacements of control, which previously were exercised by the state, both represent new models of governance and have, in an indirect way, helped facilitate such governance.

Chapters 5–7 then outline three different scenarios with regard to the diffusion of political power and the growing importance of different models of governance. Chapter 5 describes a scenario in which the state reasserts control, reclaims displaced bases of control and once again takes a higher profile in society. Chapter 6 looks at what might appear to be the opposite development, that is, one in which the state lets other regimes and groups of actors such as subnational institutions or transnational organizations lead governance. However, given our belief that the state remains more powerful than is often assumed, we see these developments as changes allowed and sometimes even encouraged by the state rather than as indications of the decline of the state. In Chapter 7, we explore governance in the context of deliberative democracy and communitarianism. Here, what is basically at stake is governance with a minimum of involvement of political institutions. Instead, communitarianism and related philosophies argue that collective interests can be pursued directly by citizens involved in and committed to their community.

4

Governance at Three Levels

Governance, in different shapes and forms, is nowadays a common feature at all levels of government and to some extent also between institutions at these levels. In the global and international arenas, voluntary forms of state cooperation have traditionally been linked to national, collective goals of security (see Jervis, 1983). More recently, similar – if not more extensive and institutionalized – forms of transnational organization have emerged in response to the globalization of private capital. Regulating trade has long been a core area of states' international engagements. However, the reconstruction of GATT (General Agreement on Tariffs and Trade) into the WTO (World Trade Organization) as well as the consolidation of the EU and other transnational organizations such as ASEAN (Association of South East Asian Nations) and APEC (Asia–Pacific Economic Cooperation) all signalize a growing need among states to operate collectively in a wider range of issue areas than international security. These new issues which are subject to transnational governance are, for example, promoting common regional interests, addressing issues and problems which by their very nature are not confined to individual states such as environmental protection, and serving as a counterweight to global private capital (Gamble and Payne, 1996; Hoekman and Kostecki, 1995; Wallace, 1996).

Governance – or multi-level governance – also characterizes much of the decision-making within the European Union and the relationship between EU institutions and institutions in the member states (Marks *et al.*, 1996; Scharpf, 1997; Wallace, 1996). As is the case with other transnational arrangements of state-collaborative efforts, the (still) relative weakness of formal transnational institutions, coupled with the negotiated nature of the links between these institutions and domestic ones, necessitates other and less formal arrangements to promote collective interests and to resolve political problems in the absence of a single authority.

Governance at the level of the nation state has also become much more important over the past decade or so. The emergence of governance has been propelled by both endogenous and exogenous forces and developments. The combined effects of shrinking financial resources, growing opposition to taxes (coupled with global pressures to keep taxes at a modest level not to scare off foreign investment – see Boyer and Drache, 1996; Vogel, 1995), reduced control of elected officials over the public service, and devolution of institutional capacity to subnational government have induced the state to develop alternative instruments and channels for 'steering' society and for the production and delivery of its services.

If the state, in the 'reinventing government' language of Osborne and Gaebler (1992; see Peters, 1997b) is too weak to 'steer' and, by the same token, should not 'row', then what seem to remain for the state are essentially two critical roles. One role is setting goals and making priorities. The other remaining role for government in governance is achieving some degree of coordination of resources, drawn either from public and private sources or from institutions at different governmental levels, to support the pursuit of these goals. This strategy, in turn, is predicated on a certain degree of diffusion of power from the centre of the governmental apparatus to those institutions which relate directly to key actors in the surrounding society. Institutional changes such as the introduction of agencies and NGOs serve these objectives, as does decentralization (or 'empowerment') of lower echelons of government.

Finally, a key component of governance at the nation-state level is networks. The notion of informal public–private communication through which the state imposes its will on its external environment is essential to contemporary governance. However, networks sometimes become powerful enough to resist state influence (Marsh and Rhodes, 1992). The extent to which networks can be strategically employed by the state or, conversely, evolve as coalitions held together by resistance to pressures from state institutions depends on a number of contextual factors.

At the local level, finally, new forms of governance, manifested in a more inclusive and encompassing urban policy 'style' and more elaborate public–private networks and cooperation have emerged in the UK (King and Stoker, 1997; Stoker, 1999) as well as in most other European states (Le Galès, 1997). In some ways the kind of governance which is emerging at other institutional levels is no news for local governments where formal or informal coalitions between city hall and the local business community have been a predominant feature (Dahl, 1961; Stone, 1989). This tradition of public–private cooperation lends support to local democratic theory and the notion of politically and socially homogenous communities where pooling resources is a natural way of strengthening the community (Hill, 1974).

Institutional change is both a cause and effect of the development from reliance on formal–legal powers towards different forms of governance. We have already mentioned that governance has an important institutional aspect in so far as it requires some degree of decentralization to facilitate new and closer forms of public–private exchange. However, governance could also be seen as a response to previous institutional changes such as decentralization as well as spontaneous forms of institutional development as we have witnessed at the subnational level. A case in point is the increasing number of internationalization projects which clearly fall outside of their legal domain of functions but which have been considered instrumental in boosting the local economy.

This chapter looks at three different types of displacement of state power and control: upward, towards international actors and organizations; downward, towards regions, cities and communities; and outward, to institutions operating under considerable discretion from the state. These three types of shifts in institutional capacity are combinations of planned and spontaneous changes. Allowing for international institutions to gain importance, even making decisions which override nation-state authority, has been justified by the need for transnational cooperation to resolve contemporary policy problems. Similarly, decentralization has been a common reform throughout Western Europe and has served to enhance participation and variation in public services. In both cases, however, these planned changes trigger spontaneous institutional changes which could either extend beyond what the original reform aimed at or reduce the effects of the reform. While 'organizational memory' impairs the short-term effects of most institutional changes, the long-term effect may well be greater than intended since institutions tend to seek to expand their domain.

A key argument which will be elaborated later in this chapter is that the displacement of political control between different institutional levels is not necessarily a zero-sum game, that is, institutions at one level can have their influence increased without institutions at other levels necessarily seeing their control decreasing. There are many reasons why this is the case but the most important explanation is that by granting more powers and autonomy to, for instance, subnational governments, the state loses some of its control but not as much as subnational governments increase their control. Institutional empowerment is a dynamic, sometimes even a cumulative process; empowered local governments become more attractive to societal actors at the local level (Pierre, 1994) and this, in turn, enables local authorities to enter concerted, public–private governance projects. Through such projects, local governments enhance their effective leverage to a greater extent than the displacement of state power would suggest.

Thus, contrary to much of what has been written about the alleged 'decline of the state', the emergence of governance could well in fact increase public control over society instead of decreasing it. The main difference between the conventional, zero-sum-game view on these issues and the governance perspective lies ultimately in the conception of what constitutes political and institutional power and capability. In a legal, constitutional sense, all displacement of power is a zero-sum game; you can only increase one institution's power by taking that power from some other institution. But that conception of power looks only at the legal powers these institutions have *in relationship to each other* – as is the case in state–local relationships – and not at the capabilities these institutions will have (or be enabled to generate) in relation to other societal actors.

Obviously, these issues are central to theories of governance. Emerging forms of governance tend not to operate along traditional institutional linkages or along formal points of contact between public and private actors but rather to enhance resource mobilization and coordination through other and less formal channels. Indeed, one could well make the argument that it is the ability to identify and exploit such novel forms of institutional cooperation or exchange with key actors in the surrounding society that characterizes successful governance. Formal rules and institutional systems certainly still matter but they do so more as the framework for political action than as a definition of what actions are appropriate in a given context.

Therefore, in order to be able to interpret the emerging forms of governance we need to depart from the previous established view on government. Using that slightly idealized model as a benchmark for comparison, we can bring out what types of challenges governance poses to the structures of government and their exchange with civil society. Furthermore, we need to reassess how these forms of governance relate to governance at other institutional levels and the complex interplay between governance processes at different levels of the political system.

The conventional view on government

There are two reasons why we need to depart from a conventional view on government, the state and governance. One is conceptual or ontological. The standard, idealized image of government is the only reasonably useful benchmark against which we can observe what differences the emergence of governance makes to the state's capacity to steer society.

The other reason is empirical. Conventional techniques and processes of state steering, we maintain, are still extremely important. The new, less complying, governance strategies which we see emerging are not alternative but complementary strategies to the previous models of governance. The new governance has become important mainly because traditional modes of governance are believed to have become less efficient and appropriate in some respects. Contrasting the new governance with the traditional image of government helps us uncover what differences emerging modes of governance make and what are the likely consequences of these developments.

In the conventional view of government, the state was at the self-evident centre of the governance network. The state played a variety of different roles in different types of social and political contexts. Pluralistic democratic theory portrays the state primarily as an arena for competition between different elites and with few and vague indigenous interests. Also, this view on the state assumed – although the issue was rarely explicitly addressed – that the state exercised some degree of control over the economy and that political institutions, should the need arise, could exercise considerable clout over the private sector. The fact that it did not exercise any such continuous control was more a reflection of policy choice than an incapacity to do so.

Another classical conceptualization of the state is related to corporatist models of policy-making and interest mediation. Here, the state is portrayed as one of three actors engaged in tri-partite, negotiated arrangements of interest accommodation. While organized interests have successfully encroached on the state so too has the state incorporated these interests into its sphere. Again in a traditionalist perspective, the strength of the corporatist state has been regarded as limited owing to its inability to insulate itself from societal interests.

Despite the many differences between these two perspectives, there also exist many similarities. One is that the state is conceptually and empirically separate from the rest of society. True, the corporatist model of the state emphasizes the many ways in which the border between state and society is crossed but even so the state retains unique capabilities and a societal role which no other actor can play. In the pluralist model of the state, the public–private distinction is much clearer and sustained.

Another similarity between the pluralistic and corporatist models is that states can be understood and interpreted in a non-contextual, almost clinical fashion. For pluralists, legal and constitutional frameworks give an accurate and exhausting description of what states can do and cannot do. In corporatist models of the state, there is a strong notion that the state has a limited number of roles to play but also that the capabilities of the state, on the whole, are limited by other actors. Third, states are typically seen as monolithic and value-free structures. Neither state model allows for internal conflicts and contending goals; indeed, states in and by themselves are not believed to have any other goals than those pursued by the incumbent constituency.

The conventional perspective on government and the state is highly state-centric. True, one could argue that any perspective on government by definition must be state-centric. The point we wish to make, however, is that in the conventional view on government there is little interest in how the institutional organization of the state relates to the organization of society, or how the processes of state–society exchange impact on the state. The resurgence of the state–society approach in the 1980s departed from a belief that 'bringing the state back in' into the analysis of public policy would yield new insights on the issue of what differences states make (Held *et al.*, 1983; Evans *et al.*, 1985).

The conventional view on government could be summarized in four general points; state-centrism, institutional insulation and homogeneity, state sovereignty and superiority, and a focus on constitutional arrangements. The state-centric view on government sees the state as the undisputed locus of power. The extent to which the state intervenes in markets, changes the structure of ownership in the industry, redistributes wealth among different social groups, or expands or contracts its services is a matter of policy choice. The state, in this perspective, is a set of powerful institutions which can be employed to enforce the political will of the dominant political constituency.

This view on government, in turn, is predicated on an assumption of institutional insulation and homogeneity. Institutions do not have to engage in bargaining or joint ventures with other societal actors to attain their goals and tasks but can rely on their legally defined jurisdiction. Furthermore, the conventional view on government holds that institutions are not impaired by internal tensions and conflicts. The Weberian view on the bureaucracy is, in fact, an important component in this image of government.

The third defining characteristic of the conventional view on government – state sovereignty and superiority – is to some degree derived from the previous points. The state is seen as sovereign, meaning that its powers and capabilities are absolute rather than something relative, contextual and negotiable. It is much more a matter of 'power over' than 'power to'. This also means that the state to a considerable extent could define its own powers. The state certainly has extensive exchanges with the surrounding society but conducts those exchanges largely on its own terms. Also, in the conventional view on government there was little concern with legitimacy problems or critique against taxes and involvement which could undermine the effective capabilities of the state.

The focus on constitutional issues and arrangements, finally, is an important element of the conventional view on the state because constitutions and other legal frameworks governed state actions with little or no discrepancies between rules and behaviour. Given the powerful role of written rules, constitutions – conceived of as the rules of the political game – never allowed to develop organically but were assessed more in terms of their internal logic than to what extent they were *de facto* shaping political life.

The governance perspective challenges these conceptions of the state and the sources of state capabilities. We have already discussed why we think that a state-centric approach to governance seems to offer the best analytical mileage. The governance approach, as outlined here, shares a state-centric perspective with the state–society literature of the 1980s but focuses more narrowly on public–private exchange, contextual and entrepreneurial styles of politically driven social and political change, and the ways in which these exchanges reverberate on the state. As we shift perspective from government to governance, state-centrism is a matter of analytical choice to a much greater extent than in the conventional view of government. In our view of the new governance, the state thus remains the key player albeit for slightly different reasons. The state exercises influence through coordination and steering in combination with the employment of its resources in various projects. The main difference between the two perspectives is that in the conventional view the centrality of the state is taken for granted whereas in the governance perspective the state is a *primus inter pares* actor whose capabilities are contingent on its ability to mobilize other societal actors for its purposes.

The institutional insulation and homogeneity which is the second feature of the conventional view on government does not find much support in governance theory. The monolithic view on the state is substituted for a model of the state which assumes much more institutional fragmentation and incoherence, perhaps even contradiction and tensions between and within institutions. To be sure, in order to meet the challenge of governance, most states have deliberately relaxed their organizational cohesion in order to enable different segments of the state to develop their own forms of exchange with societal actors. Furthermore, different institutions of the state – and sometimes even segments within institutions – have their own views about what should be the goals of governance. In addition to the institutional fragmentation and deconcentration, another typical feature of the contemporary state in governance is the relaxation of political steering and control. Thus, states frequently play both internally as well as externally coordinating roles. In some Third World countries it seems clear that states cannot engage in successful governance until they bring about some degree of internal institutional coherence and capacities (Hyden, 1992; Leftwich, 1994; Peters, 1998a); in the modern western advanced democracies there is a tendency to move in the opposite direction in order to increase the points of contact with the surrounding society.

The third assumption in the conventional view on government, state sovereignty and superiority, does not receive much support in theories of governance. There is a consensus that states control some types of resources which no other actors have access to, such as the legal enforcement of authoritative decisions. The main difference is that these types of resources are becoming less critical for most societal actors. Private businesses seem to be less dependent on national policies just as organized interests are less inclined to engage in close cooperation with an increasingly resource-constrained state. There still exist delicate dependencies between the state and powerful societal actors but the direction of those dependencies has shifted. Previously, industrial leaders were anxious to have a good dialogue with policy-makers and senior civil servants; now it is elected politicians who seek contact with private industry. Similarly, in the heyday of corporatism, organized interests were eager to secure access and participation in the state's decision-making processes. Today, it is the state which seeks to engage the third sector in public service delivery.

The focus on constitutional arrangements, finally, has been significantly downplayed in governance theory. In the conventional view, the constitution was the ultimate source of the state's powers. Today, constitutions define archaic borders between state and society which are seen as obstacles to governance. Also, systems of rules tend to impair political institutions in their exchange with societal actors which are more free to move resources without public monitoring. Also, since political capabilities in governance are derived from political entrepreneurialism and a political ability to read and exploit unique contexts, constitutions tell us less and less about what states can and cannot do.

Moving up: the emerging role of international organizations

One of the most profound and conspicuous developments since the Second World War with regard to alterations in state powers is the growing importance of international groups of actors or organizations. States have chosen to surrender parts of their sovereignty to such transnational arrangements in a number of policy sectors. We are still far from the final destination in this journey although we should expect to see the development towards powerful international structures to be interrupted by pendulum-like backlashes in the form of growing national sentiments (Wallace, 1996).

Different models of international regimes have been around for a long period of time, either as temporary, *ad hoc*, international negotiated agreements such as the Vienna Conference in the nineteenth century or as institutionalized and continuous patterns of international cooperation such as the League of Nations and later the United Nations. Our primary concern here is not so much with international organizations aiming at governing the global community of sovereign states but more on recent international actors with a different and broader agenda.

The development in international trade regulation is a good example of the consolidation of international institutions. Regulating trade, particularly ensuring free trade and the abolition of trade barriers, is a core concern for all exporting industrialized states. In the early postwar period, western states agreed on a General Agreement on Tariffs and Trade (GATT) which other states soon signed as well. The agreement was renegotiated at regular intervals but there was very limited continuous monitoring of states' trade policies. As part of the *régime économique* in the 1980s and early 1990s, however, GATT was increasingly seen as an ineffective instrument to regulate international trade. As a result, GATT was replaced by the World Trade Organization (WTO) which assumed the same roles as GATT played but, more importantly, also serves as a controller, investigator, and court for international trade disputes. In order to join the WTO, states have to demonstrate that they, in policy as well as in action, subscribe to the principles of free trade and non-state intervention in private industry (Hoekman and Kostecki, 1995).

Another perhaps even more intriguing example of the growing importance of international organizations is the Agenda 21 project. Laid down at the 1992 Rio Summit, the basic idea of Agenda 21 is that subnational governments – not states – are targeted as lead actors to develop programmes of sustainable economic development. Thus here is a case of international governance which aims at subnational political change without much control or interference by the nation state.

The emergence of these types of international actors is a very powerful challenge to the state. Indeed, it is little surprise that the project of voluntarily surrendering some of the state's sovereignty to transnational organizations has encountered fierce political resistance in many instances, as displayed not least in western Europe alongside the continued political and economic integration of the Union (Taggart, 1998). The obvious questions are: Why this tendency to move governance up to the international level? Why do states so willingly surrender their sovereignty to transnational institutions over which their influence is extremely limited? What are the costs and benefits associated with these developments? Can the process of internationalization be reversed, and what leeway do individual states have to choose whether or not they want to join these powerful international organizations? And through what mechanisms and instruments does international governance link with domestic governance?

There are many contributing explanations for the emergence of international organizations and actors but five overall hypotheses seem to offer a reasonably good account of this development. First of all, most of the significant problems confronting the contemporary political elites of the western world are not defined by national borders but are regional or even global in nature. In 1980, environmental protection was still in its political infancy; nowadays, it ranks among the very top political priorities throughout the western world. The bumper sticker argument 'we all live downwind' captures the notion that environmental protection can only be attained if states cooperate and global, highly specified, agreements are reached and enforced. Drug-trafficking is in many ways a similar type of policy problem: the deregulationist regime in Europe and the United States has stripped border control of many of their authorities hence some form of internationally coordinated efforts has become the only means of curbing international drug trade. Moreover, although the international community after the Berlin Wall sees only one superpower, the world has not yet presented itself as any less prone to military conflict, probably the opposite. If anything, international security has become more, not less, complicated along with the resurgence of nationalist sentiments in many of the small recently formed states in the former Soviet Union and Yugoslavia.

A second explanation for the growing powers of these international structures is that international coordination is necessary to accomplish deregulationist goals. Domestic economic growth and development are increasingly seen as contingent on the international performance of the nation's industry. While there certainly is an argument to be made against the nation-state paradigm in economic development (Reich, 1991), it probably remains the case that even the knowledge- and information-based economic ventures of the 1990s are dependent on the state with regard to a number of factors which play an important role in defining the competitiveness of these businesses.

A third set of explanations is provided by the literature on the globalization of private capital. The argument is often sustained with reference to the deregulation of financial and currency markets but has a more general scope. International trade is much more important to most developed states today than it was a couple of decades ago: domestic economic growth is primarily believed to be predicated on increased exports. This is a seemingly deceptive economic development strategy, since international trade in theory at least is a zero-sum game: all countries cannot simultaneously develop and sustain a positive trade balance. However, as the history of the capitalist economy has shown, this economic system has powerful incentives not only to dominate existing markets but also to identify and exploit new markets.

Critics of the globalization argument show that for countries like Britain international trade is no bigger today in terms of the percentage of the GNP than it was in the early twentieth century (Hirst and Thompson, 1996). Also, countries like the Scandinavian countries built much of their prosperity during the 1950s, 1960s and 1970s on export revenues. For them, globalization is no news. The key difference between the 1910 or 1920s on the one hand and the 1980s and 1990s on the other is that economic policy has shifted from demand-side to supply-side economic thinking. The commitment to anti-inflation monetarist policies forces most industrial states to keep domestic demand at a fairly low level, something which forces industry to look overseas for markets with greater demand.

A fourth reason why states support emerging international organizational structures is that policy problems are assumed to become increasingly similar among different countries and that, subsequently, developing institutions to facilitate cross-national policy learning becomes an important strategy to develop new policy concepts. The OECD has evolved into an organizational organization which serves to diffuse policy concepts in economic policy and administrative reform. The IMF and the World Bank increasingly often provide international loans which are contingent on specific economic reforms. Policy learning takes place at what seems to be a rapidly increasing number of international conferences for 'epistemic communities' (Haas, 1992) and a growing interest in bilateral exchange.

Finally, the argument has been made that the rapid strengthening of international organizations, or indeed globalization more generally, is a convenient excuse for nation-state governments not to address predominant political problems (Weiss, 1998). It is a legitimate political standpoint to argue that problems such as environmental protection, controlling the spread of epidemic diseases or fighting international crime can only be addressed by states acting in concert through some form of international efforts. At the same time, this argument also serves as a political pretext for the sometimes seemingly limited domestic political attention to these issues. Most importantly, globalization, according to this school of thought, has helped legitimate the dismantling of the welfare state and the downplaying of redistributive policies (Martin, 1996).

Moving down: regions, localities, and communities

The second major type of displacement of state power – the decentralization of state authority to regional and local institutions – has gained more attention than the strengthening of international structures. Decentralization, with significant differences in detail between different national contexts, has been implemented in a large number of western democracies over the past couple of decades. Across Western Europe and the United States there is a clear pattern that from the early 1960s onwards the growth of central government has been slower than that of subnational government (Sharpe, 1988). Also, we have seen devolution of political power to regional institutions, propelled by ethnic and cultural sentiments, in countries such as Spain, Canada and Britain (Keating, 1996).

The decentralization process has in many countries been conducted in several steps. After the institutional 'empowerment' of local governments we have seen intra-city diffusion of some powers, too. As was the case in state–local decentralization, giving neighbourhoods more influence has been coupled with greater financial responsibilities while at the same time facilitating more direct citizen participation and input on political issues. This has become important during periods of cutting back public expenditures.

This wave of decentralization has been driven by a wide range of political objectives or as responses to structural changes in the democratic state. The continued urbanization and agglomeration of cities, for instance, have necessitated financially and administratively stronger local governments. More importantly, however, the expansion of public services during the past decades have fuelled a professionalization and accumulation of expertise in subnational governments and to some extent decentralization has aimed at unleashing and capitalizing on this expertise. Another motif for decentralization is that many public services are becoming less standardized and that the need for these services to be responsive and adapted to local needs has become more important.

Decentralization has in many cases helped the nation state to bring its budget at least closer to balance and to curb the growth in public expenditure at the central government level. This has meant 'passing the buck', or displacing the problems, to subnational institutions. That said, it is interesting to note that this decentralization has not significantly been associated with an overall decrease in the size of the public sector *tout court*. Rather it is a matter of a changing division of labour within the public sector as well as changing patterns of financial and other responsibilities for public services.

Equally interesting, however, decentralization has had a number of less intended consequences which are of significant interest in a governance perspective. This is not to suggest that in individual countries these consequences were not considered by policy-makers: in Britain, for instance, developing subnational systems of institutions which were geared to serve as vehicles for different forms of governance has been important to central government. In most cases, however, these types of changes were secondary to the national objectives driving decentralization.

The most important consequence of decentralization is that it has facilitated new forms of governance, both among institutions within the public sector and between local governments and the surrounding society. For societal actors there is little point in approaching local governments who have very limited powers, limited financial resources and constrained autonomy. Decentralization makes local government an attractive target for political pressures but also as a partner in different local projects, for instance within economic development and public service delivery. Thus decentralization has probably strengthened urban regimes, normally conceived of as coalitions between the local political elite and corporate actors (Elkin, 1987; Stone, 1989). Corporate actors now see stronger incentives for working with local authorities.

Moving out: NGOs, corporatization and privatization

The third type of power displacement has been to move powers and capabilities traditionally controlled by the state to institutions and organizations operating at arm's length from the political elite. Most of the advanced democracies have helped set up a large number of non-governmental organizations (NGOs) in public service delivery, if they have not gone so far as to privatize such functions altogether. This idea of creating 'satellite' institutions has gained massive popularity and is currently used at all levels of government.

The exportation of policy activities takes a number of different forms. The simplest is creating quasi-autonomous 'agencies' in government to perform tasks previously performed by government departments. The Next Steps project in Britain, for example, saw the creation of agencies implementing policy with enhanced discretion. At a second level central governments can use subnational governments for their own implementation purposes. Finally, governments can use for-profit or not-for-profit organizations to fulfil government purposes. In some cases these organizations may have existed long before the contemporary move towards greater externalization of activities. In other cases governments have fostered the creation of these organizations, and then become their major funders.

Furthermore, a general trend across Western Europe and also Japan has been the selling off of state-owned companies, for example in the telecommunications and public transport sectors. Several arguments have been used for that privatization, ranging from the state's need to capitalize on its assets to reduce its debts to a more normative idea that states should not own companies which provide services. It is interesting to note that the justifications for bringing (or keeping) these services under state auspices, especially that they were collective goods which should be protected from corporate profit, has surrendered to the notion that the state is not well-equipped or designed to own such companies and that in order to make them more efficient they should be privatized.

There has also been a significant transfer of primarily implementation authority to non-public actors, not least at the local level. In some national contexts such as in Sweden, local governments have created companies owned by the local authority to deal with tasks and responsibilities which the city proper is not very well geared to, such as provision of water and electricity. This 'corporatization' has been criticized partly because it complicates public monitoring on how tax money is spent and partly on a normative level, arguing that local authorities should not own companies but that they should be privatized.

Finally, public–private partnerships have become a popular instrument for enhancing the capability of political institutions, primarily at the local level (Pierre, 1998a). Such a partnership could be seen as an *ad hoc* fusion of political and private resources. What critics see as questionable ways to spend public money and exercise political power in close concert with corporate interests are for others a pragmatic and efficient means of increasing the institutional 'capacity to act' (Stone, 1989). What does seem clear is that partnerships are likely to become increasingly common creatures, primarily at the local government level, as cities find themselves lacking the financial resources to fund important projects for example, in economic development and – equally important – as the targets of urban policy become less tied to its localization and hence less susceptible to formal political control.

The general idea behind these changes has been to create organizations and inter-organizational relationships that can be engaged in the policy process without some of the constraints that hinder most public sector organizations. In some instances, that may imply organizations that can function under conditions which approach market-like conditions as closely as possible, while at the same time implementing public policy. In others the organizations may operate more like private eleemosynary bodies, albeit with heavy levels of public funding. The general point is to move the activities out of the public sector.

These organizational developments are triggered in part by a need to find formats which enhance efficiency in the public sector. The inclination to experiment with different organizational solutions to these problems appears to have been much stronger at the local than at the central level. The use of private organizations is also a way of enhancing the legitimacy of certain types of activities (social work) in cases in which government has lost the respect and support of many programme recipients. These organizations also permit involving the clients of programmes to a greater extent than might be possible with public sector organizations, so that there is community involvement as well as less expense.

As has been the case with most other institutional developments described earlier, these organizational changes have been extremely important in developing new channels and instruments for public–private concerted action and exchange of resources. For most of these changes we do not believe that that aspect of organizational reform was seen as very important: it is clear that the primary goals of those reforms were cost-cutting and bringing in private-sector management philosophies. However, one of the more important consequences of the centrifugal organizational developments in the public sector has been that they have facilitated new forms of governance.

We need to think of these three shifts in formal political power – up to international regimes, down to subnational authorities and urban regimes, and out to NGOs and private organizations – in a dynamic perspective. The effective division of labour is often contextual and negotiated. In some, but far from all, cases the state still has at least a theoretical option to reclaim diffused power bases. Furthermore, different policy sectors display different patterns of power relocation. From the point of view of the state there is a risk of 'institutional stretching', that is, some of its control has been shifted upward while some of it has been displaced downward. Let us now look closer at where all this leaves the state.

What's left of the state?

Looking back at the preceding discussion about the displacement of state capabilities upward, downward, and outward, the obvious question is what areas of control and resources remain under state control. The issue, however, is not so much what specific formal areas of control the state has retained as what types of instruments and capabilities it still possesses. We believe that the new emerging governance will see traditional instruments of governance being used in new contexts alongside alternative instruments. There is a growing emphasis on getting things done and less emphasis on the role of government in that process.

The developments described here lend themselves to two different, albeit not contradictory, conclusions with regard to the future of the nation state and its role in the new governance. One scenario is that the different displacements of state power and control are irreversible processes of state decline. In this perspective the state will contract until it retains only a few core societal functions. Public services will continue to be adapted to the financial condition of the state; contracting out, privatization and third sector involvement will replace state auspices in service delivery. In the international arenas, globalized capital will gain further momentum while nation states will see a further erosion of their control over private capital.

The other scenario takes a more positive view on the future of the state. Here, recent developments are interpreted not as indicators of state decline but rather as of state transformation and successive adaptation to changes in its external (domestic and international) environments. States have historically proved surprisingly able to respond to such changes (Navari, 1991). The nation states of the late 1990s are very different from those of, say, the 1950s or 1960s, both with regard to their institutional design as well as their domestic and international capabilities (Shaw, 1997). There is also a greater degree of heterogeneity among nation states today than there was some twenty years ago due to the difference in pace and direction of administrative reform, institutional restructuring and political–economic regimes. The Anglo-American democracies seem to have gone much further than countries like Germany, France, Japan and Sweden in these respects. Thus in this scenario what we are witnessing is a process of structural and political adjustment in the state to the challenges it is now facing. Traditional sources and bases of state power are downplayed since they are less efficient and appropriate instruments of governance. Instead, collaborative instruments and a more transparent and integrative state model emerge to serve as a vehicle for the pursuit of collective interests.

A key element of governance theory is that the total sum of state

capabilities may well remain largely unchanged despite the relocation of traditional state authority. The emergence of international
regimes suggests that the state is deprived of some of its sovereignty
but that this loss to a considerable extent is matched by the state's
access to the leverage controlled by such international regimes.
Following the same 'logic of appropriateness' (March and Olsen,
1989), decentralization and subnational internationalization are
'appropriate' structural developments as the state responds and
adapts to the contemporary domestic and global society in which it
is embedded. What does change, however, is the selection of instruments and organizational arrangements through which the state
imposes its will on society and also the nature of the points of
contact between state and society. In subsequent chapters we will
look more closely at those issues.

5

Scenario 1: Reasserting Control

The new governance can be summarized as the emergence of different alternative models – defined as different political and institutional arrangements – of organizing the pursuit of the collective interest. One of the key arguments in this book is that the emergence of these patterns of governing should not necessarily be seen as indications of a weakening of the state but rather as transformations of previous models of governance into new ones which are better geared to the politics and political economy of the late twentieth century. Several contemporary observers have arrived at a similar conclusion: it is much too early to dismiss the state as a centre (if not *the* centre) of power and authority (Evans, 1997; Weiss, 1998). Thus, the main issue is not so much whether the state is declining but rather how it transforms and what contending sources and models of governance seem to be emerging.

In this and the two following chapters we look at three different scenarios regarding different state strategies to cope with the challenges of governing and alternative trajectories of governance. First we will look at a scenario in which the state reasserts some of its former control over the economy and society. In Chapter 6 we describe a scenario in which states step back and allow for other models of governance to develop. Then, in Chapter 7, we look at several different models of democracy and participation as a third conceivable scenario. The three scenarios are not mutually exclusive. We can, for instance, see states reasserting control in some sectors while letting other regimes rule in others. To be sure, the most likely development is probably a mix of all three scenarios, something which, in turn, creates governance problems. We will return to this issue in the concluding chapter.

Here, then, we shall look at a scenario in which the state takes a high profile and repositions itself as a powerful centre of governance. The point of departure in this scenario is that although recent changes such as globalization, deregulation, privatization and increased subnational autonomy all suggest that the traditional powers of the state have diminished, a closer look will reveal that the state exercised exactly those powers in bringing about these changes and, more importantly, that these developments have not disarmed the state of those capabilities. They were introduced and executed by the state and the state retains – not just in theory – the formal and effective powers and capabilities to reverse those developments when it so chooses. These changes were manifestations of the powerful pro-market regime of the 1980s and 1990s, first in the UK and the United States and later diffused to a number of other western democracies. However, there is no reason to rule out once and for all that more proactive regimes will not reemerge on the political scene.

True, we should not expect a return of the advanced welfare state regimes of the 1960s and 1970s (Esping-Anderson, 1990), largely because the financial underpinnings of such a political project are not available. But the 'rush to the market' has a potential political backlash in many countries which is fertile soil for more proactive politics (LeGrand, 1998). In Sweden, for instance, the previous strong electoral pressure for tax cuts has been significantly weakened as the effects of such cuts have become visible in the abolition of public service programmes or the deterioration of traditional strong service sectors such as education and health (Nilsson, 1998).

Similarly, the tremendous pressures exercised by global capital and currency exchange market actors over national governments around the world have probably fuelled sentiments of reregulating financial markets. Indeed, Helleiner (1996:194) suggests that 'a reversal of the liberalization trend is more likely than is often assumed'; encouraging or tolerating capital mobility has proved more politically complicated and controversial than expected in many countries, as developments in both Western Europe and more recently in Korea, Malaysia, Thailand and Japan clearly illustrate. The loss of autonomy as a result of the deregulation of financial markets is another potential impetus for considering some form of reregulation, as Milner and Keohane (1996:249) argue: 'The declining policy autonomy of states as they cede control to markets may only be a temporary phase, until new forms of intervention are demanded and discovered.' Thus, the idea of states reasserting control over financial markets is far from being just a theoretical construct: there are many indicators suggesting that such a policy change is far from unlikely.

The conclusion of the story is that no regimes last for ever and we need to begin to think beyond the current market-dominated political projects in most of Western Europe and North America. Our first scenario outlines the nature of a politically more assertive regime. The general idea, to reiterate an earlier remark, is not so much that we will witness states devising new instruments and power bases but instead that they reactivate instruments and power bases that they themselves have chosen to mothball. We should also expect states to change the mix of those instruments to make them better geared to address current policy problems and, by concerted action, eliminate the competitive advantage of 'low-road politics' (Betcherman, 1996) and hence much of the market's pressure on individual states.

Direct control

States have historically exercised direct control in a wide range of sectors of society and the economy. The instruments employed to enforce this control have varied extensively, ranging from deliberative processes of policy-making to regulations and tax incentives. The selection of policy instruments has to a great extent been made in a routine, institutionalized fashion rather than making a careful decision about what instrument is best geared to resolve a particular problem (Linder and Peters, 1989). Obviously, there are huge differences between different national contexts not only with regard to which instruments have been most frequently used but also the range of state control and encroachment of society. But even so, governments governed society and the economy through various means of direct control.

The traditional model of direct state control and the challenge of globalization to this arrangement is often misunderstood. First, the significance of direct control should be neither exaggerated nor underestimated. Sometimes, it appears as if observers of the ongoing globalization tend to exaggerate the powers and capabilities of the state prior to globalization, hence creating an image of greater changes than perhaps have actually taken place. This line of reasoning is most frequent among those who see globalization as a major threat to the autonomy of the state and the redistributive capacity of its institutions (see, for instance, Boyer and Drache, 1996).

Equally deceptive, however, is the view that current states have lost most or all of their direct control. First of all, it was states that effectively allowed for and enforced the current deregulation of finance, capital and currency markets which, as Susan Strange (1996) points out, still operate to a very large extent under the authority and auspices of the state. Furthermore, although it is an undeniable fact that the increased mobility of international capital has to a large extent been at the expense of the traditional regulatory powers of the state, this is not the same as saying that states are now devoid of political power and control. Also, as will be discussed in the next chapter, states have responded to these shifts in the political economy in a number of ways, not least by according transnational institutions more leverage. These transnational institutions, it must be remembered, are dominated by nation-state interests and hence serve primarily as institutional vehicles for the articulation of state interests at the transnational or global level. Thus, understanding recent changes within and between the political and economic arenas of society is a much more complicated exercise than the zero-sum game it is often believed to be.

A third source of error is to treat states in a fashion assuming that they all behave alike in these respects. States seem to respond and adapt to globalization in different ways, owing to differences in institutional set-up, trade dependency, political culture, and so on (Weiss, 1998). Some states, particularly smaller states that are especially susceptible to currency speculation by international capital, have led the way in seeking to develop or strengthen collective institutions to coordinate states' macroeconomic policies such as the EU and OECD. Also, a large number of states are developing new domestic – national, regional, and local – strategies and instruments of steering and cooperation rather than relying on formal powers in order to develop new modes of interaction with private capital. For instance, public–private partnerships play an increasingly important role in coordinating public and private action in local economic development in most countries (Pierre, 1998a; Walzer and Jones, 1998). At the regional level, institutional reform in Britain and Sweden has recently been implemented, aiming at providing new instruments for economic development, to a significant extent involving private actors (Evans and Harding, 1997).

It is an intriguing question to what extent different countries respond differently to globalization and, if so, what explains these differences. In the political economy literature this problem has been on the research agenda for a long time (see, for instance, Albert, 1993; Katzenstein, 1984; Gourevitch, 1978, 1986; Rogowski, 1987, 1989). We will return briefly to these questions – a full treatment would go far beyond the scope of the current analysis – in the concluding chapter.

As we have seen, many of the strategies which states have developed in response to globalization depart from notions of governance rather than 'government'. Thus, a fourth common mistake – and one which is especially present in the perennial debate on states and globalization – is to equate state strength with the formal, constitutional powers of government. Globalization has to a significant extent propelled the emergence of governance. As we discuss direct control as one conceivable scenario we should keep in mind that such control is likely to be accompanied by more subtle techniques of governance.

The capacity of the state to resist

One traditional indicator of state capacity is the ability of its institutions to resist pressures from powerful actors in its environment. One of the working definitions of 'strong institutions' is their insulation from political and parochial pressures. Such insulation has been seen as a prerequisite for the execution of policies which discriminate between different constituencies, regions or sectors of the economy (Weaver and Rockman, 1993; Weiss, 1998). Strong institutions, according to this perspective, are the trademark of strong states.

The governance perspective on policy-making and implementation challenges this notion of state strength. Governance implies, slightly paradoxically perhaps, softer and more subtle means of steering society, not least of all networks and coordinated mobilization of resources. States may maintain some of their former powers to impose their will, but supplement those with newer forms of governing. Institutional strength, in this view, is more a matter of entrepreneurial and networking skills than the exercise of regulatory or any other traditional governmental capability.

However, if governance means forging coalitions with such actors, how does that affect the capacity of political institutions to formulate and execute policies, or, to put the question in a broader perspective, to what extent does governance impair institutions' role as expressions of the collective interest? Is there a danger involved in the strategy to move closer politically to societal actors which frequently are the targets of public policy? Will a development from 'government' to 'governance' blur or confuse the collective interest? Does governance, by definition, entail what Lowi (1979) calls 'the private use of public power', or what Schmitter and Streek (1985) refer to as 'private interest government'?

This is a complicated issue. On the one hand, it appears logical that institutions which forge coalitions with powerful actors in their external environment – actors that frequently are the very targets of the policies which the institutions are implementing – must offer something of interest for these actors when brought to the negotiating table, in order for the coalition to be formed. Societal actors could be assumed to be primarily interested in access to state power, hence forging coalitions with these actors entails losing some institutional discretion and autonomy. According to this perspective, nothing can be gained in terms of control over societal actors without something – be it power, resources or discretion – being lost.

On the other hand, history is replete with examples of how such coalitions have not necessarily impaired the political institution's ability to implement its policy; this is not necessarily a zero-sum game of power. The essence of the corporatist model of policy-making in the Netherlands, Austria and the Scandinavian countries is the institutionalization of coalitions between the state and key actors in its environment. Such a model of interest representation and involvement in policy-making does not appear to have significantly weakened these states. To be sure, since corporatist models of policy-making help ensure broad societal acceptance for policies, what may be lost in leverage in the early phases of the policy process is often gained later in the implementation stage.

Similarly, the post-Second World War 'economic miracle' in

Japan was orchestrated primarily by the Ministry of International Trade and Industry (MITI) which conveyed its 'visions' to private industry through close and continuous dialogue, again without losing much of its leverage over these actors (Allen, 1981; Johnson, 1982; Okimoto, 1988). The current interest in 'trust' and 'social capital' as significant factors in understanding state–society relationships corresponds very well with this perspective on the effective capabilities of the state (Putnam, 1993; Fukuyama, 1995). The exchange between a strong state and a strong society is frequently characterized by moderate political control and relatively subtle policy instruments (Hall, 1986; Migdal, 1988; Weiss, 1998).

There are several different explanations why states and their institutions seem to be able to engage in various forms of institutionalized cooperation with societal actors without having to compromise their political leverage. One important explanation is that the dependency, especially when looking at these issues historically, between the state and the societal actors is not symmetrical. Throughout most of the postwar period, states seem to have been less dependent on support from societal actors than vice versa: gaining access to government decision-making has been more important for interest groups than acquiescence of those groups to government.

Second, states that formulate and implement policy through different arrangements of institutionalized interest representation have rarely hesitated to resort to their core regulatory powers whenever it has been deemed necessary to ensure compliance with policy. Coming back to the case of the Japanese postwar political economy, Johnson (1982:266) notes that 'MITI has on occasion retaliated with force against an enterprise that rejected its advice'. Thus, strong states only use the leverage necessary to ensure compliance; if coalitions with powerful actors sufficiently serve this end then there is little need to use political and administrative 'overkill', but the power to do so is always available. The thrust of the state's constitutional powers is probably felt and acknowledged on both sides of the table even when they are not demonstrated.

If (strong) states traditionally have been characterized by an ability to resist political, parochial and economic pressures from their external environment, we now need to explore to what extent that option is still available to them. There is much to suggest that states still can muster sufficient political and administrative powers to resist such pressures. Most importantly, the state still has a monopoly over a large number of resources and capabilities, not least regulatory powers. States may have to husband those powers rather carefully, but they do still exist.

There seem to be two main explanations for the current wave of the 'decline of the state' argument. One is simply that states are becoming increasingly reluctant to exercise their core political and administrative powers. The predominant policy style in the United States and Western Europe over at least the past two decades has strongly emphasized 'less government', deregulated markets, economic growth, and keeping a close eye on inflation. This monetarist regime, which stands in stark contrast to the welfare regime of the 1960s and 1970s (Esping-Anderson, 1990; Pierson, 1994), accords government a minimal role in the economy and society. But these policy objectives and image of government, it must be remembered, reflect policy *choices* and, as such, there is nothing *per se* dictating that they cannot be replaced by more pro-active policies and a higher profile of government. Such proactive policies are likely to be implemented with less invasive instruments – there seems to be a general tendency among western governments to replace invasive policy instruments with more subtle techniques of steering (see below) – but that should be seen more as an adaptation to the current political economy and state–society relationships than as an acknowledgement of the supremacy of the market. This is the essence of the strategy of reasserting control.

The second powerful reason why these state capabilities have been questioned is that the deregulation of international capital has triggered fierce competition for investment capital which, in turn, has started a 'race to the bottom': states compete by offering low taxes, limited redistributive policies and minimal interference in private businesses (see Boyer and Drache, 1996). No individual state can afford the risk of not joining the race since that, so the argument goes, would leave the economy uncompetitive and international businesses would flee to more cooperative nations.

Had the iterative process of change and response stopped there, those who see globalization as a fatal blow to the autonomy of the state would clearly have had a strong case. But parallel with the globalization of the economy we have also seen a number of transnational actors gain strength. The rationale for this has two components: first, that political regulation is necessary to ensure that the market operates effectively according to its own logic, and

second, that globalization means that state interests need to be articulated at the transnational level. While these transnational organizations – the EU, ASEAN, NAFTA, and so on – so far have catered
almost exclusively to market interests, there is nothing indigenous to
these institutions which dictates that they cannot embark on a more
political, state-centred project.

The state's unilateral capacity to resist has probably declined but
the capacity of states acting collectively to resist pressures from
markets is rapidly growing. Collective action, in this perspective,
serves as a guarantee that no individual country will be hit by market
speculation as has happened in the 1990s, first in Western Europe
and later in Korea, Malaysia, Thailand and even Japan. For all of its
problems and political intricacies, the EMU is a macroeconomic
mechanism that will offer an effective shield for its member states
against international speculation against the individual country's
currency exchange rate. The same logic can easily be applied to
several other manifestations of globalized capital. Furthermore, by
acting in concert in the macroeconomic policy area, states can also
greatly reduce the powers of the categorical imperative that only
states who use all their capacities to respond to business interests can
sustain their economic development in the longer term.

The capacity of the state to resist pressures from powerful actors
and interests in its environment depends, to phrase what we just said
slightly differently, to a significant extent on the development and
consolidation of transnational, or even global, governance institutions. It is no coincidence that globalization and governance have
gained attention more or less simultaneously: globalization has been
a powerful drive for the emergence of transnational economic governance. And, as we will argue later in this chapter, globalization
requires governance; historically, as well as in the contemporary
capitalist economy, there is much to suggest that markets depend
upon regulatory structures in order not to develop imperfections or
even fail. Indeed, markets are socio-political constructions based
upon law (private property, contracts, and so on) and the power to
enforce those laws.

Rethinking traditional instruments

States seeking to maintain or reclaim control in an era of economic
globalization and growing social complexities, while at the same

time wrestling with their internal fiscal problems, probably need to rethink the use of traditional policy instruments. This is partly because the nature of the policy problem is changing, and partly because solutions which were previously employed routinely are much less likely to be equally effective today. Just as 'you can not step twice into the same river, because other waters are continually flowing on', as the Greek philosopher Heraclitus once pointed out (quoted in Morgan, 1986:233), you cannot reassert control over the same society because society changes continuously.

Governmental systems change, too, both in structural terms and with regard to institutional relationships. For instance, most central governments cannot resort to the previously common strict and detailed rules to control subnational governments without being inefficient at best and counterproductive at worst. Local and regional governments have developed an extensive organizational professionalism and expertise, and also, more importantly, governance networks with key actors in their environment which it would be pointless to maintain if recentralization might occur.

The same problem applies to how policy-makers relate to the central public administration. The creation of agencies, quangos and other organizations which operate at arm's length from policy-makers has deprived policy-makers of the use of instruments to control the implementation of public policy. Indeed, much of the administrative reform in the western world during the past decade seems to have less political control and growing reliance on the bureaucracy, internal competence and capability as a common denominator (Peters and Savoie, 1998). With this type of control lost governments must look for other mechanisms for influence, and may use society itself as the source of necessary control relationships.

The examples above refer to the changing nature of intra-governmental, institutional relations but the need to rethink policy instruments is even more pronounced with regard to state–society relationships. Here, too, the nature of the policy problems is changing and states seem to become increasingly dependent on outside (national or international) collaboration to address them effectively. Governing the economy is nowadays, a very different task compared to just a couple of decades ago. The current strategy in much of the western world seems to be to rely primarily on monetarist-type instruments which are seemingly less invasive but quite efficient means to promote the type of macroeconomic policies we see in that part of the world. To be sure, monetarist policy instruments may well appear to be subtle but, as the record in the United States and Britain suggests, they are in fact very powerful indeed.

By the same token, tackling environmental problems normally requires extensive international collaboration in order to be efficient. While essentially all governments today subscribe to the importance of addressing problems derived from pollution and waste, there is much less consensus on what should be the targets and goals of such measures, as the recent conference on these issues in Kyoto demonstrated. Like many other common-pool problems (Ostrom, 1990), however, individual countries have little to gain by imposing self-denying policies, so there is the need for some form of international regime.

Thus, there are several obstacles in these policy processes which limit the use and efficiency of legal and regulatory instruments and where there seems to be a greater need for negotiation and the use of more subtle instruments. This applies to a wide range of issues such as environmental policy, macroeconomic policies, labour-market policies and law enforcement, not least internationally concerted projects to attack drug-trafficking or international financial fraud (Kapstein, 1994). The significance of all of this is that governments must reassess the appropriateness of their policy instruments in the light of the growing importance of international instead of domestic policy measures. This is not to say that reasserting control should be an impossible project but it does seem to suggest that such a strategy must depart from an analysis of what policy instruments might serve this end best.

Thus, many policy instruments have become inappropriate either because of previous policies, or because of changes in the state's environment (Woodside, 1998). Previously used instruments need to be reconsidered and new instruments may also have to be developed, not least if the state is to rely increasingly on new means of communicating its will to society such as partnerships and networks.

Rethinking the mix of instruments

Just as many of the instruments which were routinely used in the past need to be reconsidered, current governments must also rethink the mix of policy instruments as the nature of the policy targets changes. States have always sought to develop ideal mixes of instruments to ensure efficient policy implementation: relying solely on one type of instrument is rarely a sufficient strategy to ensure that policy implementation is efficient and in accordance with the policy itself. Traditional mixes of instruments were normally combinations of coercion and encouragement with substantive differences between different national contexts with regard to the relative weight of these two types of instruments.

Generally speaking, the emergence of governance would, as mentioned earlier, suggest that coercive or regulatory instruments become less important and that 'softer' instruments gain importance. In the 'reasserting control' scenario, we should expect to see states design and select policy instruments so as to ensure a maximum of compliance with a minimum of coercion; our general view on how the state regains the control it has lost is that it does so not by reverting to the state–society relationships of the 1950s or 1960s but rather by developing a strategy of reasserting control which is geared to the society and economy of the early third millennium. Redesigning the mix of policy instruments so that it attains what previous mixes attained but using less direct political and administrative force is one of several elements of this strategy.

The regulatory role of the state, which to some extent will remain important albeit in a different state–society context, will probably see an increase in law and courts. There are several reasons for this. One is that since the relationship between the state and actors and interests in society changes towards voluntary inclusion, there will be a growing need to define the rules of these partnerships or other forms of joint ventures. Another reason is that regulatory frameworks will probably replace some of the stricter policy instruments of the state, hence a need to define these frameworks and their meaning properly.

Positive interdependencies

A key aspect of the 'reasserting control' scenario is that, somewhat ironically perhaps, some degree of continued governmental control over the economy is necessary to ensure that the economy does not generate allocation losses. The point here is not that controlled or regulated markets perform better according to political criteria but that they do so according to market criteria. This view was for a long period of time a contested standpoint – and probably still is among hard-core market theorists. In the real world, however, the macroeconomic development throughout Western Europe during the postwar period clearly suggests that, overall, regulations of markets have had a positive effect on the economy (see, for example, Brenner, 1991; Galbraith, 1967; Kenworthy, 1995; Miliband, 1969; Polanyi, 1941; Schumpeter, 1975; Shonfield, 1965).

States employ a wide range of measures to increase markets' efficiency, for example, legal frameworks ensuring contract law, private ownership, and unrestrained access to markets for both consumers and producers. In addition, there are a number of related policy instruments which are equally – if not more – important to prevent market failures, including fiscal and other macroeconomic policies which help keep down inflation; labour-market policies which reduce transactions costs in the labour market; education which is a prerequisite for economic development; and research and development policies which provide venture capital and help companies cover the often huge costs associated with developing new technologies.

Some take this argument so far as to argue that the state–market division is essentially a false dichotomy because markets are dependent on regulation and control in order to function effectively (Boyer and Drache, 1996). While that remains a debatable argument, what is important to acknowledge in the present analytical context is that states obviously pursue these market-strengthening policies for a reason: it is in the immediate interest of the state that the economy is expanding, yet the state itself cannot be an actor in these markets. Therefore, the two ways in which the state can safeguard economic growth are, first, to seek to eliminate or contain sources of market failure and, second, to resolve the collective action problems which the economy tends to generate.

This view on the political economy speaks to the current discussion about the new governance in several important ways. One important conclusion is that this particular type of state-driven coordination is by no means a novel phenomenon. States have historically played critical roles in the capitalist economy by defining contract law and private property, that is, defining the basic ground rules of the economy. More recently, states have contributed positively to economic growth by providing education and infrastructure. Kenworthy (1995) argues that markets tend to discourage cooperative behaviour, which he believes is a prerequisite for a strong economic performance, but that the state, through its institutional structure can promote and encourage such behaviour. That view gives a broader and more complete illustration of this role of the state in the economy. States, and only states, can resolve the collective action problems which impair economic growth but which are caused by the capitalist economy itself (Pierre, 1997a).

Furthermore, if state intervention in markets is critical to the performance of the economy, then reasserting control as a governance scenario should not encounter any major resistance from the current market-dominated regime. This is, admittedly, a constructed argument since these political groups remain the most articulate critics of any governmental presence in the economy. But with Clinton having replaced Bush and Blair having placed Major and the Conservatives in opposition it appears as if at least the British debate on the political economy is now less dogmatic in its critique of political control of markets. As is the case with the consequences of the deregulation of financial markets, the negative consequences of a macroeconomic policy focusing strictly on boosting economic growth across the western world – the dismantling of many core social services and a two-digit unemployment rate in many countries – breed a powerful constituency which can sustain a state strategy of reasserting greater political control over the economy and society.

Finally, and something we will elaborate on later in this chapter, the coordinating role of the state in the economy is an ideal position from which the state can also promote its own interests and not just cater to the interests among economic actors in effective governance of markets. Expressed in more concrete terms, states governing the economy in order to prevent indigenous perversions of the economy such as monopolization in important sectors or a rising inflation rate can supplement appropriate macroeconomic policies with policies which express the interests of the state in the economy. Such measures could, for instance, include curbing inflation in private consumption markets in order to allow for some state spending on labour-market programmes, as we saw happening in several Western European countries during the 1970s and early 1980s. Another example is the Reagan administration's aggressive cost-cutting in the federal bureaucracy, and its dismantling of many social welfare programmes in order to strengthen the economy while at the same time spending huge amounts of resources on the Star Wars programme. Thus, what specific measures the state seeks to impose on the economy is a direct reflection of the ideological orientation of government.

Governments have always been constrained in the economic policy field, more so than in most other policy sectors. What governments want to do frequently has to yield to what they must do and is furthermore constrained by a wide range of structural factors and, not least, a very limited ability to control or guide key economic actors (Grant, 1993). True, from time to time governments embark on spending extravagances, for instance during election years (Hibbs, 1987), but these are exceptions rather than the rule. Controlling and regulating the economy is critical to any government because if those roles are not performed with sufficient consistency the economy will not produce the growth which constitutes the financial backbone of the government's programmes. Also, transnational institutions in the macroeconomic policy area are increasingly keeping a close eye on governments' economic policy. This is most clearly manifested in the context of the European Union and EMU which promises to reduce the autonomy of national economic policy rather dramatically.

This view of economic policy as an extraordinarily 'narrow' and constrained area of public policy might suggest to some that there is not much in this policy sector which fits in with the reassertion of state control scenario. However, looking at the different types of constraints in a governance perspective suggests that what in a 'government' perspective is a constraint can be thought of as a source of governance capacity. Thus, the notion that governments have limited political and administrative leverage over private capital (see, for example, Offe, 1985) is an image derived from a conventional view on government and its instruments. The governance perspective suggests that governments seeking to work in non-coercive coordination with private capital can probably attain more in terms of acquiring information and conveying views and objectives than was the case in the traditional image of government (see Khademian, 1996).

By the same token, while it is true that transnational regimes exercise tight control over economic policy in individual countries, states can extract some governance capability from these international institutions, too. Looking at the national-international exchange in a

governance perspective indicates that this is not so much a constraint as an additional leverage of government over the economy,
since national governments have an input on transnational macroeconomic norms and also enjoy a 'safety in numbers' *vis-à-vis* international currency speculation as members of the international
organization. Thus, applying a governance approach to economic
policy puts the issue of the governability of the economy and the
leverage of government in this sector in a slightly new perspective.

The role of the state in the governance of the economy cannot be
properly understood without factoring in the pace of change in the
capitalist economy (Hollingsworth *et al.*, 1994; Hollingsworth and
Boyer, 1997). Different schools of thought offer different interpretations of the relationship between the state and the economy. The
traditional, liberal view has been that the state operates and restructures largely independently of changes in the economy; this is the
essence of the constitutionalist, traditional view on government. On
the other side of the argument, neo-Marxists have long argued that
the structural organization of the state reflects – and is embedded in
– the contemporary nature of the capitalist economy and the role it
defines for the state (Jessop, 1982; Pickvance and Preteceille, 1991).
In this view, the institutional structure of the state during the 1950,
1960s and 1970s was geared to cater to the needs of the 'Fordist'
economy with its emphasis on standardization, economies of scale
and vertical organizational integration. The state is now, however,
embedded in a different model of capitalism. 'Fordism' has gradually been replaced by a 'post-Fordist' economy emphasizing flexible
production and specialization (Hirsch, 1991; Jessop, 1995; Stoker,
1990).

Both of these views are exaggerated. The liberal view that the
state can be understood without any reference to the configuration
or *modus operandi* is an idealized image of the supremacy of the state
which has few, if any, empirical illustrations. Similarly, the neo-
Marxist perspective that the state is subject to changes in the
economy and restructures mainly to accommodate the reproductive
needs of the capitalist system denies any autonomous interests or
objectives of the state and, more importantly, suggests a uniformity
in state transformation across the western world which simply is not
there. A more nuanced account would be to look at what different
types of collective action problems different forms of the capitalist
economy tend to generate and how the state can intervene to resolve

those problems. For instance, there is no economic incentive for individual corporate actors to develop their own education programmes or their own infrastructure, yet for all corporate actors skilled labour and efficient infrastructure are critical to their operations. While the nature of these collective action problems has varied along with the development of the capitalist economy, it has remained the case that states have played crucial roles in resolving these problems. This, however, is far from saying that the state is without any political direction of its own.

For the current analysis, we must also recognize that different models of capitalism require different forms of governance and that the state, arguably, is better equipped to play some of these roles than others. It would appear as if the state was better geared to govern the Fordist economy than the post-Fordist model, not least because there is a higher degree of institutional 'match' between the state and the Fordist economy; the Weberian model of the public bureaucracy is in many ways a mirror image of a Fordist economic order. Therefore, reasserting control over an economy which has developed from a Fordist towards a post-Fordist model probably requires substantive institutional change in order to be successful.

In the perspective of emerging forms of governance, there are two forms of positive interdependencies between the state and the market which should be noted. One is the observation that the state is necessary to coordinate private activity. This is a wider perspective than saying both that political intervention in markets is necessary to guarantee the efficiency of the market and that political presence in the market is necessary to safeguard political objectives. It includes the notion that the state – by virtue of its political authority – is the only structure in society which can function as an arbitrator between contending private interests, for example, in the labour market. We will return to this aspect of brokerage as a means of control later in this chapter.

Another area in which the state is likely to play an important role is mitigating and coordinating the interaction of globalization and regionalization. This is currently a high-paced development and the role of the state is probably best described as one of managing the role transition of central and subnational governments. We believe that regionalization, which will be discussed in the next chapter, neither is the final destination of the current process of institutional change, nor is it likely to 'hollow out' the state as the most extreme argument suggests (see, for example, Ohmae, 1995). A more likely scenario is that the state will transform (in fact, it is already transforming in many ways) to accommodate regionalization, just as it is transforming to respond to globalization. We mentioned earlier that what the state can do as a mitigator between globalization and regionalization might not be the same thing as it would want to do. Some governments look at regionalization with pronounced scepticism while others take a more positive view.

Brokerage as form of control

The idea that brokerage entails a form of control is not directly associated with theories of governance although it fits nicely with the governance model of political 'steering'. We need only to consider for a second the role of the state in corporatist models of interest representation and policy-making for excellent descriptions of such brokerage and the power bases it has to offer. Sometimes, this model is conceived of as a 'tripartite' arrangement of interest representation, suggesting that the state should be merely one of three parties at the negotiation table. That may well be the case on particular issues but is less the case as a general description of the role of the state in corporatist systems.

The nature of interest representation is an important factor when assessing if and how the brokerage role of the state also has political leverage to offer. The essence of the corporatist model is (or, perhaps more correctly, was) the representation of peak organized interests with strong internal organizational cohesion and control. In such 'organized democracies', as Johan P. Olsen (1983) once called them, the state has every possibility to exploit the representation of interests for its own purposes, mainly ensuring compliance for policy from the interest organizations. Here, the brokerage role, while important, was coupled with a more complex role in which there was a continuous exchange between the state and organized interests. In other models of policy-making and interest representation, the role of the state is more diversified but even in those models the state can exercise control by regulating exchange between different social actors. Thus, how much the state can use brokerage as a means of control depends to some extent on the configuration of interests in society.

Another significant factor in this context is the role of the state in society in a larger perspective. The state remains the legitimate power centre in a turbulent environment. Only the state seems to have the capacity to resist pressures from powerful social and economic actors, as we noted earlier. This notion of state 'steering' through brokerage is particularly important outside the First World. In many developing countries where civil society is weak and systems of political and social representation are still poorly developed, the state – despite frequent problems with patronage and rent-seeking behaviour – remains the only structure in society with some degree of continuity and insulation from sectoral or corporate interests.

Can the state reassert control?

In closing, we need to ask ourselves just how likely this scenario is: how willing are states to reassert control, and how able are they do it? What ends would such a strategy serve and what would be the consequences on the economy if states were to reverse the processes which are said to have reduced their control? Have not globalization and regionalization developed so far that the state, even if it were successful in reasserting control, would find that the historical roles associated with the state lost significance or have been coopted by international institutions?

Let us first discuss the political and institutional rationale for reasserting control. The most basic and essential normative justification for states to reassert control seems to be that the state – not just historically – is the undisputed vehicle for democratic government and social transformation. Since no other actor in society can assume these roles we must avoid 'hollowing out the state' of its resources and legitimacy. If globalization and regionalization threaten to do just that, then there is a normative basis for reasserting some form of state control. Such control must not be merely symbolic: since the state is the most important channel for political representation, its institutions must have real leverage over society and the economy. This is not to suggest that globalization and regionalization should be inherently 'undemocratic' developments. The point we wish to make here is that since institutional adaptation often tends to be slow we must ensure some form of adequate and meaningful political representation even under such profound institutional changes as globalization and regionalization.

Second, do states really have the powers necessary to reassert control? Well, yes and no. The point we have been stressing throughout this chapter is that reasserting control is not the same thing as regressing to the political, economic and institutional model of the 1960s or 1970s. Instead, reasserting control should be thought of as a process in which the state reclaims some of the leverage and control it has surrendered to subnational government, transnational regimes or the market, utilizing policy instruments which are better geared to the current state of the economy and society. We do not believe that states can resort to the model of regulation which was previously employed – at least not without major political and economic costs.

These questions are ultimately reflections of two broader aspects of the relationship between state and society. The first refers to the role of the state in the transformation of society, or, more specifically, to what extent the state is the conductor and coordinator of such changes or whether it merely responds to changes in its environment. This is obviously a question worthy of its own book – or even book series. The short answer is probably that we, as observers of state transformations, tend to exaggerate both the strength of the state prior to globalization and the degree to which this strength now is lost to other actors. Even if political elites and senior civil servants spend a great deal of time trying to find out how to respond to globalization and regionalization, that is far form saying that the institutions of the state are becoming obsolete.

The second aspect is to what extent states are capable of sufficiently coordinating their macroeconomic policies in order to ensure that all states present market actors with a fairly similar set of policies. If we use the European integration process as an empirical example, the record to this point has not been terribly impressive. Certainly, a high degree of coordination has been implemented but, as the debate on EMU shows, a great deal remains to be accomplished in these respects. Letting other regimes rule easily triggers anxiety both among the political elite and the man in the street, as the next chapter will discuss.

6

Scenario 2: Letting Other Regimes Rule

Along with globalization, the two perhaps most profound changes in the governance of society and the economy during the 1990s have been first the increasing importance of transnational or global systems and institutions of governance and second, the emergence of subnational governments as actors in international arenas (Fry, 1998). It is little surprise that many observers of these trends discuss the accumulated effect of globalization, strengthened global institutions and subnational governments going international in terms of the decline of the state. If the state loses control upward, downward and inward, as a result of relaxed control over agencies and other executive institutions, then what is actually left of the state, and what is left for the state to exercise control over? Much as we can see the apparent logic in these conclusions regarding the future of the nation state, a closer inspection of these developments indicates that what is happening is perhaps not so much a decline of the state as a gradual transformation of state institutions, policy preferences, domestic coalitions and, in a larger perspective, the role of the state in society (Evans, 1997; Hirst and Thompson, 1996; Keohane and Milner, 1996).

In this chapter we will discuss the second of our three scenarios of governance. This scenario conceptualizes the state as stepping back and allowing for subnational and international institutions and actors to gain importance. Unlike the scenario outlined in the previous chapter, which was cast in a somewhat hypothetical language, much of this scenario is already here, as even a quick glance through the *Financial Times* or *The Economist* substantiates. Thus, we do not need to speculate about the likelihood of this scenario although some current developments are still in process and it is hence too early to assess what the final outcome is likely to be. The key problem here is instead understanding what factors have driven this process, what is its most likely final destination, and how it will impact on the state in the longer term.

Before we go into those issues, however, we need to briefly elaborate on what we mean by 'letting' other actors or groups of actors rule. The choice of wording here is far from arbitrary. A theme running throughout this book is a state-centred approach to governance: we believe that there is no better point of departure for understanding the emergence of different forms of governance than the traditional model of government. Thus, when we say 'letting' other regimes rule we suggest that this is a conscious strategy of the state much more than a surrender to local and transnational pressures for greater control and autonomy. The growing importance of transnational or global institutions such as the European Union, the World Trade Organization or ASEAN is a process which would not have gained any momentum if it had not been sustained by national governments. Similarly, the increasing interest among subnational governments in a large number of countries to develop international networks is, too, a development which is predicated on the state's allowing for this to happen. While there is little to suggest that any government would forbid local or regional institutions to pursue internationalization, they certainly have the legal and administrative leverage to do so whenever they choose.

Thus, the word 'letting' should be read more as allowing for certain processes to take place than surrendering to them. The only slight exception to this rule is the type of regionalization which is driven by cultural or ethnic sentiments or a territorial identity which have deep historical roots. This type of regional identity, which we see in Scotland, Catalonia and Quebec, to name three prominent examples, is much older than the nation state and should therefore not be seen as something directly similar to the more current regionalization which to a significant extent is part of an economic development strategy (Keating, 1996). Further, this political mobilization is driven not by the economic logic of coping with world markets but by more primordial sentiments.

Pressures from below

To some extent, the current interest in governance, as opposed to 'government', stems from the changing relationship between institutions at different tiers of government. It appears as if the traditional model of central government control over subnational government is eroding, even in highly centralized countries (Trosa and Crozier, 1994); hence the growing interest in alternative forms of policy coordination. In the more traditional model, central government exercised fairly tight control over local government through a mix of regulation, legislation and earmarked financial resources. Much of that control is now relaxed: state grants have in many cases been lumped together into one non-categorical grant and local authorities have been granted more influence over the services they deliver. Even where general assistance to local governments has been reduced, for example in the United States, categorical grants are being replaced with block grants with fewer strings attached (Conlan, 1998).

However, at the same time as these reforms have been introduced the state remains the only institutional structure which can formulate and execute policies for the entire country; the state is still the predominant carrier of the collective interest. In the longer term we should expect there to be representative institutions either to be created, as is already happening in several national contexts (Spanish autonomies, Scotland) or adapted to their new roles and strengthened in terms of leverage and administrative capabilities. In the short-term perspective, however, regionalization has entailed a 'democratic deficit', as EU experts sometimes refer to the phenomenon: institutions that are granted more autonomy and capabilities lack the representative channels to ensure electoral input and accountability.

These developments are not as uniform across the western world as the discussion so far might suggest. In Britain – a country which has been singled out as a deviant case more than once in comparative central–local government relations – the state still exercises considerable control over subnational governments. The *ultra vires* principle dictates that local governments can only do what Parliament allows, nothing else. This centralized regulatory style stands in stark contrast to that of the Scandinavian countries where local autonomy is generously defined in the constitution and where it is the restrictions rather than the entitlements which are regulated. Furthermore, while central government's regulative control over education has been relaxed in several countries, Britain has gone the opposite way and recently introduced a national curriculum.

What is argued to be emerging in Europe is 'multi-level governance', in which there are governance activities occurring at all three levels of government – EU, nation state and subnational regions of all sorts (Marks *et al.*, 1996).

Regions bypassing the state

It is important not to account for the current process towards regionalization only through institutional politics within the framework of the nation state. Most observers would probably argue that a much more powerful driver of regionalization has been an increasing awareness within the regions that much of their future prosperity is contingent on developing a common identity with the region and thinking about economic development as a regional more than a local issue (but see Evans and Harding, 1997). The state, in this perspective, no longer has the financial resources to support regions in various ways, and, similarly, the local government system is too weak and fragmented to be able to tackle these issues and to provide adequate channels of political representation. Thus, the state is too big and too poor and cities are too small to attack these issues, therefore the region is often seen as the most powerful and appropriate organizational level to resolve the problems which are on top of the current political agenda. In the United States, for example, states have become major players in economic development in part because of their ability to transcend the single city and work on a larger canvas. Also, governors have found that 'creating jobs' is a powerful political weapon for reelection.

It is also tempting to relate the growing significance of regions and cities to overarching changes in public policy, particularly what seems to be a decline in large comprehensive programmes in most western countries and a growing emphasis on citizen engagement and 'customer-attuning' of public services (Clarke and Newman, 1997). Such a shift in public service design and delivery logically has institutional ramifications and shifts control downwards in the governmental apparatus. Also, in the United States and Canada at least, state and provincial governments are particularly apt loci for customer-driven programmes, given the range of direct services and business regulations implemented at this level of government.

This increasing subnational assertion of control is contingent on some degree of institutional strength and organizational professionalism at the regional and local levels. Interestingly, the decentralization and devolution of state functions which we will discuss later in this chapter have to a large extent provided exactly that. Indeed, in so doing, central governments in many countries 'built the perfect beast': in order to be able to implement decentralization reforms the state had to beef up subnational governments and succeeded so well in this respect that local and regional authorities developed sufficient organizational strength and professionalism to resist central government's 'steering' and control (Pierre, 1994). Instead, subnational government became a powerful institutional tool to promote regional and local interests, sometimes in some degree of conflict with the state.

Further, the emergence of regions as powerful actors has been strongly promoted by the European Union and its vision of 'Europe of the Regions' which we will come back to later in this chapter. This policy paradigm, which aims at 'empowering' the regions (Smyrl, 1997), has clearly helped drive the economic aspects of regionalization although its effect on other aspects of regionalism (see Keating and Loughlin, 1997) is more unclear. When it was launched and the extent of financial resources associated with it became evident, regions which were poorly coordinated and fragmented saw strong incentives to develop organizational coherence and formulate policies and programmes that were palatable to the EU Commission and the Structural Funds (Adshead and Quinn, 1998).

Thus, the development towards stronger subnational government is partly the result of previous policies aiming at decentralizing the public sector and partly the outcome of more spontaneous processes at the subnational level. This strengthening of subnational government, in turn, provides a good part of the explanation for these governments bypassing the state and their interest in exploring international networks (Fry *et al.*, 1989; Hobbs, 1999). In addition, we are witnessing a growing political and economic dynamic at the local and regional level. Strategies for economic development have increasingly included international contacts as a means of boosting the local economy, a process that generally bypasses the nation state.

What must be noted, however, is that the regionalism we now see emerging is, for the most part, a new and different type of regionalism that is much more market-driven than historical notions of regionalism. To a large extent, the current regionalism sees political institutions primarily catering to the needs of businesses in the city or the region, for example, by developing networks with cities and regions where businesses can find markets. Previous international networks created by subnational actors such as sister cities sought primarily to promote cultural exchange. Thus, it is probably only a slight exaggeration to argue that while cities and regions previously promoted economic contacts as a means to facilitate cultural exchange, today they promote cultural exchange as a means of boosting their business sector.

Again, the key exception to this pattern is the type of regionalism which is based in strong ethnic and cultural sentiments (Malmström, 1998). That having been said, it also seems clear that such regions – Quebec being a case in point – also pursue an aggressive strategy to boost the regional economy, for instance by opening up overseas representation offices (Keating, 1996). Regionalization in these cases may not be motivated by economic concerns but once it is activated politically that regionalization may well be manifested through some economic development programmes.

States devolving functions

As already mentioned, almost the entire western world has seen states – including what historically should be categorized as 'strong states' – conduct extensive decentralization and devolution of functions and programmes previously associated with the state. Sometimes, this decentralization has been implemented on an *ad hoc* basis, as is the case when a single public service programme is transferred from central to subnational government. More often, however, we can see a more distinct shift in overall value systems guiding the institutional politics of the state. There has been a devolution to both local and regional governments. Much of the early devolution was from the state to local government and more recent reforms have aimed at strengthening the regional level of government. These latter reforms have included both some devolution of state functions and the creation of institutions to increase coherence, coordination and, in some cases, political representation at the regional level.

Thus, the Mitterrand government in France in the early 1980s initially executed fairly wide-ranging decentralization reforms, delegating authority primarily from the central state to the *départements* and later also to the local level (Loughlin and Mazey, 1995). While the pace of decentralization slowed down during the late 1980s, it now seems to have picked up again. At about the same time there was a similar across-the-board wave of decentralization in the Scandinavian countries. There has also been institutional reform implemented in Spain and Italy over the past couple of decades aiming at strengthening the regional tier of government (Evans and Harding, 1997). Finally, even in Japan, a historically highly centralized state, the past decade has seen decentralization take place albeit on a temporary trial basis (Horie, 1996).

There has been a similar process in many federal systems, too. Thus, in America, the Reagan administration launched 'The New Federalism' which, despite its seductive labelling, consisted mainly of drastic reductions in the federal administration and a shift downward in the institutional system of financial responsibilities of a large number of public service programmes, not least in the welfare sector. This pattern of decentralization has been furthered in the Clinton administration, most notably through the welfare reform of 1996. And in Germany – a system already extensively decentralized – there has been a further reliance on the *Länder* and cities as administrative reform has attempted to bridge the distance between citizens and the public sector (Derlien, 1995).

The developments in Britain have played out slightly differently, owing mainly to the extraordinarily strong British *étatiste* tradition (Dyson, 1980) and the politicization of regional autonomy, primarily with respect to Scotland. Ironically, as Dunleavy (1989) points out, we should not expect 'statism' to be so strong in a state featuring such strong centrifugal forces, nor would anyone have predicted that the Thatcher government would be able to change much of this in a limited period of time.

The past two decades have seen three different types of devolution in the UK. The first wave of reform was conducted during the 1980s and aimed at opening up local authorities to various forms of partnerships with private businesses, a project which several Labour-dominated cities regarded with great suspicion. Here then is a case of devolution in which historically highly constrained local authorities were granted more powers which they were hesitant to assume but for the most part did, forming what Harding aptly refers to as 'shotgun partnerships' (Harding, 1998).

The second and more recent devolution dates back to 1994 and the creation of the Government Offices for the English Regions (Mawson and Spencer, 1997). The purpose here was to strengthen the regional institutional level, facilitate a higher degree of political and administrative coordination and to develop a single interface between regions and Whitehall. Some observers see the reform as 'one of the most significant developments of Whitehall/ regional machinery for some considerable time' (Mawson and Spencer, 1997:83). Others, not least some central government structures like the Trade and Industry Committee in the House of Commons, are more sceptical about the reform (see Mawson and Spencer, 1997).

The third sector of regional institutional reform has been the creation – or, more correctly, recreation – of a Scottish Parliament. This is the outcome of a sustained discussion between advocates of greater Scottish autonomy and independence and central government and thus represents a very different type of regional institutional reform compared to the Scottish Offices existing in Whitehall and in Edinburgh. However, there is a similarity in so far as both reforms are concerned with the poor democratic representation at the increasingly important regional level of government (see Evans and Harding, 1997).

In Europe, this model of devolution has been strongly endorsed by the European Union and its regional policy. The notion of a 'Europe of the Regions' clearly implies that the EU sees the regional level as the main 'paradigm' for promoting economic development and structural adjustment. As mentioned earlier, this has had a positive effect also on regions with poor coordination and a weak territorial identity: the EU strategy to allocate monies from its Structural Funds only to regions who can present proposals which are supported by partnerships between political institutions and private business has most likely served as a powerful impetus for many regions to get their proverbial 'act together'.

This brief exposé of regional institutional reform in the western world is by no means a complete account of such changes (Le Galès and Lequesne, 1998). It does indicate, however, that most advanced states have gone through more profound institutional changes than is perhaps always understood. If nothing else, these sometimes profound institutional rearrangements suggest that states are more flexible and adaptive systems than is often recognised by those who see the strengthening of subnational actors as an indicator of the decline of the state. That said, there are also several important examples of slow or insufficient institutional adaptation. As we will argue later in this chapter, 'letting other regimes rule' is a philosophy which to some extent is proof of the decreasing 'fit' between the institutional arrangements of the state and powerful changes in the state's environment.

Before we look at the consequences of these reforms in terms of greater subnational independence *vis-à-vis* the state and what models of governance they have entailed, we need to briefly discuss what has driven these reforms. We can see several reasons why so many states have implemented extensive decentralization reforms over the past couple of decades (for overviews, see Pierre, 1997b; Sharpe, 1988). The fiscal pressures on the state were exacerbated by a combination of a growing public sector and public services on the one hand and stuctural problems in the economy in the early 1970s on the other. In order to try to balance its books, central government in many countries has 'hived off' responsibilities to subnational government (Sharpe, 1988). This strategy of managing the economic crisis was often presented in terms of the need to decentralize the public sector and allow for greater local diversity in public service delivery. For most local and regional governments, however, the reforms were a mixed blessing since they had to assume a greater financial responsibility for the services and programmes over which they now had more autonomous control (Pierre, 1994).

That said, there has also been a genuine understanding within many central governments that much would be gained from capitalizing on the increasing professionalization of local government (Laffin and Young, 1990). In the early postwar period, local authorities were often poorly staffed and had little expertise on administrative and managerial matters. There was little need for such expertise since the state controlled and monitored most of the local government service delivery very closely. By the 1980s and 1990s, this picture had changed profoundly: it is fair to say that because of greater specialization within local authorities, subnational governments are just as knowledgeable about public management and service delivery as central government. For example, in the United States the federal government has been tending to borrow management ideas ('reinvention' in the Gore Report) from state and local government, rather than vice versa.

Third, decentralization can be seen as an institutional response to the growing critique against public sector bureaucratic inertia. Such frustration with large public bureaucracies swept across Western Europe and north America during the 1980s, undercutting much of the legitimacy of the public sector as a service provider. To alleviate these problems, states developed ways of closing the distance between citizens and public institutions (see Pierre, 1995b) and facilitating a greater diversification in public services. A key component of this strategy was to give lower-tier institutions more autonomy.

A fourth reason for the almost universal rush to decentralization as an institutional reform objective is the increasing tendency among nation states to see how other countries have addressed similar problems and then apply similar solutions in their jurisdiction. Such policy transfers (both substantive policy and managerial techniques) are believed to account for much of how states develop and execute policy concepts in their jurisdiction, at least in some policy sectors (Dolowitz and Marsh, 1997; Peters, 1997b).

Furthermore, some observers see a close link between regionalization and internationalization and suggest that devolution and stronger regional government are appropriate state responses to internationalization (Evans and Harding, 1997). Some scholars take this argument to the extreme and suggest that national context accounts for very little in today's global economy but that instead '"region states" ... where real work gets done and real markets flourish' (Ohmae, 1995:5) are the most dynamic and appropriate institutional arrangements.

Yet another argument holds that the recent decentralization testifies to the close relationship between public policy and institutional arrangements. The big comprehensive government programmes of the 1960s and 1970s have largely disappeared along with shrinking state finances and a strong belief in the market and non-collective solutions to societal problems. Instead, there has been a growing emphasis on localism and small and efficient public service providers offering services tailored to meet local demands and needs. Putting this slightly differently, what we are witnessing is an institutional restructuring to meet the organizational needs of the 'managerial state' (Clarke and Newman, 1997), as pointed out earlier. In an organization theory, changes in 'domain' of institutions at different levels of the state could be seen as a zero-sum game in which 'the withdrawal, albeit relative, of the state, opens up new opportunities for cities' (Le Galès and Harding, 1998:142). Thus, the higher profile of local and regional government is more the result of the state's withdrawal than of the state's deliberate strategy to allow for greater subnational autonomy.

Thus, we can identify a number of different factors which have propelled decentralization. The significance of these factors varies considerably among different national contexts, owing to different trajectories of state-building (Dyson, 1980) and the history of sub-national autonomy. Some decentralization reforms are clearly initiated and executed by the state whereas others reflect a growing assertiveness among local and regional institutions and interests. These two aspects of decentralization are, to some extent, related, to reiterate an earlier remark: the state-initiated decentralization provided much of the institutional vehicle for the more autonomous policies and strategies which regions in many countries are currently pursuing.

Subnational governments and governance

Having shed some light on what has driven the strengthening of subnational governments, we should now ask ourselves, first, to what extent these developments constitute new patterns of governance and, second, to what extent such emerging forms of governance challenge the role of the state as a source of goal-setting and coordination. Despite all the furore that has been around it may be that little has actually changed in the way that services are delivered to citizens.

The strategy which many regions are currently pursuing to position themselves internationally is more organizationally and politically challenging that is often acknowledged. Going international has become somewhat of a fad among subnational governments in a large number of countries around the world. There are several instances where internationalization projects were not properly planned, objectives were poorly defined, and where, most importantly, the city or region lacked the necessary internal cohesion and coordination and many of the structural, economic or cultural prerequisites to become an international player and to benefit from overseas contacts (Beauregard and Pierre, 1998).

Do these internationalization projects constitute a new, emerging form of governance? No, they do not, at least not yet and not in themselves. With very few, *ad hoc*, exceptions, we have not yet seen any systematic patterns of governance bypassing the nation-state paradigm, that is, with transnational institutions coordinating and directing subnational governments. The previously mentioned Agenda 21 arrangement is one of very few instances where global governance has bypassed the state and aimed directly at subnational institutions. Also, while the 'Europe of the Regions' philosophy is likely to become increasingly important as a governance style in Europe, we are still very far from seeing that arrangement fully implemented and institutionalized. States still play immensely important roles within the larger policy-formulating and implementation framework of the European Union. The fact that regions are a common target for these policies does not mean that there is a governance in the EU which connects regions directly and interactively with transnational institutions.

Phrased slightly differently, regions bypassing the state can, under specific circumstances, become components of a global–local model of governance of which we are only seeing the very first elements. Another and more important observation with regard to the connection between internationalization and governance, however, is that while such strategies do not aim at consolidating global–local patterns of governance, they are predicated on a high degree of intra-regional institutional and political coordination. Recent institutional reform in several countries could be said to serve this end; coordination within a system appears to be a precondition for effective participation in the larger transnational system. However, regional governments in Europe remain structurally weak (Le Galès and Lequesne, 1998).

Thus, subnational internationalization is not (yet) a step towards a new model of global–local governance but a type of economic development stategy which is predicated on, and strengthens, regional governance. This need for coordination and policy coherence 'trickles down' in the institutional hierarchy: as Le Galès (1998:242) argues, 'the impact of globalisation seems above all to strengthen territorial sub-regional mobilisation to resist or adapt, that is, it reinforces the political process at this level'.

Our second question is to what extent subnational internationalization interferes with state-centred governance. Again, it is difficult to give a clear-cut, definitive answer to these questions since we have not seen the final outcome of several current – and concurrent – trends and developments. That said, it seems reasonably clear that successful cases of internationalization have enabled subnational government – to a varying degree and with substantive variation across policy sectors – to escape some control from central government. Internationalized subnational institutions can extract resources which allow them to conduct projects they might not have been able to carry on within the framework of the state. Regions and cities with strong overseas networks do not have to comply with, or respond to, the state's policies in sectors such as industrial policy because they have little to gain from remaining subservient to the state and fitting into its plans. In this perspective, subnationalization does complicate state-centred governance. From the point of view of the state, this development constitutes an incentive to reconsider some of its traditional policy instruments *vis-à-vis* local and regional governments, as we discussed in the previous chapter.

But we can also put a slightly different spin on these questions and ask to what extent regions actually are being forced to choose between internationalization on the one hand and remaining an integrated participant in the governance executed by their home nation state on the other. If state-led governance *vis-à-vis* the regions aims at supporting economic development, then it is difficult to see any reason why there should be a trade-off, or a zero-sum game, between the two strategic options. Rather, the existence of the two optional arenas appears to maximize the probabilities that the subnational government will be able to achieve its ends.

To understand these issues we must look not just at governance *strictu sensu* but also at the institutional politics of governance. Some cities and regions have embarked on internationalization projects because they feel neglected or even discriminated against by central government. Cities which have been successful in positioning themselves internationally like Seattle, Atlanta, Barcelona, Osaka, São Paulo and Frankfurt have done so, to a varying extent, in opposition against central government. This opposition is frequently derived from historical and cultural patterns of territorial identity, or from political and economic rivalry between competing metropolitan regions, or from the state's regional policy. It could also be the case that these cities have little going for them within the nation state: many of them are too big to be regarded as needy of central government support, especially when the domestic competition for such support is strong, yet they are not big enough to be 'natural' global cities like London, Tokyo, Paris and New York (Knox and Taylor, 1995; Sassen, 1991). To sum up this argument, understanding internationalization and assessing its ramifications for the state's governance depends to a great extent on the degree of cooperation and contestation between central and subnational governments.

Global economic governance

Shifting perspective from subnational to global governance from one paragraph to the next might appear to be a tall order even for the intellectually flexible reader. However, as we will demonstrate, subnational and global governance share several features. They are also conceptually and empirically related in several ways that may not be obvious from their apparent disparity in scope and in the nature of the actors involved.

There are several different dimensions of global governance of which the emerging economic dimension is one (see Diehl, 1997). Notions of global governance have historically speaking been an integrated part of the international relations vernacular. The idea that some form of voluntary cooperation among sovereign states is necessary to safeguard key national interests is well-established both among political elites and academic observers. However, thinking about these issues of cooperation from a governance perspective is a fairly recent approach (for an overview, see Rosenau, 2000).

Thus, global governance is essentially a strategy for states to pursue critical goals in an environment where each state individually has a minimum of influence. In this respect, such governance could be said to highlight the limits of state power and capacity and the contingencies associated with limited control in a turbulent environment. Certainly, history provides a depressing number of cases of failures in international governance and cooperation, in the shape both of military conflict and of inabilities of international aid organizations to provide quick and appropriate support to countries or regions in acute crisis. But fortunately there are also a large number of examples of successful international governance, although they do not manifest themselves as dramatically and conspicuously as the failures; through international organizations a number of conflicts between or within states have been resolved peacefully and international cooperation has also been highly successful in providing almost immediate help to the victims of famine disasters or natural catastrophes. Further, the relative stability of the international market-place since the end of the Second World War is in part a function of the international financial regime implemented immediately after that conflict (Helleiner, 1994).

Modern global governance represents something more than conflict avoidance and concerted action to alleviate crises in different parts of the world. While these areas certainly remain important objects of such governance, much of the current international coordination of states' actions is aimed at resolving other more continuous sources of friction between states, not least in the area of economic development and trade. The economic variety of this perspective on transnational or global articulation of state interests is fairly recent but has developed at an impressive pace. To be sure, if the deregulation and globalization of private capital is one of the most salient features of the political economy of the past two decades, different – and still emerging – forms of global economic governance have become one of the most powerful institutional responses to these developments.

This is the perspective on global economic governance which we will entertain in this chapter; we see such governance as propelled by national governments, partly in pursuit of a market-based macroeconomic policy agenda, and partly in order to develop institutions with some regulative leverage over private capital at the transnational or global level. Even the most aggressive economic actors may be willing to participate in these institutions in order to have their competitors bound by the same rules or to place constraints on international capitalism, as leading international marketeers like George Soros, somewhat paradoxically perhaps, advocate (Soros, 1998).

To this admittedly West-centred view on global economic governance must be added, however, the type of governance structures that many Third World governments identify as key forums for voicing their interests in international economic and trade policy. Global economic governance faces the challenge of accommodating the interests of these countries at the same time as it seeks to resolve trade disputes among far more wealthy countries. This also has been true in other regimes, for example, the environment where less-developed countries demand the capacity to increase emissions of greenhouse gases at the same time as the more developed countries are attempting to reduce those emissions.

Thus, there are different perspectives on global economic governance. According to one view, global or transnational economic governance is yet another element of the powerful pro-market ideology. Global economic governance in this perspective serves primarily to eliminate national trade barriers and to ensure free competition in the international economy. Organizations such as the World Trade Organization (WTO) have been granted extensive powers to resolve bilateral trade disputes. The WTO also has the authority to request that countries seeking membership in the organization conform to a market-based economic system, promoting free trade and private competition. Similar objectives are pursued by regional trade organizations such as ASEAN or trade agreements like NAFTA.

The other perspective on global economic governance is that it represents a development towards a new form of international coordination of macroeconomic policies which has been set in train by national governments to ensure that their individual and collective interests are articulated and pursued at what has become the appropriate level, given the globalization of private capital. By banding together, national governments may be capable of combating the seemingly inexorable forces of the global market. We will first look more closely at these two different aspects of global economic governance. Following that, we will briefly discuss critical opinions in domestic politics towards the strengthening of transnational institutions.

Use of international institutions

An approach to understanding what has propelled the emergence of strong transnational institutions could be a policy-oriented perspective, that is, to focus on the agenda pursued by these institutions and what interests they serve. To understand these aspects of global economic governance, we need first to remind ourselves that such governance is not a new phenomenon, nor is the basic rationale upon which it rests. Early forms of transnational organizations promoting trade were already found some 600 years ago when the Hanseatic League connected cities in what is now northern Germany with other cities around the Baltic Sea, creating a strong trade network which controlled much of the trade in northern Europe for a couple of centuries. The notion that free trade leads to specialization and comparative advantages for the participating states and hence greater prosperity and economic growth is a foundation of much classic (and neo-classic) economic theory. Also, free trade helps to generate new markets and more choice in existing markets.

However, even if economic theory indicates that much is to be gained from free trade, a quick look at international trade over the past century shows that a large number of states have chosen not to follow that strategy but instead to introduce barriers against foreign trade along their borders. In Britain, the late nineteenth century witnessed a sustained political argument between advocates of free trade and protectionists. For the latter, free trade was believed to expose the domestic economy to overseas competition which would jeopardize national autonomy and wealth. There have been strong similar protectionist sentiments in the United States, too, for parts of the twentieth century. To a shifting degree, public policy against free trade in favour of some form of trade barriers has also been implemented in countries such as Australia and Japan. Thus, while most experts on these issues probably agree that free trade is good in theory, political elites in many national contexts have still – albeit for different reasons and in different historical and political contexts – opted to protect their domestic industries and markets from international competition.

The recent development towards institutionalized economic governance at the transnational or global level has been primarily market-driven and should be viewed against this historical background. The emergence of the European Union (EU) was in many ways a continuation of a number of bilateral trade agreements in Western Europe, primarily the coal and steel union between France and Germany. From the Rome treaty onwards, the EU integration process has sought to remove obstacles to economic growth by consolidating Western Europe as a cohesive economic region. Alongside these objectives, there has also been a massive institutional development to create the democratic mechanisms necessary to guide the consolidation of the Union and to provide representational linkages between EU institutions and those of the member states.

These developments, it must be remembered, have been state-driven processes. The fact that they have catered mainly to interests associated with economic development only substantiate a well-known point we are making throughout this book: states have a tremendous stake in economic growth. However, the sources of economic growth are changing. Only a couple of decades ago, industrial production and trade were to a large extent bilateral processes: goods were produced in one country and purchased in another. In the 1990s, by contrast, industrial production has increasingly become a matter of coordinating the compilation of components and semi-products from several different countries into a product which is then marketed simultaneously across a large part of the world. Or economic growth results from the use of electronic transactions that are almost disassociated from physical products. As a result, trade negotiations increasingly have become multilateral instead of bilateral affairs, as well as becoming more complex because of their subject matter.

The development of the World Trade Organization should be understood in this perspective. The WTO replaced the General Agreement on Tariffs and Trade which had played a similar role as the WTO in serving as a forum for multilateral trade negotiations. However, the WTO has significantly more capabilities than its predecessor. The WTO plays an important role in settling trade disputes. It also has forums and a wide range of other instruments for settling such disputes and promoting free trade. As Hoekman and Kostecki (1995:271) aptly put it, 'The WTO's *raison d'être* is to constrain the ongoing civil war in the polity of members regarding the trade policy stance that should be pursued.' It does so not least by influencing domestic debates on these issues: 'The WTO enters the picture by giving foreign players a voice in domestic political markets – the negotiation leverage of proliberal democratic lobbies is enhanced because foreign export lobbies will support them in multilateral trade negotiations' (ibid.).

Thus, while international institutions have evolved as a result of state interests in devising some instruments at the global level which can both resolve collective problems among sovereign states and act as a counterweight to international capital, these institutions have over time acquired a high degree of influence over domestic politics. Global governance is thus a two-way street type of phenomenon: while it offers states some potential control at the global level it also means subjecting the state to a new and powerful source of influence.

There is a tendency to associate – conceptually and empirically – these emerging forms of global economic governance with the fairly

aggressive pro-growth agenda that is being pursued in this governance. In other words, it is sometimes assumed that these institutional structures can only promote one particular agenda. In part,
this argument rests on the well-known assumption that there exists a
close linkage between institutions and interests (see, for example,
Hall, 1986; March and Olsen, 1989). That argument notwithstanding, we think that perspective is, on the whole, misleading: as
the European Union demonstrates, there can be heated argument
over these issues. In the EU the argument revolves around whether
this set of structures should be employed primarily to promote mon-
etaristic policy objectives or if they should be primarily concerned
with fighting unemployment. It is therefore probably more correct
to conceptualize global institutions as sets of economic and administrative instruments that, in theory at least, can be employed for a
variety of different political projects. As the intelligent reader has
already concluded, this is precisely the perspective and expectations
we have on domestic institutions: governments, sometimes with
vastly different political agendas, come and go but the structures of
government remain largely the same and are designed to cater to
these different ideologies.

New strategies for pursuit of state interests

Global economic governance, as mentioned earlier, should be seen
not just as a matter of reducing trade barriers but also – and equally
important – of developing some kind of levers to exercise some level
of control over international capital. These two objectives need not
necessarily collide: for instance, economic and monetary union
(EMU), which has been created to coordinate the macro-economic
and fiscal policies of the EU member states and also to introduce a
joint central bank and a common currency, will offer effective protection from international speculation against individual countries'
currencies.

Global governance and domestic discontent

Global governance is not embraced by all political elites, nor by all
constituencies in society. The idea of surrendering national sovereignty to transnational institutions is highly politically charged and
easily sets off backlashes drawing on nationalist sentiments. In many

countries in Western Europe, 'Eurosceptics' oppose further European integration (Taggart, 1998). It is interesting to note, however, how differently these issues position themselves on the left–right political spectrum in different countries in Western Europe. In the Scandinavian countries, Conservative and Liberal parties are the strongest and most articulate supporters both of the EU and EMU. These parties see EMU not least as a key element of the liberalization of markets and reduced state encroachment of the economy. Meanwhile, the Social Democratic parties appear to be torn between a general pro-EU stance on the one hand and a fear of losing control over macroeconomic levers and the possibility of growing economic inequalities on the other. In Britain, however, the growing capabilities of transnational institutions are viewed sceptically by Conservatives who see these developments as a threat against national sovereignty, autonomy and control.

Put slightly differently, the notion of 'letting other regimes rule' is not looked upon very favourably by significant groups in society. These issues are both technically complicated – for instance, there seems to be some confusion of autonomy and sovereignty involved in much of the debate; maintaining nominal sovereignty by remaining outside the EU, for instance, does not lead to a higher degree of autonomy – and they also quickly stir nationalist sentiments in many countries. Therefore, it is probably easier to generate political support for the 'reasserting control' scenario; if nothing else, that is a model of governance which is by far the most familiar to most of us.

Negative interdependencies

Just as in the previous chapter on state strategies to reassert control, we discussed the political economy of that strategy, we should now look at the same logic applied to the present scenario of letting other regimes rule. Reasserting control as a political–economic strategy could be justified fairly easily with regard to the positive interdependencies between state and market. Is there a similar logic which could sustain the strategy of letting others rule? Are there negative as well as positive interdependencies between state and market?

Global governance, it was said earlier, rests ultimately on notions of institutional insufficiency to control their environment while at the same time these institutions are extremely dependent on changes in these external environments. In some ways it appears as if the institutional machinery of government was designed and developed in a political and economic environment which is fundamentally different from the current situation. While there certainly have been extensive, sometimes profound, institutional reforms conducted in countries throughout large parts of the world, there is still a legacy of the 'strong state' of the 1950s and 1960s and the environment these states operated within. This legacy exists in the minds of many politicians as well as in the actual structures of the public sector.

This legacy manifests itself in two different ways. First, most states still display an institutional structure which is typical of an image of the state where central government is in undisputed command, where transnational systems of institutions and governance do not exist (or, to the extent that they do exist, exercise limited leverage over the state), and where subnational governments have very few political or administrative initiatives of their own. With most or all of these features having changed considerably, there is today almost an overkill of monitoring and controlling institutions in many states. True, the decentralization reforms discussed earlier have addressed these problems but they have frequently done so more by strengthening local and regional government than by abolishing central government's institutions to oversee subnational government. Similarly, although the system of state subsidies to local government has been deregulated, central government still exercises considerable legal and constitutional control over local and regional government.

Second, the design of the institutional structures of most governments is to a surprisingly large extent a reflection of – or geared to – the economy as it operated prior to deregulation and globalization. For instance, in almost all countries stock markets and currency markets are monitored by institutions whose jurisdiction is defined by national borders; yet a growing part of the transactions in these markets takes place between domestic and foreign financial actors. Similarly, central banks are still assumed to act as the ultimate instrument of currency and fiscal control; yet their effective leverage is significantly constrained by international financial actors.

One might argue that these institutional legacies only serve to illustrate the lag and inertia in the transformation of the state to changes in its environment. Also, some might suggest that perhaps the institutions of the state, normatively speaking, should not be very adaptive since their core political and democratic mission in society – articulating, defending and pursuing the collective interest – is a matter above and beyond what might be short-lived changes in the state's external environment. These arguments notwithstanding, the poor institutional 'fit' with their external environments is sufficiently conspicuous as to raise questions about the causes and consequences of this state of affairs.

Relating this issue to the 'letting other regimes rule' scenario, there are three general points that deserve mentioning. First, institutions cannot control their external environments. Admittedly, there may have been a time when the institutions of the 'strong state' related to changes in their environment in a continuous and logical way but they probably did so more by enacting their environment than by responding to changes in it (March and Olsen, 1989; Peters and Pierre, 1999). One of the consequences of the 'rolling back of the state' which we have seen taking place over the past couple of decades is that this enacting capability has been significantly impaired. At the same time, the institutions of the state have not yet developed the knowledge of how to adapt to changes in the institutions' environment. Unlike most other organizations in society, state institutions never developed a routine of monitoring, interpreting, and developing appropriate responses to changes in their environments simply because – with only very slight exaggeration – there was no need for them to do so. It could well be that what we are currently witnessing is political institutions learning how to respond to external changes.

Second, the plight of contemporary states in these respects is that they are increasingly dependent upon markets over which they have decreasing control. True, as we have discussed earlier in this book, there are strategies available to states which seek to regain some of their previous control over markets but this is a politically delicate and complex project requiring a high degree of global coordination. As a corollary to the problem of states currently learning how to respond to external changes, there is a significant problem involved in states acquiring greater control over markets because a large number of states never exercised such control to any great extent and hence lack the organizational knowledge and memory to do so in a successful way.

Finally, and derived from the previous observations, we should not be surprised to see states and central governments turning increasingly inward, allowing for subnational and transnational regimes to gain leverage and control as the institutions of the state become less significant. This development, to reiterate an earlier remark, is not the same as the state surrendering to external pressures but more a matter of policy choice to assume a lower profile in society. Further, the change may be more apparent than real, as governments learn to govern 'smarter', using less obtrusive instruments that permit substantial control without expending much scarce political capital.

Institutional adaptation or the decline of the state?

The two emerging types of governance discussed in this chapter are directly related to each other. Internationalization and global governance are, taken together, a strong impetus for regions to develop governance mechanisms and also for nation states to encourage such governance. Similarly, some form of global economic governance has become necessary to accommodate the new types of actors which are making their way on to the international stage.

To some extent, 'letting other regimes rule' is a governance scenario which reflects a policy choice based in a strategic assessment of the consequences of economic globalization and subnational political assertiveness. It is also, however, in part testimony to what appears to be insufficient institutional responses to external changes. However, asking whether these developments reflect an institutional adaptation, albeit slow and partial, or whether we are in fact witnessing the decline of the state is misleading since clearly these complex processes can not be conceptualized in an either/or kind of analysis. As we have argued several times already, the growing interest in governance should not be confused with a decline of the state but is rather proof of the state's ability to develop new strategies to maintain some degree of control. It appears to be the case that this strategic response is much quicker than the institutional changes which in the longer term will prove critical to the state.

7

Scenario 3: Communitarianism, Deliberation, Direct Democracy and Governance

In addition to challenges to traditional patterns of governance arising from globalization and from the power of networks, there is yet another set of challenges that would produce very different styles of governing. This collection of related challenges all endeavour to deinstitutionalize governance and to more directly involve citizens in making binding policy decisions. The assumptions undergirding these ideas is that the public can – and more especially should – have more direct influence over decisions than they can exercise in representative democracy. These ideas go beyond the 'new governance' ideas of using groups, networks and other intermediate social structures as mechanisms for governance to focus on citizens themselves as the principal source of governance.

These ideas then represent a populist challenge to 'big government', and seek to return governance to 'the people'. Unlike the market challenge (Self, 1993; Niskanen, 1996) to large-scale government involvement in the economy, however, the normative inclination here is collectivist rather than individualistic. Its purpose is not so much to permit the individual to retain earnings and wealth as to permit the individual to participate in a legitimate political community and to make effective decisions about their future through collective action.

These populist challenges are then more closely linked to traditional governance ideas than is the market vision of reform. In particular, these views are linked to a traditional conception of *democratic* governance. The assumption is that to govern appropriately a democratic political system must be capable of linking the demands and wishes of the public directly to policies (Rose, 1976). Further, the traditional governance view often argues that most representative institutions do not permit adequate debate and discussion but rather depend more on one side prevailing over the other with as little discussion as possible.

For both the market and the collectivist challenges the status quo of governance is considered deeply flawed, but the prescriptions tend to be diametrically opposed. Rather than dismantling most governance structures in favour of an atomistic market many of these populist reformers would build even more inclusive structures, and would require most citizens to devote greater time and energy than they now spend to the processes of collective governance. Even those collectivist reformers who do not desire to build structures *per se* do want to use a political (voting) device, rather than an economic device, to make choices for the collectivity.

Although we are discussing alternatives to governance through the public sector, the critique of government embedded within this populist challenge is actually targeted more broadly. It is a generalized critique of virtually all representative and intermediate structures in industrialized societies, including political parties and even the interest group networks that are so central to much of the 'new governance' literature (Rhodes, 1997; Kooiman, 1993). These critiques also extend beyond the public sector to include large corporations and also large labour unions, and in some cases even organized religion. The State is a central object of the critiques discussed in this volume, but the same problems are perceived difficulties in almost all social institutions that extend beyond the local community or even the family. The ideas being advocated are to reform all social institutions and to develop alternatives that will either replace or complement the more traditional structures.

There are three major variants of this populist challenge to the traditional conceptions of governance. All three versions would deinstitutionalize existing government structures, or at least would seek to augment them with more direct citizen involvement. Within the three there are still some differences in the degree to which government structures and representative democracy would be deemphasized. The least movement away from the status quo in governance appears to be represented by communitarianism. This is an emergent political philosophy, as well as a set of more practical recommendations about how to manage public problems (Etzioni, 1995).

The basic tenet of communitarianism is that large-scale society and government have outlived much of their utility and they need to be replaced by smaller units of governing. The more appropriate basis for governing is considered to be the 'community', although this term itself is open to some interpretation. In this view some of the basic mechanisms of governance by political means are not incorrect; the difficulty is with the scale on which those devices are being implemented. Large-scale decision-making, it is argued, forces the same sort of individualism associated with economic models of policy; individuals need to have their self-interest modulated by less selfish commitments to community.

The second alternative to the existing patterns of government is deliberative democracy. This alternative also has some elements of a political philosophy (Barber, 1984; Sandel, 1996) but has a somewhat stronger emphasis on the immediate reform of decision-making institutions. The logic of this approach is that representative democracy does not permit average citizens to exert adequate influence over policy decisions. Rather than being the apathetic 'couch potatoes' assumed in some contemporary discussions of governing, the public is assumed to desire to be more involved in political life. Advocates of deliberative democracy argue that citizens feel, however, that they are effectively excluded by the current institutional arrangements used for governing. This view represents one of the standard sociological definitions of alienation – the existence of ends with the absence of effective means to achieve those ends.

Establishing mechanisms for greater direct public involvement in policy-making are hypothesized to be essential for reviving democracy. This contribution to enhanced democracy is especially valid if those methods can create more numerous opportunities for the public to discuss issues and to develop more complete and nuanced understandings of those issues than is possible within existing representative institutions. Developing these institutions for discussion and deliberation is deemed to be especially important (and feasible) at the local level, having this conception in common with the communitarians. The lower level of government is believed to be a more suitable locus for developing 'genuine' deliberative democracy than are other levels of government.

Finally, direct democracy constitutes another alternative to representative democracy. Even more than the other two alternative approaches, this method of governance would supplant the existing representative institutions in favour of the public making its own decisions through mechanisms such as initiatives and referendums. In the literature supporting this alternative the assumption is that the public does not really need to have the elaborate discussion and deliberation inherent in the deliberative democracy approach. Rather, the public is argued to be capable and ready to make important policy decisions through a simple vote on the issues. Even more than that, there is an assumption in some of this literature (and practice) that the public is capable of setting the agenda for governing, as when initiatives permit the public (through petitions) to place an issue on the ballot for subsequent resolution. For example, Proposition 13 that radically reduced property taxes in California was begun as an initiative, getting the required number of signatures, and then decided in a popular vote. This conception of direct public involvement in policy is somewhat akin to the 'second face of power' (Bachrach and Baratz, 1964) in which the most important power that elites can exercise is determining what issues will, and will not, be actively considered by government.

This chapter will discuss each of these three alternatives to the conventional pattern of governance. The discussion will attempt to demonstrate some of the strengths of each alternative, but also to portray some of its weaknesses. The fundamental argument developed here is that none of these three is capable of supplying governance in the coherent and integrated manner that is required. There are some common problems in all these models that we will identify, but there are also some very particular issues that arise for each of the three. In some instances, a strength of one of these three alternatives may be a major weakness of one of the others.

We will also point out that each of the three alternatives represents useful complements to existing patterns of governance, although they are almost certainly not adequate replacements in all instances. As with all attempts to make contingent decisions about institutions or processes (Sartori, 1994), the vexing question is under what circumstances each of these alternatives is the most appropriate option. The advocates of each of these approaches tend to consider it as a general solution for the problems of governance, but our views will be contingent and more modulated. There are in our view a large number of instances in which the traditional patterns of governance are preferable, and in which the use of one of the alternatives will produce a positive loss of governance capacity.

The diagnosis

Before we embark on the detailed examination of each of the three alternatives, however, we should examine some general points of diagnosis – what do these approaches to governance believe is amiss in the conventional patterns of governing? This critique has some general points, but there are also some more specific problems raised by each of the approaches. This portion of the discussion will remain rather general, with the more particularistic points discussed in reference to each of the three alternatives. The critique of the existing patterns of governance rests on four main problems in the present governing systems: size, remoteness, displacement of goals and the adversarial nature of the institutions. These four factors are all closely interconnected but some independent effects of each factor on governance can be discerned, especially to the critics of that current system.

Size

The first critique is that existing governance structures are too large. This is true of the geographical and social space that they cover. It is also true of the range of issues about which they attempt to exercise governance, and also about their ambitions in governing. That is, governments in many industrialized democracies are argued to have taken on too many responsibilities and promised too much to their citizens, and have not been able to deliver the goods and services promised. In an argument not dissimilar to discussions of overload (King, 1975; Rose and Peters, 1976) a generation ago, the disjuncture between promises and performance has been one component of the disaffection of many citizens with their governments.

Size tends to exacerbate the problem of remoteness to be discussed below, but has negative consequences of its own for governance. Size is principally a problem for communitarians, but also poses some difficulties for the advocates of deliberative democracy. It is argued that large units of government, here often meaning any units larger than a group that would permit frequent face-to-face contact between all members, may move the definition of public problems beyond a human scale. Communities may be defined in terms of shared understandings and experiences, so that they may extend to the boundaries of a nation, if not a state, but making those common values operational may be more difficult (see Fowler, 1991, 1995).

The larger scale of discourse tends, in turn, to make individuals less responsible for their own governing and less likely to be able to conceptualize solutions. The argument is not dissimilar to the arguments Illich (1971) made about modern medicine, although the villain here is scale and not technology. Seeing themselves at the mercy of forces well beyond their control, citizens are assumed simply to opt out of political participation. The other option is that a definition of political life is developed that tends to exclude those who do not accept a particular civic virtue, or who do not fit the prevailing conception of appropriate behaviour. For communitarians the large size of contemporary governments and the absence of any sense of community makes intolerance, individualism and exclusiveness far too easy.

Larger-scale governance structures also tend to make any sort of constructive deliberation among citizens less likely, and less meaningful if it is possible to organize. Even if viable 'public spaces' for discussion are maintained in a large-scale representative democracy, deliberation becomes relatively useless: there is little or no way that meaningful discussions can occur at that larger scale of governance (Habermas, 1984). Only at the face-to-face level, in small units, is there likely to be discussion and dialogue over policy, other than in the most superficial manner (see Cohen, 1997). In a mass society individuals become atomistic and anomic and are not likely to be effective participants. In this view the general decline of participation in many democracies is a function of the alienation produced by the size and remoteness of government. The problem with that analysis is that participation tends to be lowest at the lower levels of government where it should (according to that logic) be greater. The assumptions of deliberation, such as consensus formation, appear less likely to be present in a larger-scale setting in which representative institutions and associated adversary politics appear more likely to be present (see Kelman, 1992).

Another aspect of this critique of large-scale government is that size prevents governments from developing the types of policies that are increasingly required in a 'post-industrial democracy' (Bell, 1976). That is, one of the many drives for public sector reform in the 1980s and 1990s has been to attempt to customize the policies being supplied and to make them more suited to particular segments of society, or even individuals. Although large governments, whether national or subnational, may be making numerous well-intentioned efforts to make themselves more consumer-friendly (Hood, Peters and Wollmann, 1996), the argument from the advocates of alternative forms of governance is that they will be unsuccessful simply because of their size. Having to cope with large numbers of clients, and large numbers of service providers, makes 'empowerment politics' more difficult to implement.

Remoteness

Another common complaint about the contemporary system of governance is that it is too remote from the average citizen. That average citizen encounters a very difficult time in influencing policy or setting the terms of debate about policy. Given the number of citizens that each elected delegate must represent (over half a million in the United States), he or she cannot really be said to reflect those views very closely or even be aware of most of them. This scale means that the representatives are able to make decisions on their own with little or no reference to the wishes of their publics. Further, the views in any constituency may be so diverse that the representative can pick and choose among interests and views, rather than seek to form any consensus among those ideas.

This remoteness is argued to be extremely frustrating for the citizen in democracies. Well before the creation of these various populist responses to large-scale democracy, Huntington (1974) argued that 'post-industrial' politics would be alienating. As populations became better educated and more politically efficacious the difficulties in influencing policy would become more vexing. Further, Majone (1992) argued that the public now does possess a great deal of useful information for policy-makers that officials ignore at their peril. Citizens often have information that is not possessed by official sources but is more 'street-level' knowledge that even for some technical policy issues may be crucial for making the most appropriate decisions.

Even with interest groups, as components of the networks that are so central to the 'new governance', there is a gap between the average member and the group leadership. This is one of the standard arguments about democracy in interest groups, especially trade unions, as discussed by Lipset, Trow and Coleman (1956). More broadly, it is a restatement of Michel's familiar 'Iron Law of Oligarchy'. The average organization member should not expect to exert any real influence over the policy positions of the group, with little expectation therefore that the group will actually reflect the views of the members. In short, both conventional representative institutions and the interest groups that are proposed as a substitute to those institutions in some models of democracy and governance are remote from their general publics and hence may not offer 'authentic' democratic options for individuals.

A final aspect of the remoteness of representative government from the average citizen is that this citizen believes, often with some justification, that government is dominated by money, rather than by the interests of citizens (see Nye, Zelikow and King, 1997). Eliminating the need for members of representative institutions (especially in the United States) to raise campaign money, whether it is personally or on behalf of a political party, is thought to enhance the capacity for government to better represent the concerns of the average citizen. As we will point out below, it is not always clear that the alternatives proposed to representative government will be that much less susceptible to the influences of the rich and powerful in society: both direct democracy and deliberative democracy appear to depend on the capacity of groups to influence political life and that capacity is differentially distributed. It is, however, very clear to critics that the prevailing system is not providing the type of governance they desire so that even with the potential problems, the alternatives are worth attempting.

Displacement of goals

Finally, given the remoteness of leadership in both political institutions and interest groups, there is a capacity for the leaders to pursue their own goals rather than those of the citizens or their membership. This is in part because the large-scale structures, and the low levels of information conveyed by voting, and even by occasional public meetings, are insufficient to provide guidance for even the most conscientious politician.

The above view is, however, in contrast to one of the other critiques of modern politicians that they are unwilling to make stands on their own but rather depend too heavily on public opinion polls. In the deliberative school, however, those polls are themselves deeply flawed (Fishkin, 1996). And for the less than conscientious among them there is ample latitude for self-aggrandizement, whether legal or extra-legal. This is hardly a novel critique of government and political organizations: Michel's Iron Law of Oligarchy recognized this tendency in political parties at the beginning of the twentieth century, and Merton (1940) and Downs (1967), among others, have noted its presence in public sector organizations.

The pursuit of individual goals by political elites while in office is seen in these critiques simply as a continuation of the same individualistic norms inherent in contemporary governance structures. Rather than being part of a community of any variety, the individual citizen is simply one lone individual attempting to make his or her way through this veil of tears as skilfully as possible. This perceived focus on the individual politician as a utility maximizer in matters of governance may be a case of life imitating art, as the methodological individualism of rational choice theory has come to dominate analysis in the social sciences (Green and Shapiro, 1994). This view can be contrasted to a variety of more collectivist theories about social life (see especially March and Olsen, 1984).

Citizens are often particularly critical of the political elite for vote-trading and logrolling. They see their politicians not voting even according to their own values but rather in a way that simply eases their position in the political world. The public sees this behaviour as an abnegation of their role in governance in favour of self-aggrandizement. Logrolling may be more a function of the complexity of the contemporary issues and differential benefits that policies can have for different constituencies. The public, however, sees it as just one more manifestation of the separation of the elite from the average citizen, and of the need for alternative forms of governance that are more subject to public control.

Adversarial governance

The fourth general problem with representative government institutions identified by the three alternative conceptions of governance is that these institutions tend to be adversarial. Steven Kelman (1992) has argued that one of the most important differences among various political systems is the extent to which they are adversarial, with the Westminster systems being particularly combative while more corporatist systems (Scandinavia) being more consensual (see also Lijphart, 1984). For the proponents of these alternatives (the direct democracy group are singing this chorus *sotto voce*) the differences are perhaps not worth considering, and representative institutions in general are excessively oriented toward conflict and a winner-take-all style of conflict resolution. It is perhaps not surprising, therefore, that most advocates of the alternative visions of governance are from Anglo-American systems.

The problem being identified here is that government through adversarial mechanisms divides members of the public rather than permitting the development of policies that can satisfy all of the public, at least minimally. In some instances it may be difficult to find such a policy, but the process of negotiation itself may be a significant way in which to expose fundamental issues and at least to identify the reasons for the disagreement. Further, representative institutions are almost designed to enhance adversarial and competitive behaviours, rather than consensus-building. The idea of securing a majority in parliament in order to govern, for example, is an inherently adversarial concept and, especially when a single party can win control (as in Westminster systems), tends to institutionalize the winner-take-all mentality of those systems.

As noted above, the direct democracy alternative is not as much concerned with the problem of adversarial institutions as are the other two. Indeed, the notion of voting for a proposition – usually as a 'yes or no' question – appears inherently adversarial itself. One positive point, however, is that the campaign surrounding the vote in itself may expose the issues. On the other hand, however, the necessity of having an election and its associated campaign may polarize rather than create greater consensus.

Communitarianism

The most general option for addressing the problems in democratic governance outlined above is communitarianism. As an option to the isolation and atomism of contemporary society and representative political institutions, these scholars and activists would create working communities and community governments (Etzioni, 1995, 1998; Bell, 1993). There is a working assumption that most socio-economic problems can be solved at lower levels of aggregation than at which they are currently addressed. Further, there is an implicit judgement that with the proper social engineering even large scale cities and towns, if not nations, can be made into more communal decision-making systems. There is also a belief that people are inherently communal rather than individualistic, so that contemporary structures fail to fulfil some basic needs of the public.

In the communitarian view individual autonomy is important, but it can only be understood as socially constructed, as opposed to the more complete autonomy characteristic of much liberal individual-istic thinking (Walzer, 1995). Further, in the communitarian view, personal autonomy implies substantial respect for the autonomy of other individuals, as well as preserving the process of self-actualiza-tion. Thus, actions that may be harmful to the collective welfare are not acceptable, even if they fulfil the individualistic desires of some members of the society (Etzioni, 1996:18). Full personal autonomy is also found only when there is some order in society, so that some mechanisms must be found to blend individual with collective desires (see also Bay, 1965).

In some ways it is easier to identify what the communitarians are opposed to than what they are actually for as reforms of the state (Tam, 1998). It is clear that the individualism identified as endemic and destructive in contemporary society and government are not the circumstances in which they prefer to live, but the proposals they advance appear somewhat Arcadian for countries with tens of mil-lions of inhabitants, or even for cities with a few million. Few people would not welcome closer contacts within their communities, or enhanced capacity to have a personal influence on the outcomes of policy deliberation; at least most want to achieve their goals if not to invest the necessary time in the process.

Another way to conceptualize the communitarian solution to gov-erning is to consider the now wide-spread arguments about social capital (Putnam, 1993; Perez-Diaz, 1994). When attempting to understand why democracy has flourished in some settings and not in others scholars have concluded that the existence of 'social capital' is crucial to its success. Social capital is indicated by the exis-tence of large numbers of social groups formed outside the family or the immediate clan. The formation of such groups indicates that individuals are able to identify with social entities outside the family and are willing to make some commitment to such non-familial groups. That level of social trust enables people to be involved in politics.

It is not clear just how the communitarian argument would conform with the idea of social capital. On the one hand there is a commitment to participating in some types of social organization outside the family. On the other hand, however, the communities under discussion could be quite localized and also highly particularistic and may therefore not be the type of social groupings that figure in Putnam's models of building democracy. That is, membership in the community may be tightly circumscribed, so that not just anyone may be a member. The type of more localized involvement implied by communitarianism may be simply another form of localism, and may lack the commitment to broader involvement and civicism that seems inherent in Putnam's arguments about building democracy.

The governance implications of communitarianism

By this point the implications of this pattern of thinking for governance should be clear. Their implicit, and at times explicit, plan is to decentralize government as far as possible and to make smaller 'communities' responsible for more aspects of public policy. There are some versions of this approach already in operation, and indeed rather familiar. For example, Neighbourhood Watch and similar co-production programmes have a strong affinity with the ideas of communitarianism. Attempts to create 'little city halls' and neighbourhood councils are attempts to create governments at a low level.

Communitarianism proceeds well beyond the simple desire to devolve governing to smaller governments and communities as defined in a common-sense manner. It involves as much as anything else a shift away from individualism towards a more collective sense of governing. This involves rethinking the basis on which public policy is made: rather than individual utility maximization, policy is to be made on the basis of community values, presumably held by all participants. Much as in March and Olsen's (1989) conception of a 'logic of appropriateness', the members of a community are assumed to be guided by a common set of values.

If we move away from the existing structures, communitarianism would advocate creating mechanisms that would enhance participation and facilitate the development of meaning in government. There is often more discussion of the principles of governing than the practicalities, but there are some suggestions about using the principles for actual governance.

Problems in communitarianism

As appealing as some aspects of communitarianism are, there are some significant problems when this set of ideas is taken as an approach to governance. Perhaps the most fundamental is that the theory makes assumptions about human nature that are perhaps not sustainable. There is an assumption that the average citizen wants to participate in government and to invest a great deal of time and effort in governing. It further assumes that human beings are cooperative and not the self-aggrandizing individualists that are assumed in a good deal of contemporary social and political theory. These are felicitous assumptions, but may not be sustainable in the real world of politics.

The problems of communitarianism are exacerbated when there is no clear definition of the community for which the political system is to function. That is, in a homogenous society the community and the society may be coterminous. In many contemporary countries that correspondence may not exist, and people who live next to each other may not think of themselves as belonging to the same community. A genuine sense of community appears necessary for sharing and for making the redistributive decisions necessary for most public policies. Given that it is difficult to think of a public policy that does not have some redistributive effects, then making policy across communities becomes much more difficult, and with that governance also becomes more difficult.

Can political community be created? One of the assumptions of the communitarian approach is that even when there is no natural or preexisting community, it can be created. This is in part a 'field of dreams' argument, with the assumption that if there are opportunities for community policy-making created, then the public will find it desirable to take part. In this view community can come out of interaction, rather than interaction coming from community. That view may, however, require at least some minimal level of community existing at the beginning of the virtuous spiral being assumed.

Communitarian theory also assumes that important problems can be solved at relatively low levels of aggregation. In reality, the important problems may not be solvable in very small units. For example, poverty can be seen at a low level but its causes may be economic and social forces that have their origins well outside the local community. Even if not global in their origins, these forces may not be controllable through the resources available in the local community. Even for administering programmes smaller local communities may be of inefficient sizes for delivering the services.

Deliberative democracy

In some ways ideas about deliberative democracy comprise a subset of communitarian thinking. The basic idea of creating a locus for making decisions at a low level of aggregation appears compatible with communitarian thinking. What is most fundamental to the practice of deliberative democracy, however, is a *process* of involving the public in making decisions through open debate and dialogue. This process is in contrast to representative democracy in which the public is involved only as voters selecting the elites who will later make the decisions. It is also in contrast to direct democracy in which the public make decisions themselves, but do so with little or no collective deliberation or confrontation of alternative views on the issues.

The ideal model (in practice) for deliberative democracy is the Athenian city state (Thorley, 1996) or the New England town meeting in the United States. In these systems of government all citizens enjoy the opportunity of participation through debate with their fellow citizens, and can hear and evaluate alternative points of view. There was, and is, little hierarchy among the participants in these meetings, and all are able to speak as equals. After the debate the participants can then cast a vote, with their votes ultimately determining the policy to be adopted. Both of these forms of democracy were (or are) relatively small so that all citizens could participate if they wanted to do so. As we will point out below these versions of democracy do not meet all the criteria advanced by scholars in the field, but represent perhaps the closest to those ideals that have been attained as general formats for governance.

There are several conditions that can be used to judge the extent to which any particular attempt at deliberative democracy corresponds to an 'ideal type' model (see Hunold, 1998). The first question is whether the process of deliberation is empowered to make the final decision on a policy, or whether it is only advisory to a formalized decision-making body. For example, mechanisms such as public hearings in the United States (DeSario and Langton, 1987) and public inquiries in Britain (Barker, 1995) provide an opportunity for citizens to present their views, and perhaps to hear the views of others, but in the end it is the zoning board, or a city council or some other formalized body that makes the decision. Citizens in this setting are not decision-makers but only advocates for their own points of view and passive hearers of the ideas of others.

A second criterion is whether the discussion is ongoing or is a simple one-time chance to express views. The better deliberative process is one in which there is an opportunity for discussion over some length of time, with opportunities to consider and address lacunae of information and to counter opposing arguments (Bessette, 1994). Without some continued possibilities for interaction among the participants, a deliberative process may become reduced to a simple opportunity to vent feelings rather than a genuine opportunity to make decisions. Again, the public hearing model does not permit that type of continued interaction but tends to demand that a decision be made at the one meeting; to postpone a decision is generally seen as a failure, rather than a reasonable step in making a superior decision.

Third, adequate deliberation also hinges upon how the participants are selected, or rather not selected. The ideal type of a deliberative process is one in which anyone can participate, as opposed to being selected as a representative of some interest or some segment of society. The advocates of deliberation argue that the more selective process prevents the full range of opinion from being heard and tends to bias outcomes in favour of more or less 'tame' interests. This view is especially common in feminist analyses of policy, arguing that women are often excluded from the process of decision-making within representative institutions. In this case the public hearing model tends to be rather good, given that in most instances all the citizen must do is to register in order to be able to speak. This does not mean that all speakers will be accorded equal weight, but they will be able to participate.

Finally, deliberative systems vary in the extent to which the range of options available to the participants is constrained *a priori* or not. In some deliberative processes there is a simple question to be considered and decided, with the process thereby constrained, no matter who is entitled to participate and for how long. So, in the public hearing example above, the question may be simply whether a certain piece of land will be rezoned in a certain way or not; the question of what the zoning options should be, or even if there should be zoning, is not open for consideration. In the more developed deliberative process, once the process is initiated the range of possibilities would not be so restricted. Clearly the need to make a certain type of decision will initiate policy-making, but the advocates of deliberation tend to want to have fewer constraints once the process is initiated.

This ideal model of the deliberative process is rarely, if ever, achieved in the real world. If the standard could be achieved the assumption of the advocates of deliberation is that the process would have several positive effects. One would be to enhance the actual quality of the decisions made in the process. As noted, there is an assumption that members of the public have a great deal of information that is useful for policy decisions (De Leon, 1997; Majone, 1987). More importantly, this type of process should enhance the legitimacy of the decisions that are made. The idea that this is a more genuine form of democracy than representative systems, and that face-to-face participation will enhance citizen efficacy, is fundamental to the advocacy of deliberative democracy.

Even if the ideal model is not attainable, there may be some approximations that are functioning. Even if not ideal, they may have some of the positive effects assumed to obtain from the more perfect version. The familiar public hearing is a very limited, if still effective, version of deliberative democracy and could easily be extended to a wider range of policy issues. It could also be enhanced to more closely approximate the ideal type. For example, there could be the possibility for hearings to define more of their own agendas rather than having all the issues and options determined in advance. Further, hearings need not be simply one-time events but could be reconfigured to permit some ongoing debate and discussion.

Another operating example of a deliberative process is called 'negotiated rulemaking' in the United States but is also similar to various corporate and corporate pluralist mechanisms in Europe

(Rokkan, 1967; Olsen, 1987). The idea here is for the parties affected by a regulatory regimen to be permitted to meet together to discuss and then write the relevant rules. This pattern of decision-making meets some of the requirements for deliberative democracy, but by no means all. For example, participation in the negotiations is not open but is based upon holding some position in a group selected for participation. Again, however, this may be a more open and democratic option than the more administrative means through which rules might be made ordinarily and hence may make governance more democratic than it would be otherwise.

The democratic and populist values inherent in deliberative democracy are appealing in many ways, but there are also a number of problems inherent in the model (see Stokes, 1998). Some of these problems are not dissimilar to the questions already raised concerning communitarianism, in particular how can advocates make this model premised on small (and generally homogenous) groups of people function in larger and more diverse political settings. Once the deliberative process is moved beyond the small organization or the small community, not only do the physical problems of engaging in meaningful dialogue become more evident, but also the social basis of communication may be insufficient to permit that meaningful dialogue. As the community becomes more heterogeneous the different premises for arguments and the different goals of the actors diminish the possibilities for effective dialogue. The Habermasian 'ideal speech community' (Habermas, 1973) assumes that the public forum for discussion would be available to any and all participants, while in practice more heterogeneous assemblies may find effective communications more difficult. Further, some writers question the capacity of deliberative settings to foster the type of equality assumed necessary; biases of all sorts may intrude into these arenas, just as they do in other political settings (Knight and Johnson, 1997).

Following from the above is the question of whether the general public really has much to add to a discussion of nuclear power or one on biotechnology. Experts in these fields would point to the absence of basic understandings of the technologies involved and misperceptions of risk that exist in the general population (Sunstein, 1998). The advocates of deliberative democracy would, of course, argue that these questions are too important to be left to the experts. They would also point out that the experts have been wrong about a number of major points in these fields, and that there are social and political questions arising from these technologies that extend well beyond the technological issues themselves. If the public is excluded from the discussions about the technologies then those normative points may well be excluded as well.

Finally, there are important questions about how any final decision can be reached through such a deliberative process. The underlying model appears to be that of discussion and bargaining until a consensus is reached. The model therefore assumes first that there is a consensus to be reached, and second that confronting social problems with evidence and creating understanding will make people operate against what may well be their true self-interests. There does appear to have been movement of ideas during some deliberative processes that have been mounted (Fishkin, 1996; Fearon, 1998) but it is significant that these processes have not been truly responsible for the final policy choices. When there is the possibility of making the final decision there may also be a greater tendency to protect interests and less receptiveness to the ideas of others.

Direct democracy

The third populist challenge to the conventional forms of governance is direct democracy. This is by far the simplest of the three alternative approaches, and lacks much of the philosophical underpinnings of the other two approaches. The argument is simply that the public should be empowered to make decisions about policy themselves. For the referendum option in direct democracy, the legislature, or perhaps the executive, may ask the public to consider a piece of legislation for which they do not want to be responsible themselves. It may be that the legislature does not want to take a stand on contentious moral issues such as abortion or divorce: Italy and Ireland, as predominately Roman Catholic countries, have had several referendums on these issues. Or the issue may be perceived to be in essence constitutional: a number of countries in the European Union have dealt with proposals for major changes in the European Union basic law by calling referendums and the Maastricht and Amsterdam treaties were sent to referendums in a number of countries including Denmark, France and Sweden. Finally, the legislature may be required constitutionally to submit the issue to the people. For example, in some states in the United States, any increase in the bonded indebtedness of the state or any change in the state constitution will have to go to the people, as do significant pieces of legislation in Switzerland (Kobach, 1994).

The initiative option is somewhat more complex, with the public having to mobilize first in order to get an issue on the ballot, and then again during the campaign before the election. This opportunity removes the elected legislature and executive from the process of governing almost entirely, with the public being empowered to set the agenda as well as make the final policy determination. In the relatively few localities that provide for the initiative, members of the public appear willing to tackle difficult and controversial issues that a legislature might want to avoid. These are also issues that many ordinary citizens might also want to avoid having to discuss and decide upon, but their more activist neighbours will not permit that. They do not have to vote (in most locales) or pay attention to the issues, but with political advertising through broadcast media they may not be able to avoid being bombarded with information about them.

The justification for direct democracy is simple, clear and apparently very democratic. It is that the people should be able to decide themselves on significant issues that will affect them. The definition of significance may vary in different political systems, but the basic principle is that of preventing a remote decision-making body (even if elected democratically) from determining matters of lasting importance for the public. In this conception of democracy the public is at least as capable as their elected representatives of making difficult (and the most difficult) decisions. Further, it appears that they will be expected to make those decisions on the basis of limited information and debate.

Although appealing to all our democratic sentiments there are a number of extremely difficult questions about direct democracy as a form of governance, although we should remember that this method is still phrased as a complement to the traditional mechanisms of representative democracy. The first question is how questions get on a ballot for determination. When that process is automatic, then there may be little difficulty, but when some form of signature campaign (the initiative) is required then many of the same problems of representative democracy appear to arise. That is, organizing a campaign of that sort involves the same organizational skills and the same financial resources that tend to make access to legislatures unequal. Further, the emphasis tends to be on single-issue politics, with very intense minorities tending to have a disproportionate influence over the agenda of the public sector. This may be especially true of the agenda-setting process in which those single-issue groups can focus attention on a campaign with little concern for overall governance capacities.

A second concern about direct democracy involves the generally limited information and discussion that tend to characterize the campaigns for these referendums. Again, this places a premium on the ability to get a message out through the media, and hence on financial resources. This may explain a part of the success of anti-tax referendums in the United States (Sears and Citrin, 1985) and of anti-European Union stands in Switzerland. Leaving aside the bias that may be inherent in this form of decision-making, deliberative democracy advocates would almost certainly criticize the absence of any capacity to consider the issues and to share information among members of the voting public.

Both of these crtical perspectives oppose the conventional representative institutions of governance, but may themselves have very different ideas about what the most desirable options for change would be. Because of the restricted information and general discussion, any policy decisions made through referendums may well be decided on the basis of simple, stereotypical views of the issues and may even produce anomalous results. Voters in California have passed referendums at the same election that are opposed to each other, leaving it up to the courts (perhaps the least public of all institutions) to make a final determination on policy. That is, of course, partially explained by its being California.

There are also questions of whether the most important issues can be phrased in the simple 'yes or no' style inherent in resolution through popular voting. A part of the critique of the remoteness of contemporary institutions is that their members make issues excessively complex and also are not committed to values that would motivate their voting in the ways that their constituents would have them vote. That may be true at least in part, but it also masks something of the underlying complexity of issues. The public is given to assume that there are simple answers to complex issues, while anyone who works on these issues for any time soon learns that those simple answers are more often than not misleading.

Even if the issue in question can be presented in a simple 'yes or no' manner the use of direct democracy may threaten minority rights. Legislative bodies often will make decisions that ignore those rights, but in general political elites do tend to be more tolerant than the general public. Further, legislatures do not want to be embarrassed by having their decisions overturned by courts or ridiculed by the press. In the United States state and local referendums have adopted a number of measures limiting the rights of homosexuals and other unpopular minorities, or at least not conferring upon the legal right of equal treatment guaranteed to women and racial and religious minorities. Some of these electoral decisions have been reversed by the courts, but the decisions make the point that this 'democratic' method of making policy is not always hospitable to minority rights.

Nor is direct democracy likely to be conducive to making economic redistributive decisions that would take away from the majority and give to a minority. If voters vote their self-interest, generally not a bad prediction, they are not likely to choose to give away resources readily. Interestingly, however, the other two alternatives to conventional forms of governing may be well-suited to making redistributive decisions and to coping with minority rights. The opportunity to discuss the need for such policies, and the development of community, may make it possible to adopt those difficult policies. This is especially true for redistribution *within* a community, although the opportunities for redistribution *across* communities may be much more limited.

The democratic character of direct democracy can also be questioned because of the manner in which the public appears to consider these opportunities for participation. In general, turn-out in referendums is very low unless there is an election for public office occurring at the same time. The public appears still to believe that selecting their representatives is a more important activity than deciding on particular policy issues themselves. The lack of any personal identification with the issue may be one part of the problem. It could also be argued that the absence of real opportunities to discuss the issues involved in that referendum tends to depress participation: if the public does not understand issues fully they are unlikely to participate. If this lack of understanding is an issue, then it argues for creating a hybrid model of governance in which there are opportunities for dialogue in conjunction with the opportunity to make the final decision through the referendum.

The concepts contained in 'deliberative polling' may be a means through which to overcome at least one of the problems raised by direct democracy and to create the discussion of issues needed before a referendum (see Fishkin, 1996; Stokes, 1998). In deliberative polling, instead of having the public simply respond to survey questions without any preparation, they are provided an opportunity to discuss the issues among themselves, and perhaps also with experts, before expressing their own opinion. Deliberative polling is as yet not a method of decision-making but rather a more sophisticated mechanism for public opinion polling. It certainly has the potential of augmenting the usual mechanisms of direct democracy, but as was the case with discussion and deliberation and communitarianism, finding a means to conduct these exercises for more than a small group appears difficult and perhaps extremely expensive. Focus groups have been used in something of the same way, but again can involve only a rather small number of citizens.

Summary and conclusion

These three alternatives to governing represent possible departures from the institutions common in most democratic political systems. They all assume that the current institutions of governing are flawed in important ways, and need to be reformed in ways that will permit the public to be more active participants in governing themselves. Further, two of the three are interested in promoting more genuine debate and discussion on policy issues and making policy only once the public has had the chance to think and talk about the issues.

The most fundamental point to be made about these alternatives is that the process by which decisions are made may determine the policy decisions. The representative institutions that are the targets of criticism for these three alternatives may be good at making some types of decisions, but they are not necessarily good at making all types. Further, even if the representative institutions are capable of making the decisions, the standard processes tend to privilege certain outcomes and to disadvantage other opportunities. For example, the deliberationists and the advocates of direct democracy think that a lack of inclusiveness tends to produce decisions that favour the better-organized elements of society and disadvantage the ordinary citizens. The argument is not so much that the process *qua* process has this biasing effect. Rather it is argued that the manner of selecting the participants in the process tends to bias the outcomes in favour of powerful interests in society.

As we have proceeded through this discussion of these alternatives to traditional democractic forms of governing, it should be clear that the critique of the existing systems is more coherent and compelling than the alternatives presented for reforming the system. There are certainly very important problems with existing governance systems, and the critics are successful in identifying those deficiencies. That having been said, the proposals offered for reform appear to have some genuine deficiencies of their own. The principal problems appear to be in the practicalities of taking ideas about governance that can work in small settings and attempting to make them perform equally well for mass democracy. There is no real evidence that this can be successful.

As with so many particulars in social and political life, we are faced with making a trade-off of values when discussing approaches to governance. Among other things that are being traded off are the (relative) divisiveness of representative democracy against the deliberation and due consideration of all points of view argued to characterize deliberative democracy, and to some extent communitarianism. On the other hand, however, direct democracy may be more decisive than current representative systems, and some advocates favour it because it allows a clear decision on a point of policy, without all the amendments and ambiguities that may be built into a policy by a legislative body.

Part III

Governance and the State

Introduction

Part III applies the preceding analyses to the contemporary state, not only in the advanced western democracies but also in the Asian and Latin American regions and the developing countries. It is clear that the emergence of governance forces us to reconsider many of our ways to think about the state and state strength, and it is equally clear how immensely differently this discussion plays out in countries at different levels of development. Thus, the key questions we address in this section are what are the determinants of state strength and how important is a strong state for governance. We advance a perspective on these issues which suggests that state strength is less and less a matter of being able to impose its will on society and increasingly a matter of political and social engineering, entrepreneurialism and zeal. Strong states have developed a skill to adapt to changes in the domestic and global environment. Such skill is often derived from an ability to identify and exploit cooperative patterns of public–private exchange. States that were once strong but now appear to be weaker seem to lack much of this ability whereas previously weak but now stronger states often control these skills.

The conclusion here is that it still makes much sense to talk of strong states and weak states as long as we acknowledge that what defines such types of states is probably changing. Governance becomes the centre of attention in this discussion because state strength, we suggest, is increasing becoming a matter of playing a leading role in governance.

8

States in Transition

Much of the current debate on the state revolves around the issue of how states respond to the globalization of capital and the domestic political and economic accommodation of this new type of economy. Key themes in this debate are the degree of state resilience towards international capital and how much autonomy is left to the state as a result of globalization (see, for example, Boyer and Drache, 1996; Camilleri and Falk, 1992; Esping-Andersen, 1996; Garrett, 1995; Helleiner, 1994; Hirst and Thompson, 1996; Krugman, 1994; Moses, 1994). It is worth noting, however, that just as states have been said to be facing irreversible decline for more than a century, albeit for different reasons in different time periods (Navari, 1991), states have more or less continuously been characterized by some degree of transition and change. They have been reshaping in economic, political, social and institutional – and a fair number of them even in geographical – terms. Thus, state adaptation as a phenomenon is about as old as the state itself and therefore the issue is thus not whether states are reshaping and developing but rather how they manage their transition.

That having been said, what may currently be happening – and here we are largely speculating – is that while states themselves previously orchestrated much of the change they adapted to, they are now to an increasing extent adapting to changes which they have not proactively and directly initiated. The development of the modern state was, in institutional terms, to a large extent a matter of devising structures, instruments and processes geared to assuming the responsibilities associated with the higher profile of public activity in society. The increasing encroachment on society by those state activities in turn triggered processes to which the state institutions had to respond, not least societal dependencies on different types of state actions or provisions: we need only think of an increasing dependency on the state as a welfare provider, as a customer in markets, as the chief agent for infrastructural development, as a mediator in conflict between organized interests, or as a protector of trade strategies in international negotiations. These developments were thus to a large extent predictable consequences of the policies pursued by the state.

We touched briefly upon the possible shift in the sources of change in the state's environment in the previous chapter. We believe that the development towards governance introduces a new perspective on these issues. In particular, the notion of different institutionalized forms of public–private cooperation and coordination indicates a partially new model of exchange between the state and its environment, something which, in turn, has consequences for the mechanisms through which the state acquires knowledge about changes in that environment and how it should respond to those changes.

Given the turbulence in the environment of the contemporary state, state strength (and its governance capacity) is to a growing extent a matter of two related factors. One is its capacity to adapt to external changes. Today, as we will argue later in this chapter, institutional learning is a continuous process. This has, however, not always been the case; since the state's environment increasingly changes in ways which are not easily predicted, learning and managing contingencies have become a necessity. This reaction to the environment goes beyond the simple cybernetic model discussed earlier, and implies a modification of institutions and procedures in order to maintain and enhance governance capacity.

Another key feature of state strength is its capacity to act. This perspective, which is different from more traditional notions of state strength as a set of capabilities derived from constitutional or legalistic assessments of institutions' jurisdiction, is at the core of governance theory. State action is obviously predicated on some notion of external changes: action presupposes some degree of adaptive capacity. Again, looking at these issues in a governance perspective gives a more rewarding image of the state's capacity to act since action, in this perspective, is derived less from constitutional powers and capabilities and more from the state's capacity to establish priorities and coordinate action among key societal actors in the pursuit of those goals.

It hardly requires mentioning that states are not as homogeneous as some of the previous analysis might lead the reader to conclude. Therefore, in order to shed some light on these issues, this chapter examines the trajectory of different states (and different varieties of states) in terms of their patterns of response to external and internal changes and developments. Further, there may be variations within individual states, with different organizations and policy areas demonstrating differing capacities to adapt.

State strength and adaptability

The recent globalization has led a number of scholars to reconsider the issue of state strength (for an excellent critical review of this literature, see Weiss, 1998). One perspective holds that globalization poses a major threat to state autonomy. State structures have lost considerable leverage over the economy and this, in turn, has significantly impaired their overall capacity to act. Another argument suggests that although globalization certainly is a major challenge to the modern state, states are adaptive creatures and hence we should expect – or are already seeing – states to transform to meet the challenge of globalization.

Looking more closely at the ability of states to adapt to new external circumstances and conditions, we can see different interpretations and perspectives there, too. Theda Skocpol (1979) suggests that strong states are inherently less adaptable compared to other states. This is because state strength in her analysis is the joint outcome of insulated institutions and a centralized state. Centralization reduces the number of points of contact between state and society, something which obstructs state learning about external changes, and therefore reduces the adaptive capacity of the state.

The contending view is that state adaptivity is not directly linked to state strength and hence to governance. The rationale for this proposition is that weak states are to a much higher degree penetrated by civil society and more deeply embedded in society compared to strong states. This embeddedness serves as a cluster of linkages between state and society which the state can employ both to learn about external changes and to respond to those changes (Evans, 1995). Thus, just as the fact that oaks tend to break while birches bend suggests that in fact the birch is more resilient than the oak, strong states may be seemingly more capable of adjustment but frequently turn out to be the prisoners of their own rigidity.

Thus, strength and adaptability are not necessarily two sides of the same coin. 'State strength' in Skocpol's definition is typical to the traditional view on government – governing is the capacity to impose the will of the institutions of government over society. The notion that weak states are more adaptive than strong states is, however, closer to the governance view on this issue. That is, weaker states will have to find means other than imposition for reaching their desired goals. We will return to this question later in this chapter.

Furthermore, institutional learning and adaptation is an ongoing process. There is much to suggest that the state's capacity for such learning and adaptation is increasing: for instance, much of the recent institutional and administrative reform is geared to facilitating organizational learning by reducing centralized political control and increasing the exchange between institutions and their environment (Peters and Savoie, 1995, 1998). In particular, programmes for consultation and citizen involvement (Pierre, 1998b) mean that government enhances its chances to learn from the public and from the networks deemed so important in new governance. This learning from networks does not mean control, only that there is a positive relationship with the environment.

State models, state traditions and models of governance

One approach to understanding state strength is to observe how the state conducts its exchange with the surrounding society in a dynamic perspective, that is, to focus on trends over time. Such a perspective helps bring out triggers of change with regard to state strength and governance capabilities. We will look at four different types of such developments. These four types are strong states remaining strong, strong states becoming weaker, weak states growing stronger, and weak states remaining weak. Within each category, we have made a rough selection of cases to illustrate changes in state strength. Furthermore, in each of the four versions of state development, we will look at recent changes in their governance in order to see either to what extent changes in state strength are explained by an emergence of new forms of governance or, alternatively, to what extent they have propelled new ways of thinking about governance in the different national contexts.

Strong states remain strong

In this category of countries we use as examples France, Germany and Japan. All three states were – albeit in different ways – severely damaged and incapacitated by the Second World War. Furthermore, all three – again for partly different reasons – embarked on the postwar reconstruction process in a distinctly state-led fashion (Cohen, 1977; Hall, 1986; Johnson, 1982; Reich, 1990). In Germany and Japan the war devastation was of such a scale that there probably never existed much choice other than to accord the state a leading role in the economy although in Japan at least this was an arrangement which was well-suited to the political culture. Also, the strong influx of foreign capital to support the reconstruction of Germany required a strong centre and only the state could assume that responsibility. In Japan, several aspects of the causes of the country's international conduct from Pearl Harbor onwards were ultimately associated with managing Japan's economic dependencies; as a result, rebuilding the domestic industry was defined as a matter of utmost national interest (Johnson, 1982).

When the immediate postwar reconstruction of their respective domestic economies was completed, Germany and Japan went different ways in terms of the organization of government and the degree of centralization of the state. The German constitution of 1949 emphasizes decentralization, primarily based in the *Länder* and with a distinct division of labour between the *Länder* and the federal government. This institutional arrangement has ensured a high degree of fiscal discipline combined with extensive welfare state services. Indeed, with regard to the tight control over macroeconomic policy exercised by the autonomous Bundesbank, coupled with parliamentary procedures preventing excessive public spending, and a strong legalistic tradition governing public–private exchanges, Germany comes very close to a textbook example of a strong state.

France provides a slightly different view on the sources and manifestations of state strength, although there are some similarities with Japan with regard to the extent to which the national interest is defined in terms of managing external economic contingencies. The historical *étatiste* tradition, emphasizing a centralized system of government, and a consensus sustaining the *dirigiste* role of the state in the economy explain more than acute needs for economic restructuring (Dyson, 1980; Hall, 1986). Another aspect of the strong French state is that there appears to be a high degree of political and international self-reliance: although the country has strong diplomatic bonds with its neighbours it has – historically at least – insisted on placing the national interest before collective objectives. The French decision not to participate in the NATO joint command and to develop their own *force de frappe*, and the opposition against Britain's joining the EC in the early 1970s are but a few examples of this high and autonomous international profile of the French state. All of that having being said, however, France is today together with Germany the strongest advocate of a strengthened European Union (Menon, 1998).

Thus, we could think of this type of state strength as strength through centralization. This has certainly been the case, historically speaking, in France, Germany and Japan. The political and institutional centralization has helped concentrate and coordinate resources and control and place them under the control of insulated institutions. Central government, primarily in France and Japan, has conducted extensive planning over natural resources and economic development. Subnational governments have primarily been the local and regional arms of the state; it is indicative that the whole notion of local autonomy has been viewed with considerable scepticism by the political elite in Japan (Muramatsu, 1997).

That having been said, it is interesting to note that strength derived from centralization seems to be more a historical than a current feature. Moreover, such strength appears to be indigenous not least to 'developmental states'. Such states display tremendous capacities in mustering and coordinating national resources, public and private, to promote economic goals which are seen as core national interests (Johnson, 1982; Weiss, 1998). The strong centripetal forces which are typical of 'developmental states' generated a governance model which, although highly state-centred, clearly recognized that the state was almost completely dependent on the corporate sector to attain the top-priority goals of economic growth and industrial development. As Weiss and Hobson (1998:174) argue:

initiating policy and carrying it through involves a process far more intricate than the simple question of 'who dominates' allows. We argue that it is not a question of bureaucratic domination but of *coordination*. (emphasis in original)

This political dependency on extra-state actors – or what Weiss (1998) calls 'governed interdependencies' – fostered a reliance on subtle steering mechanisms instead of strict regulatory or intervening instruments. It is a type of dialogue between politics and business which in many ways is part and parcel of the Japanese and South East Asian culture (Johnson, 1982; Okimoto, 1988) but perhaps less so to the German *modus operandi*.

Thus, boosting state strength through centralization, it appears, was primarily a viable strategy before the emergence of globalization; before the fiscal crisis of the state; before the growing emphasis on a managerial state delivering diversified and customer-attuned services; and before the development of institutionalized influential international regimes exercising some degree of control over national governments. If that is the case – that is, if a centralized system of government was an option before these changes emerged – then why did not all states 'choose' to develop a strong state? A large part of the answer is that a number of populaces, for ideological, cultural and in some cases also for historical reasons, preferred the state to be relatively weak in order to prevent public power from becoming too big and uncontrollable. In addition, state strength must be understood in context (Evans, 1995; Gourevitch, 1986): it is embedded in, and the outcome of, a historical process which to a very large extent defines what policy options are appropriate today (March and Olsen, 1989).

A centralized state, like any other state model, has its strengths and weaknesses. The strengths have already been discussed and we now need to look more closely at its weaknesses. One apparent weakness is that centralization reduces the points of contact between the state and the surrounding society, domestically and internationally. This lack of contact becomes a problem as the pace of change increases in the external environment of the state, or when the main drivers of change are no longer political but economic. In the conventional view of government discussed earlier, the state was the main source of political, economic and social change. This view is not altogether outdated but it is not as valid as it once was, either. States have assumed a lower profile in society since the 1980s and this has forced them, metaphorically speaking, to become learning rather than teaching organizations.

Another important weakness of the centralized state model is that it, relatively speaking, is less capable of capitalizing on the knowledge, expertise and professionalism it possesses. The expansion of the state in most countries during the postwar period – not least France and Germany – has entailed a substantive growth of expertise and professionalization of the staff at the regional and local levels of the political system which in many ways match that which is found in central government. Most importantly, subnational government staff have an insight into how central (federal) programmes play out 'on the ground', something which implementation research in the 1970s found was conspicuously absent when programmes were designed (Pressman and Wildavsky, 1976).

These weaknesses of the centralized state have become more accentuated over the past two decades along with the increased pace of change in the state's external environment. States have acted in accordance with this changing relationship between state and society, as we saw in Chapter 6: throughout the western world, states – for a variety of reasons – have been restructuring in ways which increase the points of contact with the surrounding society. However, the main feature of state–society relationships over the past couple of decades has been a rolling back of the state and allowing the market to play a greater role in society, in terms of both an allocating mechanism and a heralding philosophy of private enterprise and individualism. These developments probably account for more of the new emerging relationship between state and society than the restructuring of the state itself. The changes in overarching value systems have typically portrayed the private sector as the 'principal agent' in society while the public sector increasingly is seen as subordinate to the market. Recent institutional changes in the state should be viewed in this perspective.

We now need to assess to what extent decentralization indicates – or entails – a weakening of the state or whether can we speak of state strength through decentralization. There is much to suggest that decentralization has been instrumental in sustaining the strength of the states discussed in this section. Thus, in France the recent decentralization has invigorated subnational government and politics. Local governments have used their greater discretion to embark on impressive reforms aiming at making the public sector more accessible, for instance, by simplifying citizens' exchange with authorities and by introducing websites and email as a means of communication between citizens and the public service (Meininger, 1998; Rouban, 1998).

The decentralization reforms have also been important in redefining the main roles of central government. With most of the operative – sometimes also the financial – responsibilities for public services decentralized to subnational authorities, central state institutions have become able to focus more on long-term strategic issues. These issues include the growing cluster of domestic–international networks and mitigating and coordinating global–national–subnational exchanges. In these ways, decentralization has helped reconfigure the state to address issues and problems which are typical to the environment the state finds itself situated in at the end of the second millennium, with deregulated financial markets and a growing role of both transnational and subnational regimes, as was discussed earlier in this book.

Similar developments are clearly visible in both Germany and Japan. In Germany, the division of labour between the federal government and the *Länder* has shifted even further towards the regional level. Most importantly, perhaps, economic development is primarily promoted at the *Länder* or city levels while central government focuses more directly on macroeconomic policies and managing the large number of issues related to reunification as well as transnational issues related to the further consolidation of the EU. Even in Japan, central government appears to be focusing more on core policy issues while the prefectural and city governments are operating increasingly autonomously from Tokyo. Certainly, central government still exercises a very tight control over subnational authorities by most international comparisons but the development towards some degree of subnational autonomy is fairly clear. The current deep financial crisis has probably further induced central government to focus on these critical issues, leaving an increasing discretion to prefectures and cities. The only tendency working against this slight diffusion of power in Japan is the continuous focus on economic development as a matter of national security. For instance, Tokyo still evaluates subnational internationalization largely in terms of how it affects the Japanese trade balance and uses powerful instruments to prevent cities and prefectures from pursuing policies which are not in the interests of central government.

There are two important conclusions coming out of this brief discussion on the logic of state strength. First of all, strong states remaining strong are, in fact, just as flexible and adaptive as states undergoing some type of change in their strength. Their enduring strength is not so much the result of *status quo ante* in terms of the utilization of sources of state strength as the outcome of a successful redefinition of those sources and their application in public policy. Thus, these are states which have resisted the temptation of continuously relying on traditional sources of power and capabilities and instead explored new and less coercive bases of institutional capability. Indeed, we can take this argument one step further and suggest that given the increasing pace of change of the state's environment, state strength *is the result* of adaptability. Globalization and regionalization have redefined the sources of state strength and, subsequently, the role of the state and government in governance.

Second, building state strength through centralization or decentralization – to the extent that there is a real choice here – are not concurrent choices. The two state models are logically embedded in different external environments and therefore strength is derived from different institutional configurations at different points in time. True, a synchronic analysis of the structure of states will reveal that they display a tremendous variety in terms of centralization although they are seemingly embedded in the same international environment, something which would suggest that the degree of centralization is not explained by the nature of the state's environment. A closer inspection, however, will show that much of the variation in these respects is accounted for by the historical development of the state and the trajectory of state formation and consolidation (Dyson, 1980).

A number of studies have shown that in the context of political economy, state strength depends not so much on formal capabilities of state institutions but more on their ability to work effectively with corporate actors and that, in turn, the governing capability of the state to a significant degree depends on the configuration of society (see, for example, Atkinson and Coleman, 1989; Berki and Hayward, 1979; Evans, 1995; Gourevitch, 1986; Hall, 1986; Kenworthy, 1995; Weiss, 1998). This points to a dynamic relationship between the state and private business and a need for the state to reconsider its institutional arrangements along with the restructuring of private capital. This is obviously only one of several different types of external factors to which the state must respond to maintain (or increase) its governing capacity: we need only think of the growing strength of transnational regimes or changes in the domestic civil society to see the need for some degree of institutional flexibility within the state.

Strong states becoming weaker

Most 'globalization advocates' would undoubtedly place a large number of countries, or even all countries, in this category. As we have argued earlier, however, we are not convinced that there exists a zero-sum game relationship between globalization and state strength: such a theory is predicated both on a high degree of uniformity in state organization and governance structures and on an image of states as structures incapable of adaptation and transformation. The interesting research problem, in our view, is rather how different state models and governance structures have responded to globalization.

The group of previously strong states becoming weaker should have some interesting insights to offer to such a discussion because it should help us discover something about the foundations about state strength and the politics of accommodating change. We have chosen to use five countries to illustrate this type of state development: the four Nordic countries (Denmark, Finland, Norway and Sweden) and Britain. The Nordic countries on the one hand and Britain on the other have highly different paths of development but nonetheless they share a relative decrease in state strength.

Scandinavia – or, if we include Finland, the Nordic region – is often believed to be a group of countries ideally suited for a 'most similar systems' research design (Przeworski and Teune, 1970; Peters, 1998c). While there may be some historical truth to that, there is also reason to suggest that the four countries now differ in such fundamental respects that clustering the four Nordic countries into a 'Scandinavian model' is misleading (Grönnegård Christensen, 1997). Most importantly perhaps, the countries differ tremendously in almost all aspects of their political economy: their economic bases are vastly different, with Norway capitalizing on its oil richness, Denmark specializing in advanced agriculture and industry, and Finland and Sweden still having their economy based in manufacturing industry albeit with growing sectors in future-oriented sectors such as telecommunications and the medical sector.

The postwar trajectory of the Nordic states – primarily Denmark, Norway and Sweden – is impressive in terms of the rapid development of a comprehensive welfare state. At the same time, the state has refrained from any major long-term encroachments on the corporate sector, largely because of the decisive role private businesses play in sustaining the economy. In all three countries there has been – and still exists – a delicate dependence on export revenues, hence the corporate sector needs to be internationally competitive (Katzenstein, 1985). The result of these has been an interesting model of political economy (incorrectly) referred to as a 'mixed economy'. This type of political economy features extensive redistribution and public services, high taxes (more so on income and consumption than on corporations), and a market-conforming industrial policy and political economy. Thus, it is more a matter of co-existence than of a true mix of the political and economic spheres of society.

The historically speaking strong Scandinavian states are an extension of the collectivist political culture in the region. Together with strong notions of proportional representation, this culture has also fostered strong organized interests and a distinct corporatist model of policy deliberation and implementation. Much of the historical strength of the Scandinavian states thus rested on their ability to generate consent for their policies among all key political and societal constituencies. This consent was generated both through the electoral process and through the process of interest group involvement in policy.

Thus, these states share a legacy of a strong state apparatus which recently has come to display many signs of being weakened. With the exception of Norway, whose economy has been tremendously boosted by the oil and gas revenues and the associated off-shore industry, the Scandinavian states – primarily Finland and Sweden – have proved susceptible to international speculation against their currencies. The combination of a high degree of export dependency and problems with maintaining fiscal discipline (Hinnfors and Pierre, 1996; Weaver, 1987) has made these economies extraordinarily prone to international speculation.

To some extent, the weakening of the Scandinavian states is explained by the particular type of 'peaceful co-existence' which has evolved between the Social Democratic dominated state and the corporate sector. Following Weiss (1998), what she refers to as 'governed interdependencies' are more easily managed if the corporate sector has strong interest organizations and if these organizations are in some way integrated with the political elite. In the Scandinavian countries there are a large number of organizations representing private business but the networks between these organizations and the state are mostly weak, informal and intermittent. In the heyday of corporatism, business organizations were continuously involved in different capacities in the policy process. But in Sweden at least there is much to suggest that these corporatist arrangements have lost most of their leverage over the past couple of decades (Rothstein, 1992; Weiss, 1998).

Another potential source of decline is related to the linkage between changes in the external environment of these states and their domestic arrangements for policy-making. Some observers argue that corporatist models of policy-making are not very efficient in adapting to international or global change (Gourevitch, 1986; Olson, 1982). Others, like Peter Katzenstein (1984), suggest that corporatist systems in some ways are at least as efficient as other models of policy-making and interest representation in accommodating and responding to change. What is lost in terms of how swiftly these systems respond is gained in terms of broad social consent for the measures taken in accommodating external changes. Austria and Switzerland, Katzenstein (1984:245f.) notes,

> are distinctive in that they calibrate the requirements of economic flexibility with those of political stability. Switzerland encourages economic flexibility while making some political concessions. Austria organizes policy around political concessions without neglecting the requirements of flexibility. In linking flexibility with stability, both countries have chosen to live with the costs of change.

One could probably – and not without some degree of success – argue that the patterns observed by Katzenstein reflected the political economy of corporatism prior to the globalization of capital and markets. While that seems to be the case, it must also be noted that these small industrialized democracies have a long history in operating successfully on international markets with all that that entails in terms of adapting to external changes (see Weiss, 1998). In sum, therefore, it appears as if corporatism as a governance system is not in and of itself less capable of providing steering and leadership through the process of responding to external turmoil. However, the recent weakening of the Scandinavian corporatist systems has also meant a decline in the strength of these states. Somewhat ironically, while corporatist systems seem to respond fairly swiftly to economic changes, states tend to respond slowly to the decline in corporatism. Developing new governance structures to replace the corporatist model of interest inclusion is a long-term process.

The decline in corporatism has manifested itself in several different ways. The wage-bargaining process has been decentralized and there is an overall decreased reliance on organized interests in the policy process although many policy sectors still feature strong and influential interest organizations. While there is much in current styles of political participation in Scandinavia to suggest that involvement in mass organizations has become much less attractive compared to a couple of decades ago (Katz *et al.*, 1992; Listhaug, 1989; Petersson *et al.*, 1998; Widfeldt, 1997), we do not believe that the main causes of decline in corporatism are found inside the voluntary associations. Instead there are two powerful external changes which have posed a serious challenge to this type of interest representation. One is the fiscal crisis of the state: there is now much less to bargain for – but more to be held responsible for – compared to the heyday of Scandinavian corporatism. Furthermore, the consolidation of the European Union has introduced a new mode of devising and enforcing regulations to which organized interests still seem to be searching for an effective counter-strategy. Similarly, unions are gradually strengthening their international cooperative efforts as a response to the internationalization of private corporations (Elvander and Seim Elvander, 1995).

Thus, in retrospect it seems as if the domestic political arrangements and governance structures in Denmark, Sweden and Finland have not been very efficient in tackling the problems associated with financial and ideological change and the internationalization of the economy. This may appear counter-intuitive in some ways, given the long tradition of trade dependency in these countries. Again, the problems are not primarily caused by changing patterns of international economic dependency but rather by a combination of a reduced growth in the domestic economy on the one hand and growing volatility on the political scene on the other. The previously dominant Social Democratic parties have been significantly weakened. At the same time, new parties have made their entry into parliament. The result has been growing complexities in securing parliamentary support for the Cabinet's proposals. As Weaver (1987) points out, minority governments – which have been common in all three countries – have not been geared to resolving financial problems or imposing severe austerity programmes.

However, all three countries are now members of the EU and are likely to join the EMU albeit at different times. This membership will have profound effects on the traditional governance structures. While corporatism probably will continue to be a defining feature of the political process, organized interests will have to learn to operate within a political economy with very fixed limits on budgetary deficits and inflation (Hinnfors and Pierre, 1996). Corporatism has already been significantly weakened by the general waning of budgetary resources in these countries, but may have to be eroded, or changed, even further.

Norway, by contrast, has chosen to go it alone. One might think that Norway's not joining the EU is grounded in a belief that their oil revenues give them the financial leverage to develop their economy outside the EU–EMU frameworks. However, Norway has a long political and cultural tradition of catering to its peripheries (Rokkan, 1966), something which was brought out very clearly in conjunction with the referendum on whether the country should join the EU in 1994. Much of the successful campaign against membership argued that Norway would be a net loser in the European Union and that membership would exacerbate imbalances between different regions in the country.

However, Norway faces the same problem as her Scandinavian neighbours in developing strong parliamentary majorities, helpful if not necessary for governance capacity (Lijphart, 1984). In addition, it has proved difficult to manage the oil-based economy; given its powerful growth, inflation and an excessive wage development are perennial problems. Norway has been successful in protecting the economy from becoming a 'Kuwait economy', that is, an economy completely dominated by one source of revenue. But governing the economy to ensure both these objectives while at the same time curbing inflationary tendencies requires distinct policy instruments and an unambiguous parliamentary support to enforce such measures. Neither of these requirements is met satisfactorily.

Interestingly, not joining the EU–EMU has probably forced the Norwegian state to rely on more coercive policy instruments to a greater extent than countries who are already inside the Union.

Turning now to Britain for another example of previously strong states which appear to become weaker, the Thatcherite project was clearly predicated on a strong state but, ironically, aimed at reducing the overall stateness of British society. As Dunleavy (1989) points out in a discussion about the British 'ungrounded statism', there is much to suggest that Britain never should have had a strong state: there exist powerful centrifugal tendencies in the United Kingdom and the British political economy has seen more deliberate separation than integration between the state on the one hand and the corporate and financial sectors on the other.

Moreover, the administrative institutional arrangements have been restructured in ways which suggest that they have lost substantive leverage. While institutional reforms such as the introduction of QUANGOs and agencies, or the privatization of state-owned industry and several service-producing institutions, all appear to indicate a desire to relax political control and bring in market-like mechanisms into the public sector, they also deprive the political elite of some of its instruments to govern society and the economy. Again, this was the deliberate objective of these reforms: the state was seen as too intervening and controlling. That said, the massive institutional reforms in Britain over the past two decades are indicative of what a British senior civil servant has described as the 'British disease: applying institutional solutions to organic problems' (quoted in Evans and Harding, 1997:28); while there have been other types of reforms, too, the British seem to have a stronger belief in surgery than medicine when it comes to reformulating the role of the state in society.

The capabilities of the British state are also said to have been impaired by strong sectoral networks (Marsh and Rhodes, 1992; Rhodes, 1994). This is obviously a very different type of development than the deliberate weakening of state structures although in retrospect it appears likely that the institutional changes discussed earlier have helped to perpetuate and consolidate sectoral networks. The growing strength of such networks is a good indicator on the decline in state strength. Finally, we must acknowledge that state strength is also affected by changing institutional relationships. As Andrew Gamble recently noted:

a prospect is emerging in which the national level of policy-making may become less important, while the European level and the local level become more important. The Thatcher government tried to weaken the local level and block moves towards a stronger European level. But that is only likely to have delayed the process. (Gamble, 1994:224)

Thus, to the extent that we can speak of a decline in the strength of the British state, such decline is to a very large extent the outcome of a political project aiming at precisely that: much of Mrs Thatcher's political project departed from a belief that the state played a too strong role in society and thus impaired economic growth. The main dynamic in society was not, and could not be, political, Mrs Thatcher argued, but economic, hence her politics aimed at 'unleashing' the powers of growth. Somewhat ironically, this project required all the features of a strong state in the short-term but the long-term objectives were clearly to dismantle the British state of several of its traditional sources of institutional capabilities.

Britain and Europe have lived in an uneasy relationship for decades. As mentioned earlier, Mrs Thatcher was hesitant to transfer powers of the British state to the European Union. The suspicion was mutual: de Gaulle vetoed British entry to the European Community since he was convinced that Britain was more committed to the Atlantic axis and close cooperation with the United States than to Europe. More recently, there is a much more firm and unambiguous commitment and involvement in the European Union by the present Labour government. But there still exists strong opposition in Britain towards embracing the EU–EMU project wholeheartedly, both among the political elite and the citizenry. Significant groups within the Conservative Party remain 'Euro-sceptic'. On the electoral level, parts of what Taggart (1996) refers to as the 'New Populism' draw strongly on anti-EU sentiments among British voters.

We suggested earlier that strong states remaining strong have done so to a considerable extent by successfully responding to external changes. Does that mean that strong states becoming weaker lack the adaptive capability of states which have remained strong? Well, not necessarily. It is probably true that the decline of the Scandinavian states, not least Sweden, is explained in part by a poor ability to respond to external changes. These are states which have been embedded in a prosperous economy for a very long period of time and which have allowed strong interest groups to push through programmes aiming at safeguarding the interests of their constituencies in the form of extensive regulatory and distributive reforms. Dismantling these regulatory structures has set off massive opposition from those groups who benefit from them. As Linda Weiss (1998) points out, the decline of the 'Swedish model' is more the result of domestic than international changes. As a result, Sweden has had problems keeping attractive and skilled labour and has also seen a growing number of private businesses contemplating relocating to other countries.

The UK case tells a different story. Here, weakening the state was an overarching policy objective for the Thatcher government. Thus, we must be aware of the powerful normative dimensions of state strength and also of domestic political triggers of decline, not just of the global economic changes which so often are seen as the main driver towards the weakening of the state. Further, in this one case (and perhaps others) the state itself chose to reduce its capacity for ideological reasons, believing that the society and economy should be able to make more of their own decisions. The Labour government in place since 1997 appears to be attempting to recover some of the former power of the state, including claims of the capacity to take over failing local authorities and services. It is perhaps too soon to see if that power really can be recovered.

Weak states become stronger

One pattern of change in the world of governance that might not be anticipated, given the current emphasis on the declining power and influence of the state, is that some states are actually becoming stronger. Further, some of the factors that are generally argued to weaken the state may have, within these particular circumstances, actually contributed to a strengthening of the state. The cases that we will use to illustrate these points are the Asian Tigers (Singapore, Taiwan, South Korea and perhaps Malaysia) and the United States. While these governance systems are, in many important ways, highly disparate they both appear to have been strengthened by the role of the state in international affairs: globalization has increased their power over domestic forces rather than weakening it. Further, in the case of the United States the development of networks of interest groups has also given government more power over domestic interests than in previous interest group configurations.

The Asian Tigers and the 'developmental state'   Perhaps the most obvious case of states using the international environment as a mechanism for enhancing their own power can be seen in the smaller countries of Asia. Emerging as separate entities as a result of conflicts (Taiwan, South Korea), or as a result of the termination of colonialism (Singapore, Malaysia, Indonesia) these countries were faced with the question of how to survive and compete in the international market-place. At the time of their independence their economies were either based on the export of raw materials (metal ores, oil, lumber), services (shipping) or seemingly next to nothing at all. How could they find a way to emerge from that economic state to become if not economic superpowers then certainly significant players in the world economy?

The simple answer is that they did this through creating powerful states that could then both direct foreign and internal investment and create the political stability needed to encourage foreign investment; Weiss and Hobson (1998) refer to this as 'governed interdependence'. Whereas we will see that in many other post-colonial settings governments did not develop the capacity to manage their own societies, much less be capable of shielding the economy from competition from the external environment, these countries were able to do so very effectively, and indeed, some would argue, too effectively. That is, critics of these regimes argue that their economic success has been bought at the price of a loss of civil liberties at home.

But it may not be sufficient to say that these governments became sufficiently strong to control their economies and societies. Much of the success of these states has to do with the nature of the societies they are attempting to control. In general, these societies have been rather acquiescent, with an implicit or explicit acceptance of achieving higher levels of economic growth in exchange for lower levels of individual autonomy. Further, these countries have made conscious efforts to choose economic sectors for development which could be successful on the international market and which in most cases would not upset domestic power relationships. In short, the 'little tigers' have been able to promote change internally while maintaining the essence of their domestic social and economic structure. Further, at least in Singapore (Quah, 1987) and to some extent in other cases, a top-down version of the welfare state has been created so that all classes in the society benefit to some degree from economic expansion.

The United States – weak state as superpower? One of the (many) apparent contradictions in contemporary political life is that the United States, often described as a weak state, or as a 'stateless society' (Stillman, 1991), is at the same time the only remaining superpower. Like so many contradictions in political life this is more apparent than real. This is true primarily because although the rhetoric of American politics is often that of maintaining a weak government, and the contractarian nature of American political thought denies the state much existence of its own, American government has actually developed mechanisms for effective policy and management. Those mechanisms may be built on coordination and bargaining, rather than imposition, but they do work. Further, despite a strong decentralizing ethos, much of the power of the state has come to reside in the federal government. State and local government still do most of the heavy lifting in US government when it comes to implementation (Derlien and Peters, 1997), but policy-setting has become more often than not driven from the centre.

The entire structural logic of the founding fathers was to create a highly fragmented and decentralized form of government in the United States. These constitution writers were very clever men and were largely successful in their institutional design. The system is divided vertically by federalism and horizontally by the separation of powers and, especially when the presidency and Congress are of different political parties, divided government is more often than not the order of the day (Fiorina, 1996; Sundquist, 1993). Although structurally divided, American government has become a more powerful influence over its society and has learned to cope rather successfully (when it desires to) with its divisions. The growth of a more centralized form of policy-making in American government, and the recent growth of a powerful American state, has several roots historically. The most obvious source of that power was the Cold War and the attendant need to maintain a large military force to combat the perceived threat of Communism. In the past the United States had mobilized to fight wars but then always returned to a very small peacetime army (Peters, 1985). Although President Eisenhower warned in his valedictory of the dangers of the emerging military industrial complex as a threat to the traditional values of American government, the practical effect of the Cold War was to justify a larger (measured in terms of taxing, spending and public employment) government in Washington (see Hooks, 1993). A standing military establishment of over two million men and a civilian Defense Department of half that size became common features of government during the Cold War, and national defence became a means of justifying other government interventions, for example, the National *Defense* Highways Act, and the National *Defense* Education Act.

The retreat from the traditional posture of isolationism in foreign policy has persisted after the end of the Cold War, and includes more than just a military role in international politics (although that certainly remains a crucial aspect of more centralized government). American government is also a major international economic actor, despite sometimes failing to provide all the funds due to international organizations. The central role of the USA in IGOs such as the International Monetary Fund and the World Trade Organization has maintained the strength of American government in the international arena, and has also tended to make the President a more powerful actor in domestic politics. The international economy now influences the American economy in ways that would have been unexpected just a few years ago, and Washington has derived domestic powers from its central international economic role. In this case economic globalization appears to have strengthened, rather than weakened, the governance capacity of a state.

Another centralizing aspect of American politics has been money, and the capacity of the federal government to raise more of it more easily than have states and especially local governments (Anton, 1980; Peters, 1992). Federal grants in aid became a way for subnational governments to provide services to their publics without having to endure the political pain of raising taxes. The federal government utilized the grants not only to assist their lessaffluent cousins, but also to impose federal priorities over those governments and their policies (Posner and Levine, 1985). When the capacity of the federal government to mandate state and local action (Posner, 1998) is added to the power of the purse, the federal government can be seen to have shifted the balance of power in American federalism substantially over the past several decades. Larry Mead (1996) argues, for example, that the recent welfare reform in the United States is actually a component of state-building by imposing more powerful national regulatory criteria on states and on recipients. The centralization of the system has taken place despite overt efforts by powerful politicians to reduce that shift and to restore what they consider to be the appropriate balance within the federal system.

As argued above, the development of policy networks has also tended to increase the autonomous power of American government, rather than to diminish it. Hugh Heclo (1974) made the seminal statement on the changes in the interest group universe in the United States, and his assessment of the widening range of involvement of interest groups in political activity through issue networks has proved to be very accurate. Whereas the famous 'iron triangles' once dominated this avenue for political influence in the USA, there is now a much wider range of involvement of groups of all sorts (Petracca, 1992), and with that some possibility for government to choose among competing views of policy.

In the iron triangle pattern of governing, government (or at least agencies of government) was obliged to select a single legitimate representative of the interests within a policy area (Freeman, 1967). This selection gave that one interest a great deal of power over government, politically as well as in terms of the policy advice being offered. With a more diverse set of interest groups, including increasingly active public interest groups (Rothenberg, 1992), government agencies have more possible partners in making and implementing policy. The range of information available to agencies is also substantially wider, so that agencies can make more of their own decisions. This does not mean that there are not well-trodden paths that agencies will continue to go down, arm in arm with their favourite interest group, but it does mean that there are also real options if the agency wishes to break out of the pattern.

A final point here is that ethnicity, that also has been a source of declining power of the state in many countries, has actually been a source of power for Washington. Given that ethnic minorities tend to be relatively widely spread across the United States, there have been few demands for regional governments based on these characteristics. Beginning in the 1950s with struggles over desegregation and the state's rights, central government tended to advocate policies (coming in part from the court system) and to use its power (including at times military power) to enforce civil rights rulings and later legislation. Again, rather than weakening the state, ethnic differences in the case of the United States appear to have strengthened the state. This was in large part because the constitutional notion of equal protection demanded (or so it was assumed) racial integration, rather than the then existing separation, of the ethnic groups, a strategy quite dissimilar to that adopted in most other multi-ethnic societies.

We should not assume that the United States has become a centralized state on the European model: the founding fathers did their job too well for that to happen in any foreseeable time period. There are still immense problems of bargaining and assembling workable coalitions across institutions and levels of government, but there is also evidence that the system has learned to cope with those problems. Further, there are continuing pressures for decentralizing American government even further, coming especially from Congressional Republicans (Conlan, 1998). On the other hand, as well as being decentralized, American government is also pragmatic, so that one of its features is that the participants spend a good deal of time trying to make it work, and often do succeed. It is also important to note that the building of the American state is not totally the result of the Cold War, as is often assumed, but also a result of a number of other domestic political pressures.

Weak states remain weak

Finally, some states have remained weak, or have been weakened further by changes in the global political economy. These states can be found primarily in Latin America and Africa. Although there are marked differences between the fortunes of the countries in those two regions (see Hyden and Bratton, 1992; Collier and Collier, 1991), and also between countries within each region, they share the common pattern that most countries have been failing to keep pace with changes in the rest of the world, either politically or economically. In some instances the failure of these states is relative, with some now much better off economically than they were several decades ago. In other cases, however, the failure is more absolute, with levels of economic development and governing capacity actually falling compared with only a few years previously.

Further, in these cases the relative lack of strength of the state at the beginning of the period does not appear to be associated with increased adaptive capacity, as was suggested by some of the earlier discussions of this relationship. Rather, these states apparently have not been able to utilize the flexibility that might have been available to them. This has been in part because of their own internal political weaknesses and in part because of the severe demands being placed upon them by the need to adjust to rapidly changing environmental conditions. It may be that states such as these that are so much at the mercy of the international political economy may not have any advantage from flexibility.

The reasons for the apparent decline of the governing capacity of these regimes are manifold and complex. Especially for Africa, part of the reason for decline stems from the patterns of colonialism and the nature of the states created out of the former colonies (Tordoff, 1993). Leaving aside whether the colonial powers had prepared the new regimes for governing effectively before granting independence, it is clear that the boundaries created by colonialism had little or nothing to do with preexisting social or economic regions in Africa. Rather, they were the product of political power and/or of the use of geographical borders to define the colonial holdings. This pattern meant that the internal tribal and religious divisions that have plagued countries such as Rwanda, Burundi, the Congo, the Sudan and Nigeria were built into these systems. Even the most effective governments in the world would have difficulty governing effectively with these loads placed on them.

These governments also face severe challenges from the international environment. Economically they are largely dependent upon the sale of primary commodities and, despite numerous efforts to industrialize, remain at the mercy of fluctuations in the international environment. In some cases, for example Brazil and Mexico, there has been some progress in creating a more industrial economy, but most countries remain tied to the sale of commodities. Further, unlike many Asian countries there has been less movement into light industry such as manufacturing clothing. Most of these countries have not experienced the economic roller-coaster ride that has afflicted Asia since 1998, but rather there has been stagnation and a continuing decline in the economy for most African countries, and for a large number of Latin American countries. Again, these external economic challenges would threaten the legitimacy of the most effective governments in the world.

But these governments are not the most effective ones in the world. In addition to the severe loads being placed on these governments they have their own internal problems in governing. Again, this is more apparent in Africa than in Latin America, although the instability of many Latin American countries points to some governing problems there as well. Part of the apparent problem is that their social divisions are translated almost directly into political action. Thus, political parties are in many ways stalking-horses for tribal and other social groups. This strong social linkage makes compromise and forming effective coalitions difficult or impossible, so that politics becomes 'winner take all' rather than a more constrained competition for office. Further, once in office, the political party tends to utilize that position as a means to reward their supporters and further reinforce the position that government is more about promoting the interests of one social group than it is about governing.

The above patterns have been characterized as a predatory state, a marked contrast to the developmental state discussed above for the 'little tigers'. One of the important aspects of the difference appears to be in the relationship between the state and its civil society. In these weaker patterns the state is at once a victim of the civil society and a predator on it. It is victim in the sense that the underlying social divisions in the societies tend to drive much of the politics, and the absence of 'encompassing groups' (Olson, 1982) means that politics is almost always a zero-sum game. The state is the predator in that the occupants of power, generally lacking an overarching civil commitment, may use their positions for self-aggrandizement rather than collective advancement.

The rigidity implied by this commitment of political parties to particular social groupings inhibits compromise, and with that adaptability. The failure to adapt to changing conditions is particularly evident in Latin American countries which in the late nineteenth century were more advanced economically, and in social policy (Papadopolous, 1992), than in much of North America. These countries were not able to maintain their position in the world but gradually dropped behind. The relative incapacity to adapt was to some extent related to the same patronage commitments as described for Africa above. In Latin America, however, the linkages that have tended to restrain adaptability have been through more personal, clientelistic relationships rather than through linkages with social groups. In both cases, however, the state may be used less as a means of governance and more as a means of providing benefits to particular segments of society.

In some ways many of these nominally weak states can be conceptualized as being extremely powerful. They are certainly autonomous, sharing few common goals with their people or with the international environment (Callaghy, 1984; Wunsch and Olowu, 1995). They are also often able to obtain those desired ends, assuming that the ends have more to do with predation than with change or development. Further, these states have been able to mobilize substantial military forces in order to pursue certain ends selected at the elite level, and hence have the trappings of power of nineteenth century, if not contemporary twentieth century, world powers. What makes their regimes so weak is the absence of legitimacy in a modern world in which at least the forms of consent, if not always the substance, appear crucial for governance (Hyden, 1997).

In a somewhat paradoxical way the inherent difficulties in governing in these regimes have been exacerbated by attempts on the part of the international community to produce change. Some of this has been a function of the varying, and sometimes contradictory, strategies being used. More importantly, however, an emphasis in much of the past work on developing civil society, while ultimately an important part of governance (Gyimah-Boadi, 1996), has diminished any emphasis on building and improving institutions of governance.

What explains changes in state strength, or lack thereof?

We have now examined a varied set of political systems and described their adaptations to changes in the socio-economic environment. The discussions of each of the groups of countries produced some preliminary generalizations that were descriptive of the development within that group. Are there, however, any generalizations that could extend to all these countries and could also be used as a basis of a wider-ranging theory of governance? Or are the circumstances of each group, or even each country, so particular that there is no real possibility of such a general theory?

There are several major candidates for explaining the relative success of these countries in responding to the environment. First, the principal source of explanation may be political, and the structural and behavioural elements of governments themselves may predict the ability of governments to adjust. We have noted, for example, that centralized regimes may not be able to adjust to altered circumstances as well as more decentralized systems, whether formally federal or not. The explanations go beyond simply the political, and social and economic factors, as well as the international environment itself, must be considered.

Political factors?

Although stated more implicitly than explicitly, the central hypothesis of this chapter has been that political factors are central in explaining the changing power of the state in these societies. We are, however, conceptualizing politics broadly here to include the nature of the surrounding society and its capacity to relate effectively with actors in the state. Much of the capacity of states to function depends upon their ability to cope effectively with, or to mould, or suppress, societal pressures. On a value basis we certainly would prefer that governments reflect, or even shape, societal values, but in terms of sheer effectiveness suppression has proved to be all too successful in enhancing the governing capacities of regimes.

In some cases the political factors involved are conscious choices by governments. For example, the decisions concerning privatization and agentification in the United Kingdom amounted to a conscious rejection of a strong state capacity. In some cases, elites have chosen paths, or reinforced paths, that have enhanced the capacity of states to govern. The United States is perhaps most interesting in this regard, given that decisions that have enhanced state capacity have been chosen without explicit references to that outcome; rather they have come about to cope with the international environment, or to cope with deep social divisions within the country. Had there been a more explicit understanding of the emerging role of the centralized state, the decisions taken might have been rather different.

Domestic political mobilization may also affect the capacity of states to govern effectively. The absence of significant levels of political mobilization in the 'little tigers' in Asia is one of the major factors enabling those governments to impose their somewhat Draconian policies on the societies. In other instances political mobilization of some sort may actually enhance the capacity of the state. For example, in the United States the mobilization of racial groups was key to enhancing the power of the federal government *vis-à-vis* the state governments and the society as a whole. Similarly, the mobilization of unions and other groups in France and Germany on behalf of *services publiques* has tended to prevent their governments from downsizing the welfare state to the extent found in other countries (Pierson, 1997).

Social factors?

These political factors are closely related to a social phenomenon which have a significant impact on governance. In most developing countries the state has not been able to govern through civil society because of the almost complete absence of a civil society. A large number of the less-developed countries are still ridden with domestic conflict – sometimes fierce conflict – which has largely pre-cluded the development of intermediate structures through which the state can govern society. International institutions such as the IMF and the World Bank have concluded that the development of a civil society in these jurisdictions is of primary importance, hence their recent emphasis on 'good governance' (Leftwich, 1994) as a strategy to increase the governing capacity of these weak states.

Economic factors?

Economic factors cannot be dismissed easily in understanding the changing governance capacity of the state. As we will point out below, some of the more significant economic factors are imposed from the international environment. There are, however, also some important domestic economic factors that have shaped the role of the state. One of the more important of these factors has been the structure of the domestic economy and the pattern of industrial organization. That is, states with more cooperative patterns of inter-action between labour and management, and between sources of finance and industry (essentially Rhineland capitalism), appear to have been more successful in adapting to socio-economic change than have more liberal, Atlantic patterns of economic relations.

Another domestic economic factor, albeit closely linked with the international environment, is the dependency of economies on primary economies. This dependency relationship produced one important model for understanding economic and political underdevelopment in less-developed countries (Frank, 1971). As well as strengthening one sector of the economy at the expense of others, this economic pattern tended to strengthen rural, traditional landowners at the expense of other social and political forces in the society. This, in turn, has perpetuated the clientelism that dominates political relationships in these societies and which is often assumed to inhibit political change. If a clientelistic pattern dominates, then producing effective governance in any modern form becomes extremely unlikely. Government becomes a mechanism for distributing patronage and for preserving power relationships as much as a means of actually delivering service efficiently and effectively.

The international environment

Finally, we must remain cognizant of the role of international factors in shaping the capacity of the state to govern. Much of the premise for writing this book is that globalization and the increasing significance of the international environment have diminished the power of the nation state. We have acknowledged the importance of that position, but also have pointed out that the impact of globalization on the state is neither monolithic nor simple. Indeed, in some cases (the United States and the Asian Tigers – at least until recently) globalization may actually have enhanced the power of the state *vis-à-vis* domestic actors. Further, the impact of globalization should be seen in terms of individual policy sectors rather than as a general phenomenon: what is true for controlling capital flows may not be true for manufacturing industries.

The impact of the international environment can be seen most clearly in control over economic policies, especially those most closely linked with international finance. Thus, for countries that are the most exposed to the international financial market there should be less capacity to control the impacts of the environment on their own economy. This may be true even for more affluent countries that have a large international trade and finance sector. In the past these countries used a variety of mechanisms such as corporatism to control their internal economies (Cameron, 1978). The greater global competitiveness may not, however, permit some of the inefficiencies built into corporatist systems to survive.

Further, the increasing importance of international regimes in a variety of policy areas may decrease the importance of domestic policy considerations, relative to the power of those international collectivities. Even for the states that we have identified as remaining powerful, or attaining greater capacity for exercising power, the international environment has come to exercise a good deal of influence over their behaviours. For the economically powerful the World Trade Organization and other international organizations have a substantial influence over economic success, and other international regimes influence decision-making in health, the environment and other policy areas (Rittberger, 1993). For the 'little tigers' an emerging regime in human rights and democratization is beginning to affect their capacity to act as autonomously in domestic politics as they might have in the past. In short, there are policy influences from outside the state itself that are almost unavoidable, no matter how autonomous and autarkic a regime may appear to be.

Summary

If we examine the governance capacities of states, we find that there are few simple explanations for the relative success or failure of regimes. There is some evidence in favour of political, economic and international factors. There is also some evidence that appears to refute arguments in favour of each of these factors. The final conclusion, therefore, must be that the governance capacity of a political system is the product of a number of complex relationships with the economic, political and international contexts of the state, as well as with the internal structuring of the state itself. No simple model, such as those arguing that globalization has destroyed the capacity of states to govern, is likely to do justice to the complexities that actually exist in the world of governance.

9

Conclusions: Rethinking States and Governance

So far, we have discussed governance in the context of state transformation and alternative ways to think about state strength and state capacity to govern. We have conducted this inquiry mainly with regard to three different scenarios: power being decentred to subnational actors and institutional systems, the emergence of transnational governance structures, and the search for local, purportedly apolitical, systems of communitarian governance. This inquiry has begun with an assumption that the best way to think about governance is to begin with the state, and to then understand what has happened to the simple model of state dominance.

However, we must be cautious not to confuse the emergence of these different patterns of governance with changes in the types of challenges that confront nation states. While we believe there is some degree of correspondence between alternative governance structures (or systems) and the definition of political problems, this linkage is far from self-evident. Further, any correspondence is far from uniform across countries, or even across policy areas. We also need to discuss how and why different national contexts offer different choices or developments with regard to the models of governance.

We will use most of this concluding chapter to address these issues of differentiation and comparison, both by country and by policy area. First, however, we need to summarize briefly some of the principal observations concerning state strength and state development that have emerged from the analysis to this point.

Redefining the state in a governance perspective

One of the purposes of this exercise has been to advance a state-centric image of governance. The reasons for choosing this perspective have already been discussed: states still matter a great deal in steering society and, furthermore, the state-centric image of government and society is the best benchmark against which we can assess the consequences of the development towards alternative formats for governance.

But even in this perspective, it is clear that we need to rethink our conceptualizations of the state and the sources of state strength. More than anything else, perhaps, looking at contemporary states and the policies and strategies they pursue as well as their *modus operandi* in these respects indicates that state strength has become something contextual and entrepreneurial rather than, as was previously the case, something derived from the constitutional and legal strength of state institutions.

This observation, in turn, leads us to ask how we can describe the state–society relationship in the governance perspective. What changes in this relationship have occurred as a result of the new *modus operandi* of the state?

From formal powers to political capabilities

The emergence of governance models has seen the state place less reliance on coercive policy instruments and instead begin to rely more on subtle techniques of imposing – or conveying – its will on the surrounding society (Woodside, 1998). This development has slightly different explanations depending on which segment of the policy environment of the state we are examining. Within the system of political institutions themselves, the state has become much less controlling over subnational governments. Block grants are used to an increasing extent, and we have seen massive decentralization taking place throughout most of the western world. The state apparently has less need to control local and regional governments in detail compared to just a decade or so ago, or perhaps it believes itself to be less able to exercise tight control (see Posner, 1998). This is partly because the overall nature of the political project throughout the western world has changed from expansion and the launching of new state-driven programmes towards managing budgetary problems, as well as managing problems of consent. Also, states appear to be increasingly willing to accept and capitalize on the expertise and professionalism which has evolved within subnational governments.

We can identify even more profound changes in the relationship between the state and private capital. The current regimes in most of the western world emphasize a relaxation of regulatory frameworks *vis-à-vis* private businesses and financial markets. It is only a very slight exaggeration to illustrate the changes in the mood of elected officials by saying that twenty years ago they were primarily concerned with how private businesses should submit to their political project, whereas at the turn of the twenty-first century their main concern seems to be how that project should be designed to be as unobtrusive and helpful as possible to the private sector. Globalization is often said to effectively deprive the state of its coercive powers over private capital, although some suggest that this is a myth promoted by states themselves as a pretext for not intervening in the economy more forcefully (Weiss, 1998).

The state has also restructured its own institutions, creating agencies, quangos and other institutional forms which operate at considerable distance from control by the political elite. There is a widespread notion that policies and operations should be separate; managers should be given considerable discretion in order to be able to produce and deliver public services as efficiently as possible, rejecting previously powerful notions concerning the specificity of the public sector and the necessity of hierarchical accountability to ensure proper performance (Aucoin, 1999).

There are two basically different ways of thinking about these changes and developments. One interpretation holds that what we are witnessing is a series of incremental or discrete changes which taken together point at the decline of the state. State structures are increasingly submitting to the corporate sector; they are less able to control subnational governments, and their policies aim to a large extent at dismantling its former sources of power in order to allow for the private sector to reclaim exclusive control over the economy and to boost economic growth. While it is true that the heyday of 'big government' appears to be gone for ever, we do not have to look very far to see that states as centres of governance continue to play a defining role in the economy, in international relations, and in many areas of domestic politics and policy.

The contending interpretation, which is the one supported by the present authors, is that the state is restructuring in order to be able to remain a viable vehicle for the pursuit of the collective interest in an era of economic globalization and increasing subnational institutional dynamics. It is certainly the case that states are increasingly relying on fairly subtle policy instruments in their exchange with society but that does not necessarily mean that they are any less efficient compared to more coercive techniques of steering. By the same token, it is true that the corporate world is becoming more globalized by the day, but a surprisingly large number of private companies are still 'domestic' in terms of market orientation. As Hirst and Thompson point out when discussing business relocation and internationalization, the important question is not why one company out of ten chooses to do so but rather why nine companies out of ten opt not to do so (Hirst and Thompson, 1996).

Most importantly, we cannot see any serious rival to states as sources of democratic, accountable governance (March and Olsen, 1995). While contemporary politics provides numerous examples of how states increasingly operate more in terms of governance than 'government', it is difficult to imagine how a system of governance which does not provide institutionalized systems of accountability can be sustained in the longer term (Boston, 1999; Rhodes, 1997; Thomas, 1998). It is indicative that one of the main problems facing the advocates of the New Public Management philosophy is how to define a robust system of accountability. The 1995 Cave Creek accident, killing fourteen students as a viewing platform collapsed, and the break-out of several high-security prisoners from an Isle of Wight prison facility in 1995 are but two incidents which highlighted the tremendous complexities in identifying who is responsible in a market-designed system of public service delivery (Gregory, 1998; Polidano, 1999).

The powers of the state are gradually transforming from 'power over' towards 'power to' (see Stone, 1989). This perspective highlights concerted public–private efforts, shared and accumulated resources across the public–private border, cooperative rather than adversarial policy strategies and instruments, relaxed institutional relationships with distinct jurisdictional boundaries, institutionalized links between the state and civil society in service production and delivery, and an institutional adaptation which recognizes the 'multi-organizational' nature of public organizations. These developments, it should be noted, do not offer a universal, once-and-for-all fix to the problems which are indigenous to alternative perspectives and models of government. For instance, the gradual transformation of the state described above is likely to entail a potential accountability problem which in some ways is similar to that triggered by New Public Management reforms: it makes elected accountable actors and institutions dependent on non-accountable actors for the execution of public policy. The big difference between the 'decline' and the 'transformation' perspectives, however, is that while the 'decline of the state' theory has very little to offer in terms of the future of government, governance and, indeed, democracy, the 'transformation' view outlines a reformed state guided by political choice made by accountable actors. This is obviously not a matter of wishful thinking: to reiterate an earlier remark, we believe that the state remains *the* most powerful structure in society and it would be erroneous to think that it would be incapable of transforming itself to address the political and economic situation of the 1990s and the early 2000s.

This view on the current changes within the state and the state's exchanges with its external environment portrays the state as the centre of governance albeit with significant contingencies *vis-à-vis* other centres of resources and capabilities in society. What makes the state a *primus inter pares* in these exchanges is that it is the only player in the governance process which can rightfully claim to have a political, legitimate mandate. Furthermore, this perspective on the state focuses more on the political capabilities of the state than on its formal powers. In the final analysis, the best proof of the state's leverage and its political capabilities is not whether it can accomplish desired changes in society by itself but whether it is able to muster the resources and forge the coalitions necessary to attain those goals at all.

Paradoxes of state strength

Taking these arguments one step further, it appears as if the institutional features of what we traditionally identify as strong states – insulated institutions, a strong political centre, and so on – in some ways work against the broader societal exchanges which characterize state-led governance. Similarly, many of the defining characteristics of what we often refer to as weak states – institutional fragmentation, a decentralized institutional structure, and so on – appear to be better geared to coordinate governance than strong states because of their more developed points of contact with the external environment. Theories of governance, it seems, put much of our traditional thinking about state strength on its head.

These apparent paradoxes, we argue, can be explained by what appears to be a slightly misleading or confusing conception of state strength which dominates much of the literature. Comparing our ways of thinking about the strength of local institutions to our image of state institutional strength suggests how we should reconsider our definition of state strength. Traditionally, state strength was the product of the legal capabilities of its institutions. Strong states were insulated from parochial pressures; they had the capability to impose their decisions on society; and they could implement policies and programmes which discriminate between different segments of society. The introduction of governance gives a slightly new meaning to that concept: here, strong states are those which are able to coordinate and set the priorities of various joint public–private projects. Thus, legal and constitutional powers are gradually being replaced by such factors as entrepreneurial skills, political zeal and brokerage abilities. This is a view on the state which has been advanced in the comparative political economy literature for quite some time (Gamble, 2000; Gourevitch, 1986; Katzenstein, 1978; Krasner, 1984).

Another paradox in the current debate on the development towards governance as an alternative to traditional government is that pursuing the collective interest through different forms of governance on and between different institutional levels requires a strong centre. Thus, government and governance are not altogether each other's opposites: governance can never be successful or give an accurate interpretation of political preferences among the populace unless it involves to a significant extent representative structures and an institutional means of translating these preferences into political and administrative action. Only the state can play these roles, and only the state can give meaning, objectives and direction to governance. But in order to be able to do so, the state must transform itself and rethink its performance, downplaying tight political and administrative control and employing less coercive instruments. The authority of the state is ultimately a construct of society, not the state itself, and to uphold that authority the state must emerge in a fashion that suggests it is appropriate to address the current problems. Much of the recent changes in western states could be seen as a huge project aiming at the modernization of the state.

Thus, the new governance is much about managing and responding to change. The 1990s have seen substantive changes within the state – in terms of structural design, resource base, exchange between policy-makers and bureaucrats, and so on – as well as in society and the economy. The conventional model of government discussed earlier in this book reflected a type of equilibrium between state and society; the emergence of the new governance could be seen as a development towards a new equilibrium.

Thus, alongside rethinking the structural arrangements of the state we also need to consider alternative models of the state–society relationship. A move towards governance is predicated on a decreased significance of the public–private distinction in a variety of ways, whether we conceive of governance as networks (Rhodes, 1997) or as more or less improvised types of public–private cooperation. The overall emphasis is on closer, more continuous and more informal contacts between political institutions and their environment. For some political cultures this model of state–society relations is quite familiar: we need only think of the smaller industrialized democracies in Europe such as the Netherlands, Austria and the Scandinavian countries. For national cultures where the distinction between the public and private spheres of society is more distinct, such as in the USA, developing these points of contact might be more difficult. But even there, various forms of joint public–private projects have a long history, particularly at the local level (see, for example, Beauregard, 1998; Stone, 1989).

Towards embedded autonomy?

The notion of embedded autonomy was coined by Peter Evans in his elegant study of the political economy of high-speed-growth economies (Evans, 1995). Evans's argument in brief is that these states display an interesting mix of autonomy and embeddedness which has allowed them to play a significant role in promoting economic development; they are autonomous enough to be capable of implementing efficient industrial policies and macroeconomic policies but at the same time sufficiently embedded in society that they can develop a wide variety of links between themselves and key societal actors.

State autonomy and embeddedness reflect deeply rooted cultural views and values on what is the appropriate role of the state and private capital in society and how they should interact, and hence are not easily manipulated. Furthermore, most large corporations are increasingly operating in international markets and are less accessible for domestic political institutions and, arguably, less needy of domestic political action. Corporate actors will only engage in state-led governance if they see an incentive to do so, in part because larger corporations are continually involved in other forms of governance such as 'corporate governance' which may be of greater strategic importance than mainatining a partnership with political institutions (O'Brien, 1994; Rhodes, 1997; Williamson, 1996). We should therefore not expect any major changes in the relationship between the state and big business. However, in most countries these large corporations, while obviously important to the state in terms of export revenues and jobs, account for only a surprisingly small part of the total group of businesses. For the vast number of small and medium-sized businesses, incentives to engage in various forms of cooperative projects with political institutions should be much more tangible.

The contingencies of governing

We mentioned earlier that governance entails important political and institutional contingencies between the state and resourceful actors in the surrounding society. The management of such contingencies depends to a great extent on two sets of factors. One is the predominant governance style pursued by the state. Governance style includes both what Jeremy Richardson and his associates refer to as 'policy style' (Richardson, 1982) and the process through which the state secures societal approval of its policies. Different national contexts display significantly different governance styles and hence different strategies of managing the contingencies of governing.

The other set of factors which help define the management of governance contingencies is the nature of the specific policy problems being addressed by government. Problems defined by state functions, by social factors or by political objectives – to use a crude typology – point in different directions with regard to what links with society the state should draw on in order to address the problem and consequently what contingencies it will be forced to manage (see Peters, 1998b). In particular, this definition may help to explain the capacity of the state to insulate its policy activities from direct political involvements.

Let us now look more closely at the concept of governance style and the different types of policy problems.

Governance styles

There is a long and honourable concern in the literature with options for governing, even if that discussion has not been carried on in the rubric of governance *per se*. One of the fundamental questions that has arisen is the relative virtues, and relative importance, of markets in the process of governing a society. This debate goes back at least to the seminal work of Dahl and Lindblom (1953), and can be also seen in some of Lindblom's later work on markets (1977). In the European context the even earlier work of Schumpeter and the more recent work of the so-called Austrian School have contrasted the capacity of states and markets to govern.

This debate is in part ideological and in part empirical. On one side of the ideological debate the market is often praised (if in an idealized form) for its ability to allocate resources in an efficient manner and to maximize freedom for individuals. Hierarchies are in turn damned as awkward, inefficient and as substituting one view of good policy for the efficiency of the market. On the other side of the argument markets are said to produce large-scale inequalities and to neglect issues of social need in their pursuit of a narrowly defined version of efficiency (Self, 1993). In many critiques of market allocation, hierarchies (generally in the form of bureaucracies) are not regarded much more highly than they are by the advocates of the market, but rather appear as necessary evils to overcome the inequalities resulting from the operations of unregulated markets.

The emerging alternative to both markets and hierarchies is networks (Jacques, 1990; Kooiman, 1993). In this view more or less autonomously forming relationships among groups and individuals can substitute for the weaknesses of both markets and hierarchies. We have already pointed out that networks may have their own weaknesses and inadequacies as mechanisms for allocation, but it is important to recognize their existence, even if they are not a certain cure for problems in governing. In particular, networks may be able to enhance the capacity of markets to utilize criteria that are not strictly economic, while also enabling hierarchies to permit more participation.

One of the components of a contingency approach to governance is the style through which governing groups, whether nation states or not, attempt to influence policy and control outcomes. Few countries could be characterized by only one of these styles, and to some extent all are being implemented simultaneously. Still, we can identify some dominant choices when looking at particular national cases.

The first style to identify is one in which the state leads policy-making and is asserting, or reasserting, its position as a major actor in the process of governing. We have already shown that some states have been quite successful in establishing their central position in governance, even in the face of globalization, regionalization and the increasing use of networks as mechanisms for governance. It is perhaps less surprising that there are such reassertions than that there are relatively few of them, even among states such as the United Kingdom with a history of substantial strength and central-ized management of policy. It appears that many states have either willingly abdicated some ambitions of control, or have simply accepted what appear to be the inevitable outcomes of larger socio-economic processes.

Other strategies depend upon decentring control in a variety of ways. In some cases control is being decentred up or down to other forms of government. This pattern is perhaps most evident in Europe where the increasing power of the European Union and of regional governments have tended to squeeze the capacity of the state itself to govern, and to create a pattern of multi-level gover-nance (Marks *et al.*, 1996). In a number of cases policy control is also being decentred outward to private sector actors of all sorts. This may be through private sector firms, or through networks of interest groups, or to the 'third sector' of not-for-profit organizations (Salamon, 1981). What is clearly happening, however, is that govern-ment in these cases is losing control and governance capacity, albeit often doing so willingly.

Policy problems

Finally, we need to look at the manner in which policy problems are defined for solution through a governance process. There is by now a large literature on the importance of policy 'framing' in setting the parameters for subsequently solving social problems (Schon and Rein, 1994; Dery, 1996). The basic point here is that in order to be addressed, a problem must be defined, and further that the nature of the definition of the problem will determine the nature of the resources brought to bear on it.

In this particular analysis we will focus on three alternative definitions of problems. The first of these is defining problems through the function or activity of government. Is this a regulatory problem? Or is it a problem of providing subsidies, or just what is it? These functional definitions tend to emphasize the nature of the instruments at the disposal of government (Peters and Van Nispen, 1998), as well as the formal structure of government departments and agencies. It also points out that framing defines the organization to be responsible for the problem as well as the resources needed to solve it.

Problems may also be defined by social factors, such as the target populations, or the forces mobilized to produce the policy change (Ingram and Schneider, 1991). Rather than emphasizing the structure of government itself, a definition based on social factors emphasizes the nature of society and the relationship between the public and private sectors in shaping and then solving problems. Finally, problems may also be defined by political objectives. That is, what is the reason for investing political capital and real resources into a possible solution for a problem? How is this going to improve society, or what political forces will it placate? Are those goals achievable, or is the policy merely window-dressing to prevent other types of political mobilization and more fundamental changes in the society?

Linking governance style to problems

We can now relate the three different governance styles to the three different models of policy problems. This analysis yields a typology of nine different (predicted) policy outcomes, each featuring its own particular set of internal contingencies. Thus, even though we can make some broad generalizations about the linkages among these factors, there are still important variations within each category.

Table 9.1
Policy styles and types of problem definition: conceivable policy outcomes

Policy style	Problem definition		
	By function	*By social factors*	*By political objectives*
State-led, reassertive	Steering	Redistribution	Intervention
Decentred down	Mobilization	Diversification	Participation
Decentred out	Marketization	Entrepreneurialism	Efficiency

Problems defined by core governmental functions in the context of state-led governance style tend to generate policies characterized by the most distinct state-centred steering of society and the economy in the taxonomy. In many ways, this is the governance type which comes closest to the traditional conception of 'government'. But this type of steering and control is not what it once was: the targets of steering, whether they are private businesses, subnational governments or constituencies, are seemingly less dependent on the state and therefore less easily controlled. True, the state could resort to employ firm regulatory policy instruments to ensure compliance but executing such a strategy *vis-à-vis* larger corporations, for instance, may well turn out to be counterproductive in a globalized economy. Such regulation may create incentives for these actors to relocate to less economically hostile environments.

State-led governance to address problems defined by social factors usually includes some redistributive objectives. The state remains the appropriate institutional level for redistributive policies, given its capacity to impose costs on any or all segments of society through taxes and regulations. The key contingency here is in relationship to the losers in the redistributive game: the past several decades have witnessed a rapidly growing electoral discontent with redistributive regimes throughout the western world (Kaase and Newton, 1996). Also, global competitiveness for private investment is sometimes said to rule out redistribution because it is predicated on tax levels which (purportedly) will scare off professionals and skilled labour.

Thus, state-led governance is basically an encroaching and imposing governance style. Driven by political objectives, this is a governance style which has been developed to provide a vehicle for interventionist policies. Interventionism as a governance strategy is associated with traditional left-wing politics which we do not see much of at the end of the twentieth century. The notion of 'scaring' volatile investment capital has become the standard argument against such policies, ironically at the same time as a growing number of observers – including top marketeers such as George Soros – bemoan the developments after capital and currency markets were deregulated. Further, this style may be a reaction to observed societal problems arising when government withdraws from policy areas such as health or poverty.

The 'decentring down' governance style applied to problems defined functionally could be said to promote mobilization of resources, broadly defined. It is a strategy which helps the state to capitalize on the capacity of subnational governments to deliver public policies, as well as the greater legitimacy of the lower levels of government in many countries (Nye *et al.*, 1997). To some extent, this strategy entails a trade-off between policy coherence and coordination on the one hand and resource mobilization on the other; diffusing policy capacity in order to draw on a wider resource base could leave the centre with less control over more money.

Applying the same governance style to socially defined problems generates diversification and hence better 'customer attuning' of public services: this is one of the traditional normative underpinnings of local government and local autonomy. Again, this may solve some problems at the same time as it creates others. The extent to which this is an attractive strategic option to state institutions depends largely on which policy sector is being considered and the importance of national coordination as a goal for that sector.

Decentring down enhances participation which is another traditional core value associated with local government (Hill, 1974). While decreasing levels of political involvement have become a widespread problem in many countries in the western world, high levels of participation in urban politics tend to challenge informal coalitions between city hall and the business sector elite (Swanstrom, 1985). Thus, here is another complex trade-off between different policy objectives which must be addressed by the state; what may be an important instrument of urban governance could interfere with the state's overarching policy objectives.

The third governance style, decentring authority 'out' to agencies and similar institutions operating at arm's length from the political centre, leads to 'marketization' when applied to functionally defined problems. This is precisely the purpose of this governance style which in these respects draws to a considerable extent on New Public Management-style organizational design and management philosophies (Pollitt, 1990; Self, 1993). Public services should only be delivered when they are demanded by 'customers' on the market. This is in many ways a seductive way of looking at public service delivery. On closer inspection, however, 'marketization' and the conversion of citizens into 'customers' has potentially serious consequences on the notion of citizenship and the relationship between the state and the individual which citizenship describes (Pierre, 1995a).

Decentring out socially formulated problems could be said to encourage individual entrepreneurialism. The basic idea here is that many social problems have their root and cause in a widespread dependency on public service provision and distributive programmes. Enhancing values associated with private enterprise and entrepreneurialism becomes an important objective, as much of the ideological shift in Britain and the United States during the 1980s suggests. This development would appear to be a fairly straightforward state strategy of reducing its responsibilities, and its costs, in society. It remains a normative assessment whether the exacerbated inequalities generated during this decade are a good example for other countries to follow (see Fawcett, 1998).

The governance style of decentring out applied to political objectives, finally, is assumed to be able to increase public sector efficiency. If public sector organizations are able to operate with greater autonomy it is assumed that they will be more efficient than when tied to political management. But efficiency is achieved at no little cost: administrative cultures with a strong legalistic tradition find it difficult to increase efficiency without compromising core values and standards.

Thus, the 'decentring down' and 'decentring out' governance styles entail value shifts of some degree, and it is difficult to think that such shifts can be implemented without a strong centre (that is, the state) leading and legitimizing that process. This may be a transitional phase in building these styles of governance, and therefore a short-term problem, but even so the first steps in these kinds of reforms tend to be the most critical ones.

Towards a research agenda

This book has discussed a number of features of the governance literature, as well as of the emerging patterns of governance in contemporary societies. That having been said, there is still a great deal of research that needs to be done in order to more completely comprehend governance and the capacity of States to steer in a more globalized and networked environment. The following is a partial list of the challenges that remain for governance research.

Governance in different national contexts and different policy sectors

We suggested earlier that different national contexts tend to display, or at least favour, different governance styles. There is a need to look at these issues in a comparative perspective. For instance, we need to know more about to what extent there is a tendency for some types of states – unitary versus federal, centralized versus decentralized, small versus large, developing versus developed, and so on – to seek to implement particular models of governance. It could also be that different governance styles or models of governance are typical to specific policy sectors. Again, this is something which can only be studied cross-nationally, although the major variable may be the policy sector rather than the nation (Freeman, 1985).

Governance failure

The ontological aspect of governance failure is intriguing and complex. How do we detect and observe non-events? What expectations do we have about governance that permit us to say that it has not appeared in a particular setting? Another way of looking at this issue would be to suggest that efficient governance will manifest itself in some clear ways, and that the absence of such indicators should provide a clue for where to find cases of governance failure. For instance, cities with comparatively poor economic development could be assumed to have failed in developing and sustaining efficient governance. Similarly, countries whose economy is lagging in growth compared to similar economies could be assumed to have governments experiencing difficulties in conveying its goals to society.

Governance and conflict management

We should also be reminded that governance is not as cosy and consensual as it is sometimes made out to be. Governance is to a significant degree about defining goals and making political priorities and there is little reason to expect those decisions to be any less controversial in a governance perspective than it was in the conventional view of government. As Weaver and Rockman (1993:468) argue, 'The capacity of government to manage conflict must be weighed against its capacity to steer and direct change.'

As is sometimes the case in network analyses, studying governance means essentially observing something that works. As argued above, governance failure is difficult to observe because it can only be studied by observing its consequences, not the phenomenon itself (but see Bovens and t'Hart, 1996; Gray, 1998; Sieber, 1981). If a party involved in a voluntaristic, concerted project finds that it disagrees with the goals or strategies of that project, leaving the project may often be a smoother way of managing the situation than taking issue, given the informal nature of the project. Conflict in governance is therefore often more likely to result in 'exit' than in 'voice', to use Hirschman's conceptual framework (Hirschman, 1970).

Ways ahead

This is one of those books which ends up raising more questions than it has answered. Research on governance is at the time of writing just getting under way and the research agenda outlined here identifies but a few themes where our knowledge is particularly limited. One of the most intriguing cluster of questions is what the development towards the new governance actually means to the state in terms of its choices with regard to institutional arrangement, administrative reform, policy instruments, intergovernmental relationships, relationship to transnational organizations, inclusion of organized interests and strategy for economic development, to give just a few examples of research problems.

These are state-centric problems. This book has paid most attention to the 'new governance' from the perspective of the state looking out; we now need to reverse that perspective and focus on the internal consequences on the state of the emergence of these new forms of governance. It is here, we believe, that most of the salient research problems for political scientists are located. This is not to say, however, that these are the only relevant research problems in the context of governance. We believe that the leadership and coordination of society are likely to be increasingly characterized by different forms of governance; the field is open for research from a large number of perspectives, and that research is needed as a basis for forming more effective ways of governing.

References

Adshead, M. and B. Quinn (1998) 'The Move from Government to Governance: Irish Development Policy's Paradigm Shift', *Policy and Politics*, 26:209–25.

Albert, M. (1993) *Capitalism Against Capitalism* (London: Whurr).

Allen, G. C. (1981) *The Japanese Economy* (New York: St Martin's Press).

Anton, T. J. (1980) *Moving Money: An Empirical Examination of Federal Expenditure Patterns* (Cambridge, Mass: Oelgeschlager, Gunn & Hain).

Ashford, D. E. (1982) *Policy and Politics in France: Living With Uncertainty* (Philadelphia, Pa: Temple University Press).

Atkinson, M. M. and W. D. Coleman (1989), 'Strong States and Weak States: Sectoral Policy Networks in Advanced Capitalist Economies', *British Journal of Political Science*, 19:47–68.

Aucoin, P. (1996) *The New Public Management: Canada in Comparative Perspective* (Montreal: Institute for Research on Public Policy).

Aucoin, P. (1999), 'Accountability In Public Services: Making Performance Count', in B. G. Peters and D. J. Savoie (eds), *Revitalizing the Public Service* (Montreal: McGill/Queens University Press).

Bachrach, P. and Baratz, M. S. (1964) 'Decisions and Non-Decisions: An Analytical Framework', *American Political Science Review*, 57:632–42.

Barber, B. (1984) *Strong Democracy* (Berkeley: University of California Press).

Barker, A. (1995) *The Public Enquiry of British Policy Making* (unpublished paper, Department of Government, University of Essex).

Bay, C. (1958) *The Structure of Freedom* (Stanford, Calif: Stanford University Press).

Beauregard, R. A. (1998) 'Public–Private Partnerships as Historical Chameleons: The Case of the United States', in J. Pierre (ed.), *Partnerships in Urban Governance: European and American Experience* (London: Macmillan), 52–70.

Beauregard, R. A. and J. Pierre (1998) 'Disputing the Global: The Other Side of International Initiatives' unpublished manuscript, Milano Graduate School of Management and Urban Policy, New School for Social Research, New York City.

Bell, D. (1976) *The Coming of Post-Industrial Society: A Venture in Social Forecasting* 2nd edn (Harmondsworth: Penguin)

Bell, D. (1987) 'The World and the United States in 2013', *Daedalus*, 116:1–31.

Bell, D. (1993) *Communitarianism and its Critics* (Oxford: Oxford University Press).

Berki, R. N and J. Hayward (1979) 'The State of European Society', in J. E. S. Hayward and R. N. Berki (eds), *State and Society in Contemporary Europe* (Oxford: Martin Robertson), 253–64.

Bessette, J. R. (1994) *The Mild Voice of Reason* (Chicago, Ill.: University of Chicago Press).

Betcherman, G. (1996) 'Globalization, Labour Markets and Public Policy', in R. Boyer and D. Drache (eds), *States Against Markets* (London and New York: Routledge), 250–69.

Birch, A. H. (1982) 'Overload, Ungovernability and Delegitimation: The Theories and the British Case', *British Journal of Political Science*, 14:135–60.

Boston, J. (1999) 'Organizing for Service Delivery: Criteria and Opportunities', in B. G. Peters and D. J. Savoie (eds), *Revitalizing the Public Service* (Montreal: McGill/Queens University Press).

Boston, J., J. Martin, J. Pallot and P. Walsh (1996) *Public Management: The New Zealand Model* (Auckland: Oxford University Press).

Bovens, M. A. P. and P. t'Hart (1996) *Policy Fiascos* (New Brunswick, NJ: Transaction).

Boyer, R. and D. Drache (eds) (1996) *States Against Markets: The Limits of Globalization* (London and New York: Routledge).

Brenner, Y. S. (1991) *The Rise and Fall of Capitalism* (Aldershot: Edward Elgar).

Brittain, S. (1975) 'The Economic Contradictions of Democracy', *British Journal of Political Science*, 5, 129–60.

Budge, I. (1997) *The New Challenge of Direct Democracy* (Oxford: Polity Press).

Callaghy, T. M. (1984) *The State–Society Struggle: Zaire in Comparative Perspective* (New York: Columbia University Press).

Cameron, D. R. (1978) 'The Expansion of the Political Economy: A Comparative Analysis', *American Political Science Review*, 72:1243–61.

Camilleri, J. A. and J. Falk (1992) *The End of Sovereignty* (Aldershot: Edward Elgar).

Campbell, J. L., J. R. Hollingsworth and L. N. Lindberg (eds) (1991) *Governance of the American Economy* (Cambridge and New York: Cambridge University Press).

Cargill, T. F., M. M. Hutchison and T. Ito (1997) *The Political Economy of Japanese Monetary Policy* (Cambridge, Mass: MIT Press).

Cawson, A. (1986) *Corporatism and Political Theory* (Oxford: Basil Blackwell).

Christensen, J. Grønnegård (1997) 'The Scandinavian Welfare State: The Institutions of Growth, Governance, and Reform. Review article', *Scandinavian Political Studies*, 20:367–86.

Clarke, J. and J. Newman (1997) *The Managerial State* (London and Thousand Oaks, Calif: Sage).

Cohen, M. D., J. G. March and J. P. Olsen (1972) 'A Garbage Can Model of Organizational Choice', *Administrative Science Quarterly*, 17:1–25.

Cohen, S. S. (1977) *Modern Capitalist Planning: The French Model* (Berkeley and London: University of California Press).

Collier, R. B. and D. Collier (1991) *Shaping the Political Arena: Critical Junctures, the Labor Movement and Regime Dynamics in Latin America* (Princeton: Princeton University Press).

Conlan, T. (1998) *From New Federalism to Devolution: Twenty-Five Years of Intergovernmental Reform* (Washington, DC: The Brookings Institution).

Crozier, M., S. Huntington, and J. Watanuki (1975) *The Crisis of Democracy* (New York: New York University Press).

Dahl, R. A. (1961) *Who Governs? Democracy and Power in an American City* (New Haven, Conn: Yale University Press).

Dahl, R. A. and C. E. Lindblom (1953) *Politics, Economics and Welfare* (New York: Harper & Row).

Dalton, R. J. (1996) *Citizen Politics in Western Democracies*, 2nd edn (Chatham, NJ: Chatham House).

Damgaard, E., P. Gerlich and J. J. Richardson (eds) (1989) *The Politics of Economic Crisis* (Aldershot: Avebury).

De Leon, P. (1997) *Democracy and the Policy Sciences* (Albany, NY: State University of New York Press).

Demers, M. (1998) *Government and Governance* (Ottawa: Canadian Centre for Management Development).

Derlien, H.-U. (1995) 'Public Administration in Germany: Political and Societal Relations', in J. Pierre (ed.), *Bureaucracy in the Modern State* (Aldershot: Edward Elgar), 64–91.

Derlien, H.-U. and B. G. Peters (1997) *Who Works for Government and What Do They Do?* (Bamberg: Lehrstuhl für Verwaltungswissenschaft, University of Bamberg).

DeSario, J. and S. Langton (1987) *Citizen Participation in Public Decision-Making* (New York: Greenwood Press).

Deutsch, K. (1963), *The Nerves of Government* (New York: Free Press).

Diehl, P. F. (ed.) (1997) *The Politics of Global Governance: International Organizations in an Interdependent World* (Boulder, Colo and London: Lynne Rienner).

DiIulio, J. J. (1994) *Deregulating Government* (Washington, DC: The Brookings Institution).

Dolowitz, D. and D. Marsh (1997) 'Who Learns What from Whom?: A Review of the Policy Transfer Literature', *Political Studies*, 44, 343–57.

Dowding, K. (1995) 'Model or Metaphor: A Critical Review of the Policy Networks Approach', *Political Studies*, 43:136–58.

Dowding, K. and D. S. King (1995) *Preferences, Institutions and Rational Choice* (Oxford: Clarendon Press).

Downs, A. (1958) *An Economic Theory of Democracy* (New York: Harper & Row).

Downs, A. (1967) *Inside Bureaucracy* (Boston, Mass.: Little, Brown).

Downs, G. W. and P. D. Larkey (1986) *The Search for Government Efficiency: From Hubris to Helplessness* (Phildelphia: Temple University Press).

Dror, Y. (1986) *Policymaking Under Adversity* (New Brunswick, NJ: Transaction).

Dunleavy, P. (1989) 'The United Kingdom: Paradoxes of Ungrounded Statism', in F. G. Castles (ed.), *The Comparative History of Public Policy* (Cambridge: Polity Press), 242–91.

Dyson, K. (1980) *State Traditions in Western Europe* (Oxford: Polity Press).

Easton, D. (1953) *The Political System* (New York: Knopf).

Easton, D. (1965) *A Systems Analysis of Political Life* (New York: Wiley).

Easton, D. (1979) *A Framework for Political Analysis* (Chicago, Ill.: The University of Chicago Press).

Elkin, S. L. (1987) 'Twentieth-Century Urban Regimes', *Journal of Urban Affairs*, 7:11–28.

Elvander, N. and A. Seim Elvander (1995) *Gränslös Samverkan: Fackets Svar på Företagens Internationalisering* (*Cooperation Across Borders: The Unions' Response to the Internationalization of Private Corporations*) (Stockholm: SNS Förlag).

Esping-Anderson, G. (1990) *The Three Worlds of Welfare Capitalism* (London: Polity Press).

Esping-Andersen, G. (ed.) (1996) *Welfare States in Transition: National Adaptations in Global Economies* (London: Sage).

Etzioni, A. (1995) *New Communitarian Thinking: Persons, Virtues, Institutions and Communities* (Charlottesville: University Press of Virginia).

Etzioni, A. (1998) *The Essential Communitarian Reader* (Lanham, Md.: Rowman & Littlefield).

Evans, P. (1995) *Embedded Autonomy: States and Industrial Tranformation* (Princeton, NJ: Princeton University Press).

Evans, P. (1997) 'The Eclipse of the State? Reflections on Stateness in an Era of Globalization', *World Politics*, 50:62–87.

Evans, P., D. Rueschmeyer and T. Skocpol (eds) (1985) *Bringing the State Back In* (Cambride, Mass.: Cambridge University Press).

Evans, R. and A. Harding (1997) 'Regionalisation, Regional Institutions and Economic Development', *Policy and Politics*, 25:19–30.

Fawcett, H. (1998) 'Prisoners of History: Policy Transfer, Welfare Reform and Welfare Regimes', paper presented at an SOG conference, Lady Margaret Hall, Oxford University, 10–12 July.

Fearon, J. D. (1998) 'Deliberation as Discussion', in J. Elster (ed.), *Deliberative Democracy* (Cambridge: Cambridge University Press).

Fiorina, M. P. (1996) *Divided Government*, 2nd edn (Boston, Mass.: Allyn & Bacon).

Fishkin, J. (1996) *Democracy and Deliberation* (New Haven, Conn.: Yale University Press).

Flora, P. and A. J. Heidenheimer (1981) *The Development of Welfare States in Europe and America* (New Brunswick, NJ: Transaction).

Fowler, R. B. (1991) *The Dance With Community: The Contemporary Debate in American Political Thought* (Lawrence, Kans.: University Press of Kansas).

Fowler, R. B. (1995) 'Community: Reflection on Definition', in A. Etzioni (ed.), *New Communitarian Thinking* (Charlottesville: University Press of Virginia).

Frank, A. G. (1971) *Capitalism and Underdevelopment in Latin America* (Harmondsworth: Penguin).

Freeman, G. (1985) 'National Styles and Policy Sectors: Explaining Structured Variation', *Journal of Public Policy*, 5:441–96.

Freeman, J. L. (1965) *The Political Process: Executive Bureau-Legislative Committee Relations* (New York: Random House).

Fry, E. H. (1998) *The Expanding Role of State and Local Governments in U.S. Foreign Policy Affairs* (New York: Council on Foreign Relations Press).

Fry, E. H., L. H. Radebaugh and P. Soldatos (eds) (1989) *The New International Cities Era: The Global Activities of North American Municipal Governments* (Provo, Utah: David M. Kennedy for International Studies, Brigham Young University).

Fukuyama. F. (1995) *Trust: Social Relations and the Creation of Prosperity* (London: Hamish Hamlyn).

Galbraith, J. K. (1967) *The New Industrial State* (London: Penguin).

Gamble, A. (1994) *Britain in Decline*, 4th edn (London: Macmillan).

Gamble, A. (2000) 'Economic Governance', in J. Pierre (ed.), *Debating Governance: Authority, Steering and Democracy* (Oxford and New York: Oxford University Press).

Gamble, A. and T. Payne (eds) (1996) *Regionalism and World Order* (London: Macmillan).

Garrett, G. (1995) 'Capital Mobility, Trade, and the Domestic Politics of Economic Policy', *International Organization*, 49:657–87.

Goldsmith, M. and K. Newton (1993) 'Central–Local Relationships: The Irresistible Rise of Centralized Power', *West European Politics*, 6:216–33.

Gourevitch, P. (1978) 'The Second Image Reversed', *International Organization*, 32:881–912.

Gourevitch, P. (1986) *Politics in Hard Times: Comparative Responses to International Economic Crises* (Ithaca, NY and London: Cornell University Press).

Grant, W. (1993) *The Politics of Economic Policy* (New York and London: Harvester Wheatsheaf).

Gray, P. (1998) *Policy Disasters* (London: Routledge).

Green, D. P. and I. Shapiro (1994) *Pathologies of Rational Choice Theory: A Critique of Applications in Political Science* (New Haven, Conn.: Yale University Press).

Gregory, R. B. (1998) 'A New Zealand Tragedy: Problems of Political Responsibility', *Governance*, 11:231–40.

Gurr, T. R. and D. S. King (1987) *The State and the City* (London: Macmillan and Chicago: The University of Chicago Press).

Gyimah-Boadi, E. (1996) 'Civil Society in Africa', *Journal of Democracy*, 7:118–32.

Haas, P. M. (1992) 'Introduction: Epistemic Communities and International Policy Coordination', *International Organization*, 46:1–35.

Habermas, J. (1973) *The Legitimation Problems in Late Capitalism* (Cambridge: Polity Press).

Habermas, J. (1984) *Theory of Communicative Action: Reason and Rationalization in Society* (London: Heinemann).

Hall, P. A. (1986) *Governing the Economy: The Politics of State Intervention in Britain and France* (Oxford and New York: Oxford University Press).

Halligan, J. A. (1997) 'The Paradoxes of Reform in Australia and New Zealand', paper presented at Conferences on Paradoxes of Administrative Reform, Centre for Comparative Government, Berlin, May.

Handler, J. (1996) *Down from Bureaucracy: The Ambiguity of Privatization and Empowerment* (Princeton, NJ: Princeton University Press).

Harding, A. (1998) 'Public–Private Partnerships in the UK', in J. Pierre (ed.), *Partnerships in Urban Governance: European and American Experience* (London: Macmillan), 71–92.

Heclo, H. (1974) *Modern Social Politics in Britain and Sweden* (New Haven, Conn.: Yale University Press).

Held, D. *et al.* (eds) (1983) *States and Societies* (Oxford: Basil Blackwell).

Helleiner, E. (1994) *States and the Reemergence of Global Finance* (Ithaca, NY and London: Cornell University Press).

Helleiner, E. (1996) 'Post-Globalization: Is the Financial Liberalization Likely to be Reversed?', in R. Boyer and D. Drache (eds), *States Against Markets* (London and New York: Routledge), 193–210.

Hernes, G. (ed.) (1978) *Forhandlingsökonomi og blandingsadministrasjon (A Negotiated Economy and a Mixed Administration)* (Oslo: Universitetsforlaget).

Hertier, A. (1998) *Ringing the Changes in Europe* (Berlin: De Gruyter).

Hibbs, D. A. (1987) *The Political Economy of Industrial Democracies* (Cambridge: Cambridge University Press).

Hill, D. (1974) *Democratic Theory and Local Government* (London: George Allen & Unwin).

Hinnfors, J. and J. Pierre (1996) 'Autonomi, Suveränitet och Ekonomisk Politik: EMU-medlemskapets Inverkan på Svenskt Politiskt Beslutsfattande' ('Autonomy, Sovereignty, and Economic Policy: The Impact of an EMU Membership on Swedish Political Decision Making'), *SOU 1996:158*, Appendix 18 (Report from a Royal Commission).

Hinnfors, J. and J. Pierre (1998) 'The Politics of Currency Crises in Sweden: Domestic Policy Choice in a Globalized Economy', *West European Politics*, 21:103–19.

Hirsch, J. (1991) 'From the Fordist to the Post-Fordist State', in B. Jessop *et al.* (eds), *The Politics of Flexibility: Restructuring State and Industry in Britain, Germany and Scandinavia* (Aldershot: Edward Elgar), 67–81.

Hirschman, A. O. (1970) *Exit, Voice and Loyalty* (Cambridge, Mass.: Harvard University Press).

Hirst, P. and G. Thompson (1996) *Globalization in Question* (Cambridge: Polity Press).

Hobbs, H. H. (1994) *City Hall Goes Abroad: The Foreign Policy of Local Politics* (Thousand Oaks, Calif. and London: Sage).

Hoekman, B. and M. Kostecki (1995) *The Political Economy of the World Trading System* (Oxford and New York: Oxford University Press).

Hollingsworth, J. R. and R. Boyer (eds) (1997) *Contemporary Capitalism: The Embeddedness of Institutions* (Cambridge and New York: Cambridge University Press).

Hollingsworth, J. R., P. C. Schmitter and W. Streek (eds) (1994) *Governing Capitalist Economies* (Oxford and New York: Oxford University Press).

Hood, C. (1991) 'A Public Management for All Seasons?', *Public Administration*, 69:3–19.

Hood, C (1984) *The Tools of Government* (Chatham, NJ: Chatham House)

Hood, C. (1998) *The Art of the State* (Oxford: Oxford University Press).

Hood, C., B. G. Peters and H. Wollmann (1996) 'Sixteen Ways to Consumerize the Public Service', *Public Money and Management*, 16:43–50.

Hooge, L. and G. Marks (1997) 'Contending Models of Governance in the European Union', in A. W. Cafruny and C. Lankoski (eds), *Europe's Ambiguous Unity* (Boulder, CQ: Lynne Rienner).

Hooks, G. (1993) 'The Weakness of Strong Theories: The U.S. State's Dominance in the Post World War II Investment Process', *American Sociologial Review*, 58:37–53.

Horie, F. (1996) 'Intergovernmental Relations in Japan: Historical and Legal Patterns of Power Distribution Between Central and Local Governments', in J. S. Jun and D. S. Wright (eds), *Globalization and Decentralization* (Washington, DC: Georgetown University Press), 48–67.

Horn, M. (1995) *The Political Economy of Public Administration* (Cambridge: Cambridge University Press).

Howard, C. (1997) *The Hidden Welfare State* (Princeton, NJ: Princeton University Press).

Hunold, C. (1998) 'Deliberative Democracy and Nuclear Waste Sitings: A Comparative Analysis', unpublished Ph.D. Dissertation, University of Pittsburgh.

Huntington, S. P. (1974) 'Post-Industrial Politics: How Benign Will it Be?', *Comparative Politics*, 6:164–92.

Hyden, G. (1992) 'Governance and the Study of Politics', in G. Hyden and M. Bratton (eds), *Goverance and Politics in Africa* (Boulder, Colo.: Lynne Rienner), 1–26.

Hyden, G. and M. Bratton (1992) *Governance and Politics in Africa* (Boulder, CO: Lynne Reinner).

Illich, I. (1971) *Medical Nemesis* (New York: Pantheon).

Inglehart, R. (1977) *The Silent Revolution: Changing Values and Political Styles in Western Publics* (Princeton, NJ: Princeton University Press).

Inglehart, R. (1991) *Culture Shift in Advanced Industrial Systems* (Princeton, NJ: Princeton University Press).

Ingram, H. and A .B. Schneider (1990) 'Improving Implementation Through Framing Smarter Statutes', *Journal of Public Policy*, 10, 67–87.

Jacques, E. (1990) 'In Praise of Hierarchy', *Harvard Business Review*, 127–33.

Jervis, R. (1983) 'Security Regimes', in S. Krasner (ed.), *International Regimes* (Ithaca, NY and London: Cornell University Press).

Jessop, B. (1982) *The Capitalist State* (Oxford: Martin Robertson).

Jessop, R. (1995) 'The Regulation Approach, Governance and Post-Fordism: Alternative Perspectives on Economic and Political Change', *Economy and Society*, 24:307–33.

Johnson, C. (1982) *MITI and the Japanese Miracle* (Stanford, Calif.: Stanford University Press).

Jones, C. O. (1984) *Introduction to the Study of Public Policy*, 3rd edn (Monterey, Calif.: Brooks/Cole).

Jordan, A. G. (1981) 'Iron Triangles, Woolly Corporatism and Elastic Nets: Images of the Policy Process, *Journal of Public Policy*, 1:95–123.

Jordan, A. G. (1990) 'Policy Community Realism vs. "New" Institutionalist Ambiguity', *Political Studies*, XXXVIII:470–84.

Kaase, M. and K. Newton (1996) *Beliefs in Government* (Oxford: Oxford University Press).

Kapstein, E. (1994) *Governing the Global Economy: Internaitonal Finance and the State* (Cambridge, Mass. and London: Harvard University Press).

Katz, R. S. *et al.* (1992) 'The Membership of Political Parties in European Democracies, 1960–1990', *European Journal of Political Research*, 22:329–45.

Katzenstein, P. J. (ed.) (1978) *Between Power and Plenty* (Madison: University of Wisconsin Press).

Katzenstein, P. J. (1984) *Corporatism and Change* (Ithaca, NY and London: Cornell University Press).

Katzenstein, P. J. (1985) *Small States in World Markets* (Ithaca, NY and London: Cornell University Press).

Katzenstein, P. J. (1987) *Germany: Policymaking in the Semi-Sovereign State* (Philadelphia, Pa.: Temple University Press).

Kavanagh, D. and P. Morris (1994) *Consensus Politics from Attlee to Major*, 2nd edn (Oxford: Blackwell).

.eating, M. (1996) *Nations Against the State* (London: Macmillan).

.eating, M. (1998) 'Commentary: Public–Private Partnerships in the United States from a European Perspective', in J. Pierre (ed.), *Partnerships in Urban Governance: European and American Experience* (London: Macmillan), 163–74.

.eating, M. and J. Loughlin (eds) (1997) *The Political Economy of Regionalism* (London: Frank Cass).

.elman, S. (1992) 'Adversary and Cooperationist Institutions for Conflict Resolution in Public Policymaking', *Journal of Policy Analysis and Management*, 11:178–206.

.enworthy, L. (1995) *In Search of National Economic Success* (Thousand Oaks, Calif. and London: Sage).

.eohane, R. O. and H. V. Milner (eds) (1996) *Internationalization and Domestic Politics* (Cambridge and New York: Cambridge University Press).

.ettl, D. F. (1992) *Deficit Politics: Public Budgeting in Its Institutional and Historical Context* (New York: Macmillan).

.ettl, D. F. (1993) *Sharing Power: Public Governance and Private Markets* (Washington, DC: The Brookings Institution).

.hademian, A. (1996) *Checking on Banks: Autonomy and Accountability in Three Federal Agencies* (Washington, DC: The Brookings Institution).

.icket, W. (1994) 'Autopoesis and the Science of Public Administration: Essence, Sense and Nonsense', *Organisation Studies* 14, 226–46.

.ing, A. (1975) 'Overload: Problems of Governing in the 1970s', *Political Studies*, 23:284–96.

.ing, D. S. and G. Stoker (eds) (1997) *Rethinking Local Democracy* (London: Macmillan).

.night, J. and J. Johnson (1997) 'What Sort of Equality Does Deliberative Democracy Require?', in J. Bohman and W. Rehg (eds), *Deliberative Democracy* (Cambridge, Mass.: MIT Press).

.nox, P. L. and P. J. Taylor (eds) (1995) *World Cities in a World-System* (Cambridge and New York: Cambridge University Press).

.obach, K. W. (1994) *The Referendum: Direct Democracy in Switzerland* (Aldershot: Dartmouth).

.ooiman, J. (ed.) (1993) *Modern Governance: New Government–Society Interactions* (Newbury Park, Calif. and London: Sage).

.ooiman, J. (2000) 'Societal Governance: Levels, Modes and Orders of Social–Political Interaction', in J. Pierre (ed.), *Debating Governance: Authority, Steering, and Democracy* (Cambridge and New York: Cambridge University Press).

.rasner, S. (1983) *International Regimes* (Ithaca, NY: Cornell University Press).

.rasner, S. (1984) 'Approaches to the State: Alternative Conceptions and Historical Dynamics', *Comparative Politics*, 16:223–47.

.rugman, P. (1994) *Currencies and Crises* (Cambridge, Mass.: MIT Press).

.affin, M. and K. Young (1990) *Professionalism in Local Government* (Harlow: Longman).

.ane, J.-E. (1983) 'The Concept of Implementation', *Statsvetenskaplig Tidskrift*, 86:17–40.

.asswell, H. D. (1935) *Politics: Who Gets Waht?* (Chicago: University of Chicago Press).

.eftwich, A. (1994) 'Governance, the State and the Politics of Development', *Development and Change*, 25:361–86.

Le Galès, P. (1997) 'Urban Governance and Policy Networks',paper presented at the American Political Science Association conference, Washington, DC 28–31 August.

Le Galès, P. (1998) 'Conclusion—Government and Governance of Regions Structural Weaknesses and New Mobilisations', in P. Le Galès and C Lequesne (eds) *Regions in Europe* (London and New York: Routledge), 239–68.

Le Galès, P. and A. Harding (1998) 'Cities and States in Europe', *West European Politics*, 21:120–45.

Le Galès, P. and C. Lequesne (eds) (1998) *Regions in Europe* (London and New York: Routledge).

Le Grand, J. (1998) *A Revolution in Social Policy: Quasi-Market Reforms in the 1990* (Oxford: Polity Press).

Lehmbruch, G. (1979) 'Liberal Corporatism and Party Government', in *Trend Toward Corporatist Intermediation*, ed. P. C. Schmitter and G. Lehmbruch, pp 147–53, Beverly Hills, CA: Sage.

Lijphart, A. (1984) *Democracies: Patterns of Majoritarian and Consensus Government i Twenty-One Countries* (New Haven, Conn.: Yale University Press).

Lindblom, C. E. (1977) *Politics and Markets* (New York: Basic Books).

Linder, S. H. and B. G. Peters (1989) 'Implementation as a Guide for Polic Formulation: A Question of "When" Rather than "Whether"', *International Review of Administrative Sciences*, 55:631–52.

Lipset, S. M., M. Trow and J .S. Coleman (1956) *Union Democracy* (Glencoe, Ill Free Press).

Listhaug, O. (1989) *Citizens, Parties and Norwegian Electoral Politics 1957–198* (Trondheim: Tapir).

Loughlin, J. and S. Mazey (1995) 'The End of the French Unitary State? Te Years of Regionalization in France (1982–1992)', *Regional Politics and Policy*, 4 3 (special issues).

Lowi, T. J. (1979) *The End of Liberalism*, 2nd. edn (New York: Norton).

Maier, C. S. (1987) 'Introduction', in C. S. Maier (ed.), *Changing Boundaries of tr Political* (Cambridge, Mass. and New York: Cambridge University Press 1–26.

Majone, G. (1987) *Evidence, Argument and Persuasion in the Policy Process* (New Haven, Conn.: Yale University Press).

Majone, G. (1994) 'Independence and Accountability: Non-majoritaria Institutions in the European Union', in J. Hesse (ed.), *European Yearbook of Publ Administration and Comparative Government*, vol. 1 (Oxford: Oxford University Press).

Malmström, C. (1998) *Regionerna, Makten och Härligheten: Regionala Partier Västeuropa* (Regions, The Power and the Glory: Regional Parties in Wester Europe) (Stockholm: SNS Förlag).

Mann, M. (1997) Has Globalization Ended the Rise and Rise of the Natior State?', *Review of International Political Economy*, 4:472–96.

March, J. G. and J. P. Olsen (1989) *Rediscovering Institutions* (New York: The Fre Press).

March, J. G. and J. P. Olsen (1995) *Democratic Governance* (New York: Free Press).

Marks, G., L. Hooghe and K. Blank (1996) 'European Integration since th 1980s: State-Centric versus Multi-Level Governance', *Journal of Commc Market Studies*, 34, 341–78.

Marsh, D. and R. A. W. Rhodes (eds) (1992) *Policy Networks in British Government* (Oxford: Clarendon Press).

Martin, A. (1996) 'What has Globalization to with the Erosion of the Welfare State?: Sorting out the Issues', Working Paper No. 17 Oslo: ARENA.

Mawson, J. and K. Spencer (1997) 'The Government Offices for the English Regions: Towards Regional Governance?', *Policy and Politics*, 25:71–84.

Mead, L. (1996) 'Welfare Policy: The Administrative Frontier', *Journal of Public Policy Analysis and Management*, 15:587–600.

Meininger, M.-C. (1998) 'Public Service, the Public's Service' in F. Gallouédec-Genuys (ed.), *About French Administration* (Paris: La Documentation Française).

Menon, A. (1996) 'France and the IGC of 1996', *Journal of European Public Policy*, 3, 231–52.

Merton. R. K. (1940) 'Bureaucratic Structure and Personality', *Social Forces*, 18, 3–18.

Micheletti, M. (1994) *Det civila samhället och staten* (The Civil Society and the State) (Stockholm: Fritzes).

Mierlo, H. J. G. A. van (1986) 'Depillarisation and the Decline of Consociationalism in the Netherlands, 1970–85', *West European Politics* 9:97–119.

Migdal, J. S. (1988) *Strong Societies and Weak States: State–Society Relations and State Capabilities in the Third World* (Princeton, NJ: Princeton University Press).

Miliband, R. (1969) *The State in Capitalist Society* (London: Wiedenfeld & Nicolson).

Milner, H. V. and R. O. Keohane (1996) 'Internationalization and Domestic Politics: A Conclusion', in R. O. Keohane and H. V. Milner (eds), *Internationalization and Domestic Politics* (Cambridge and New York: Cambridge University Press), 243–58.

Morgan, G. (1986) *Images of Organization* (Beverly Hills, Calif.: Sage).

Moses, J. (1994) 'Abdication from National Policy Autonomy: What's Left to Leave?', *Politics and Society*, 2:125–48.

Muller, W. C. and V. Wright (1994) 'Reshaping the State in Western Europe: The Limits of Retreat', *West European Politics*, 17:1–11.

Muramatsu, M. (1997) *Local Power in the Japanese State* (Berkeley: University of California Press).

Navari, C. (1991) 'On the Withering Away of the State', in C. Navari (ed.), *The Condition of States* (Milton Keynes and Philadelphia, Pa.: Open University Press), 143–66.

Nielsen, K. and O. K. Pedersen (eds) (1989) *Förhandlingsökonomi i Norden* (*The Nordic Negotiated Economy*) (Copenhagen: Jurist- og Ökonomforbundets Forlag).

Nilsson, L. (1998) 'The Scope of the local welfare state in Sweden: Citizens' Attitudes Towards Privatization and the Public Sector', unpublished manuscript, Department of Political Science, University of Gothenburg.

Niskanen, W. A. (1996) *Bureaucracy and Public Economics* (Aldershot: Edward Elgar).

Nye, J. S., P. D. Zelikow and D. C. King (1997) *Why People Don't Trust Government* (Cambridge, Mass.: Harvard University Press).

O'Brien, P. (1994) 'Governance Systems in Steel: The American and Japanese Experiences', in J. R. Hollingsworth, P. C. Schmitter and W. Streek (eds),

Governing Capitalist Economies (Oxford and New York: Oxford University Press, 1994), 43–71.

Offe, C. (1985) *Disorganized Capitalism* (Cambridge, Mass.: The MIT Press).

Ohmae, K. (1995) *The End of the Nation State: The Rise of Regional Economics* (London: HarperCollins).

Okimoto, D. (1988) *Between MITI and the Market* (Stanford, Calif.: Stanford University Press).

Olsen, J. P. (1983) *Organized Democracy* (Oslo: Universitetsforlaget).

Olsen, J. P. (1987) 'Popular Sovereignty and the Search for Appropriate Institutions', *Journal of Public Policy*, 7, 341–70.

Olson, Mancur (1982) *The Rise and Decline of Nations: Economic Growth Stagflation and Social Rigidities* (New Haven, Conn.: Yale University Press).

Osborne, D. and Gaebler, T. (1992) *Reinventing Government* (Reading, Mass.: Addison-Wesley).

Ostrom, E. (1990) *Governing the Commons: The Evolution of Institutions of Collective Action* (Cambridge: Cambridge University Press).

Papadopolous, J. J. (1992) *Seguridad social y politica en el Uruguay* (Montevideo: CIESU).

Payne, A. (2000) 'Globalisation and Modes of Regionalist Governance', in J. Pierre (ed.), *Debating Governance: Authority, Steering, and Democracy* (Oxford and New York: Oxford University Press).

Perez-Diaz, V. (1994) *The Return of Civil Society* (Cambridge, Mass.: Harvard University Press).

Peters, B. G. (1985) 'The United States', in R. Rose *et al.*, *Public Employment in Western Countries* (Cambridge: Cambridge University Press).

Peters, B. G. (1992) *The Politics of Taxation* (Oxford: Blackwell).

Peters, B. G. (1993) 'Managing the Hollow State', in K. Eliassen and J. Kooiman (eds), *Managing Public Organizations* (London: Sage), 46–57.

Peters, B. G. (1996) *The Future of Governing* (Lawrence, Kans.: University of Kansas Press).

Peters, B. G. (1997a) 'Globalization and Governance', paper presented at Conference on Globalization and Politics, University of Birmingham, April.

Peters, B. G. (1997b) 'Shouldn't Row, Can't Steer: What's a Government to Do?, *Public Policy and Administration*, 10(2), 34–60.

Peters, B. G. (1998a) 'Governance in Africa', paper presented at United Nations Conference on Governance in Africa.

Peters, B. G. (1998b) 'The Problem of Policy Problems', paper presented at the annual meeting of the Southern Political Science Association's Annual Conference, Atlanta, Georgia, 28–31 October, 1998.

Peters, B. G. (1998c) *Comparative Politics: Theory and Methods* (London: Macmillan).

Peters, B. G. (1998d) '"With a Littel Help From Our Friends" Public–Private Partnerships as Institutions and Instruments', in J. Pierre (ed), *Partnerships in Urban Governamce: European and American Experience* (London: Macmillan), 11–33.

Peters, B. G. and J. Pierre (1998a) 'Governing without Government: Rethinking Public Administration', *Journal of Public Administration and Theory*, 8, 223–42.

Peters, B. G. and J. Pierre (1986b) 'Institutions and Time: Problems in Conceptualization and Explanation', *Journal of Public Administration Research and Theory*, 8, 565–84.

Peters, B. G. and D. J. Savoie (eds) (1995) *Governance in a Changing Environment* (Montreal: McGill/Queens University Press).

Peters, B. G. and D. J. Savoie (1998) *Taking Stock: Assessing Public Sector Reform* (Montreal and Kingston: McGill-Queen's University Press).

Peters, B. G. and F. K. M. Van Nispen (1998) *The Study of Policy Instruments* (Cheltenham: Edward Elgar).

Petersson, O., J. Hermansson, M. Micheletti, J. Teorell and A. Westholm (1998) *Demokrati och Medborgarskap* (*Democracy and Citizenship*) (Stockholm: SNS).

Petracca, M. (1992) *The Politics of Interests* (Boulder, Colo.: Westview Press).

Pickvance, C. and E. Preteceille (eds) (1991) *State Restructuring and Local Power: A Comparative Perspective* (London: Pinter).

Pierre, J. (1994) *Den Lokala Staten* (*The Local State*) (Stockholm: Almqvist & Wiksell).

Pierre, J. (1995a) 'The Marketization of the State: Citizens, Customers and the Emergence of the Public Market', in B. G. Peters and D. J. Savoie (eds), *Governance in a Changing Environment* (Montreal and Kingston: McGill/Queens University Press), 47–69.

Pierre, J. (ed.) (1995b) *Bureaucracy in the Modern State* (Aldershot: Edward Elgar).

Pierre, J. (1997a) 'State Models and Economic Development: Controversies, Convergencies and Consequences', paper presented at the International Political Science Association conference, Seoul, Korea, 17–21 August.

Pierre, J. (1997b) 'Decentralisering av Politik och Politikens Decentralisering' 'The Decentralization of Politics and the Politics of Decentralization', in B. Rothstein (ed.), *Politik som Organisation* (*Politics as Organization*), 2nd edn (Stockholm: SNS Förlag), 118–38.

Pierre, J. (ed.) (1998a) *Partnerships in Urban Governance: European and American Experiences* (London: Macmillan).

Pierre, J. (1998b) 'Public Consultation and Citizen Participation: Dilemmas of Policy Advice', in B. G. Peters and D. J. Savoie (eds), *Taking Stock: Assessing Public Sector Reform* (Montreal: McGills/Queens University Press), 137–63.

Pierre, J. (ed.) (2000) *Debating Governance: Authority, Steering, and Democracy* (Oxford and New York: Oxford University Press).

Pierson, P. (1994) *Dismantling the Welfare State?: Reagan, Thatcher and the Politics of Retrenchment* (Cambridge and New York: Cambridge University Press).

Pierson, P. (1998) 'Irresistible Forces, Immovable Objects: The Post-Industrial Welfare States Confront Permanent Austerity', *Journal of European Public Policy*, 5, 539–60.

Polanyi, K. (1941) *The Great Transformation* (Boston, Mass.: Beacon Press).

Polidano, C. (1999) 'The Bureaucrat Who Fell Under a Bus: Ministerial Responsibility, Executive Agencies and the Derek Lewis Affairs in Britain', *Governance*, 13, 201–30.

Pollitt, C. (1984) *Manipulating the Machine: Changing Patterns of Ministerial Departments 1960–83* (London: Allen & Unwin).

Pollitt, C. (1990) *Managerialism in the Public Service* (Oxford: Basil Blackwell).

Porter, M. J. (1990) *The Competitive Advantage of Nations* (New York: Free Press).

Posner, P. (1998) *Unfunded Mandates* (Washington, DC: Georgetown University Press).

Posner, P. and C. Levine (1981) 'Austerity and the Intergovernmental System, *Political Science Quarterly*, 96, 67–86.

Power, M. (1997) *The Audit Society: Rituals of Verification* (Oxford: Oxford University Press).

Pressman, J. L. and A. Wildavsky (1973) *Implementation* (Berkeley: University of California Press).

Przeworski, A. and H. Teune (1970) *The Logic of Comparative Social Inquiry* (New York: Wiley-Interscience).

Putnam, R. D. (1988) 'Diplomacy and Domestic Politics', *International Organization*, 42, 427–60.

Putnam, R. D. (1993) *Making Democracy Work: Civic Traditions in Modern Italy* (Princeton, NJ: Princeton University Press).

Quah, J. S. T. (1987) *The Government and Politics of Singapore* (rev. ed.) (Singapore: Oxford University Press).

Reich, R. B. (1991) *The Work of Nations* (New York: Vintage).

Reich S. (1990) *Fruits of Fascism: Post-War Prosperity in Historical Perspective* (Ithaca, NY: Cornell University Press).

Rhodes, R. A. W. (1994) 'The Hollowing Out of the State', *Political Quarterly*, 65:138–51.

Rhodes, R. A. W. (1997) *Understanding Governance: Policy Networks, Governance, Reflexivity and Accountability* (Buckingham: Open University Press).

Richardson, J. J. (ed.) (1982) *Policy Styles in Western Europe* (Boston, Mass. and London: Allen & Unwin).

Rittberger, V. (1993) *Regime Theory and International Relations* (Oxford: Oxford University Press).

Rockman, B. A. (1998) 'The Changing Role of the State', in B. G. Peters and D. J. Savoie, (eds), *Taking Stock: Assessing Public Sector Reforms* (Montreal and Kingston: McGill-Queen's University Press), 20–44.

Rogowski, R. (1987) 'Trade and the Variety of Democratic Institutions', *International Organization*, 41:203–23.

Rogowski, R. (1989) *Commerce and Coalitions: How Trade Affects Domestic Political Alignments* (Princeton, NJ: Princeton University Press).

Rokkan, S. (1966) 'Norway: Numerical Democracy and Corporate Pluralism', in R. A. Dahl (ed.), *Political Oppositions in Western Democracies* (New Haven, Conn.: Yale University Press).

Rokkan, S. (1966) 'Votes Count But Resources Decide', in R. A. Dahl, (ed.), *Political Oppositions in Western Democracies* (New Haven: Yale University Press).

Rose, R. (1976) *The Problem of Party Government* (London: Macmillan).

Rose, R. and T. Karran (1994) *Governing by Inertia* (London: Routledge).

Rose, R. and B. G. Peters (1976) *Can Government Go Bankrupt?* (New York: Basic Books).

Rosenau, J. N. (2000) 'Change, Complexity, and Governance in Globalizing Space', in J. Pierre (ed.), *Debating Governance: Authority, Steering, and Democracy* (Oxford and New York: Oxford University Press).

Rosenau, J. N. and E.-O. Czempiel (eds) (1992) *Governance without Government:*

Order and Change in World Politics (Cambridge and New York: Cambridge University Press).

Rothenberg, L. (1992) *Linking Citizens to Government: Interest Group Politics at Common Cause* (Cambridge: Cambridge University Press).

Rothstein, B. (1992) *Den korporativa staten* (*The Corporatist State*), (Stockholm: Norstedts).

Rouban, L. (1998) *La modernisation de la gestion des collectivités locales de plus de 10 000 habitants* (*The Modernization of the Management of Locales bigger than 10,000 Inhabitants*) (Paris: CEVIPOF).

Salamon, L. (1981) 'Rethinking Public Management: Third Party Government and the Changing Forms of Government Action', *Public Policy*, 29, 255–75.

Salamond, L. M. and M. Lund (1987) *Beyond Privatization: The Tools of Government Action* (Washington, DC: Urban Institute Press).

Sandel, M. (1996) *Democracy's Discontents: America in Search of a Public Philosophy* (Cambridge, Mass.: Belknap Press).

Sartori, G. (1994) *Constitutional Engineering* (New York: New York University Press).

Sassen, S. (1991) *The Global City: New York, London, Tokyo* (Princeton, NJ: Princeton, University Press).

Savoie, D. J. (1994) *Thatcher, Reagan, Mulroney: In Search of a New Bureaucracy* (Pittsburgh, Pa.: University of Pittsburgh Press).

Saward, M. (1998) 'In Search of the Hollow Crown', in P. Weller, H. Bakvis and R. A. W. Rhodes (eds), *The Hollow Crown* (London: Macmillan).

Scharpf, F. W. (1988) 'The Joint-Decision Trap: Lessons from German Federalism and European Integration', *Public Administration*, 66:239–78.

Scharpf, F. W. (1997) 'Introduction: The Problem-Solving Capacity of Multi-level Governance', *Journal of European Public Policy*, 4:520–38.

Scheuch, E. (1976) *Wird die Bundesrepublik Unregierbar?* (*Will the Federal Republic become Ungovernable?*) (Köln: Arbeitgeberverband der Metallindustrie).

Schmitter, P. C. (1974) 'Still the Century of Corporatism?', *Review of Politics*, 36:85–131.

Schmitter, P. and W. Streek (1985) *Private Interest Government* (London: Sage).

Schon, D. G. and M. Rein (1994) *Frame Reflection: Resolving Intractable Policy Issues* (New York: Basic Books).

Schumpeter, J. A. (1975 [1942]) *Capitalism, Socialism and Democracy* (New York: Harper & Row).

Scott, A. (ed.) (1997) *The Limits of Globalization* (London: Routledge).

Sears, D. O. and J. Citrin (1985) *Tax Revolt: Something for Nothing in California* (Cambridge, Mass.: Harvard University Press).

Seidman, H. (1998) *Politics, Power and Position*, 5th edn (New York: Oxford University Press).

Seigfried, A. (1940) *France: A Study in Nationality* (New York: A. A. Knopf).

Self, P. (1993) *Government by the Market?* (London: Macmillan).

Sharpe, L. J. (1988) 'The Growth and Decentralisation of the Modern Democratic State', *European Journal of Political Research*, 16:365–80.

Shaw, M. (1997) 'The State of Globalization: Toward a Theory of State Transformation', *Review of International Political Economy*, 4:497–513.

Shepsle, K. A. and B. R. Weingast (1995) *Positive Theories of Congressional Institutions* (Ann Arbor: University of Michigan Press).

Shonfield, A. (1965) *Modern Capitalism* (Oxford and New York: Oxford University Press).

Sieber, S. (1981) *Fatal Remedies* (New York: Plenum).

Skocpol, T. (1979) *States and Social Revolutions* (Cambridge: Cambridge University Press).

Smith, B. C. (1986) *Decentralization: The Territorial Dimension of the State* (London: George Allen & Unwin).

Smyrl, M. E. (1997) 'Does European Community Regional Policy Empower the Regions?', *Governance*, 10:287–309.

Soros, G. (1998) *The Crisis of Global Capitalism: Open Society Endangered* (London: Little, Brown).

SOU 1990:44, *Demokrati och Makt i Sverige. Maktutredningens huvudrapport* (*Democracy and Power in Sweden: The Final Report from the Royal Commission on the distribution of power in Sweden*).

Spulbar, N. (1995) *The American Economy: The Struggle for Supremacy in the 21st Century* (Cambridge: Cambridge University Press).

Stillman, R. J. (1991) *Preface to Public Administration: A Search for Themes and Directions* (New York: St Martin's Press).

Stoker, G. (1990) 'Regulation Theory, Local Government and the Transition from Fordism', in D. S. King and J. Pierre (eds), *Challenges to Local Government* (London: Sage), 242–64.

Stoker, G. (1998a) (ed.), *The New Management of British Local Governance* (London: Macmillan).

Stoker, G. (1998b) 'Public–Private Partnerships and Urban Governance', in J. Pierre (ed.), *Partnerships in Urban Governance: European and American Experience* (London: Macmillan, and New York: St Martin's Press), 34–51.

Stoker, G. (2000) 'Urban Political Science and the Challenge of Urban Governance', in J. Pierre (ed.), *Debating Governance: Authority, Steering, and Democracy* (Oxford and New York: Oxford University Press).

Stokes, S. C. (1998) 'Pathologies of Deliberation', in J. Elster (ed.), *Deliberative Democracy* (Cambridge: Cambridge University Press).

Stone, C. N. (1989) *Governing Atlanta* (Lawrence, Kans.: University of Kansas Press).

Strange, S. (1986) *Casino Capitalism* (Oxford: Basil Blackwell).

Strange, S. (1996) *The Retreat of the State: The Diffusion of Power in the World Economy* (Cambridge: Cambridge University Press).

Sundquist, J. L. (1993) *Beyond Gridlock? Prospects for Governance in the Clinton Years and After* (Washington, DC: The Brookings Institution).

Sunstein, C. R. (1998) 'Health–Health Trade Offs', in J. Elster (ed.), *Deliberative Democracy* (Cambridge: Cambridge University Press).

Swanstrom, T. (1985) *The Crisis in Growth Politics* (Philadelphia, Pa.: Temple University Press).

Taggart, P. (1996) *The New Populism and the New Politics* (London: Macmillan).

Taggart, P. (1998) 'A Touchstone of Dissent: Euroscepticism in Contemporary West European Party Systems', *European Journal of Political Research*, 33:36388.

Tam, H. B. (1998) *Communitarianism: A New Agenda for Politics and Citizenship* (New York: New York University Press).

Thelen, K., F. Longstreth and S. Steinmo (1992) *Stucturing Politics: Historical*

Institutionalism in Comparative Analysis (Cambridge: Cambridge University Press).

Thomas, P. J. (1998) 'The Changing Nature of Accountability', in B. G. Peters and D. J. Savoie (eds), *Taking Stock: Assessing Public Sector Reform* (Montreal: McGill/Queens University Press), 348–93.

Thorley, J. (1996) *Athenian Democracy* (London: Routledge).

Tilly, C. (1985) *Big Structures, Large Processes, Huge Comparisons* (New York: Russell Sage).

Tordoff, W. (1993) *Government and Politics in Africa*, 2nd edn (Bloomington: Indiana University Press).

Trosa, S. and M. Crozier (1994) *Moderniser l'administration: Comment font les autres?* (Paris: Les Editions d'Organisation).

Tsebelis, G. (1990) *Nested Games: Rational Choice in Comparative Politics* (Berkeley: University of Calfiornia Press).

't Veld, R. (1993) *Autopoesis and Configuration Theory* (Dordrecht: Kluwer).

Vogel, D. (1995) *Trading Up: Consumer and Environmental Regulation in a Global Economy* (Cambridge, Mass.: Harvard University Press).

Wallace, H. (1996) 'Politics and Policy in the EU: The Challenge of Governance', in H. Wallace and W. Wallace (eds), *Policy-Making in the European Union*, 3rd edn (Oxford and New York: Oxford University Press), 3–36.

Walzer, M. (1994) *Spheres of Justice* (Oxford: Blackwell).

Walzer. N. and B. D. Jacobs (eds) (1998) *Public–Private Partnerships for Local Economic Development* (Westport, Conn. and London: Praeger).

Weaver, R. K. (1987) 'Political Foundations of Swedish Economic Policy', in B. P. Bosworth and A. M. Rivlin (eds), *The Swedish Economy* (Washington, DC: Brookings), 289–317.

Weaver, R. K. and B. A. Rockman (eds) (1993) *Do Institutions Matter? Comparing Capabilities in the U.S. and Abroad* (Washington, DC: The Brookings Institution).

Weaver, R. K. and B. A. Rockman (1993) 'Institutional Reform and Constitutional Design', in R. K. Weaver and B. A. Rockman (eds) *Do Institutions Matter?: Government Capabilities in the United States and Abroad* (Washington, DC: The Brookings Institution), 462–82.

Weiss, L. (1998) *The Myth of the Powerless State* (Cambridge and New York: Cambridge University Press).

Weiss, L. and J. M. Hobson (1998) *States and Economic Development* (Oxford: Polity Press).

Widfeldt, A. (1997) *Linking Parties with People? Party Membership in Sweden, 1960–1994* (Gothenburg: Department of Political Science, University of Gothenburg).

Wildavsky, A. (1979) 'Policy as its Own Cause', in A. Wildavsky (ed.), *Speaking Truth to Power* (Boston: Little, Brown).

Williamson, O. E. (1975) *Markets and Hierarchies* (New York: Free Press).

Williamson, O. E. (1996) *The Mechanisms of Governance* (Oxford and New York: Oxford University Press).

Wilson, G. K. (1990) *Business and Politics*, 2nd edn (Chatham, NJ: Chatham House).

Wood, D. B. and R. Waterman (1994) *Bureaucratic Dynamics* (Boulder, Colo.: Westview).

Woodside, K. (1998) 'The Authority and Visibility of Policy Instruments', in B. G. Peters and F. K. M. Van Nispen (eds), *The Instruments of Public Policy* (Cheltenham: Edward Elgar).

Wright, V. (1994) 'Reshaping the State: Implications for Public Administration', *West European Politics* 17, 102–34.

Wunsch, J. S. and D. Olowu (1995) *Failure of the Centralized State*, 2nd edn (San Francisco: ICS Press).

Zifcak, S. (1994) *New Managerialism: Administrative Reform in Whitehall and Canberra* (Buckingham: Open University Press).

Index

227